CW00323227

The
Economist
Guide

CHINA

The
Economist
Guide

CHINA

The
Economist
Books

Hutchinson

Published by Hutchinson Business Books, an imprint of Century Hutchinson Limited 20 Vauxhall Bridge Road, London SW1V 2SA

The publishers welcome corrections and suggestions from business travellers; please write to The Editor, The Economist Guides, Axe and Bottle Court, 70 Newcomen Street, LONDON SE1 1YT

Series Editor Stephen Brough
Assistant Series Editor Brigid Avison
Editors Jane Carroll (*first edition overview*);
Paul Holberton (*first edition travel*)
Jane Carroll and John Beyer (*second edition overview*)
Andrew Shaw (*second edition travel*)
Designer Alistair Plumb (*first edition*)
Alison Donovan (*second edition*)
Sub-editors Isla Maclean, Eleanor Van Zandt
Production Controller Shona Burns
Editorial Assistants Mary Pickles, Bettina Whilems
Indexer Fiona Barr

Contributors *Overview* John Beyer, Susan Ware, Dick Wilson; *travel* Christopher Catling, Elizabeth Morrell

Consultants Ken Davies, Derek Elley, Elizabeth Wright

First edition published in Great Britain 1988
Second edition published in Great Britain 1990

Copyright © 1988 and © 1990 The Economist Publications Limited and Webster's Business Traveller's Guides Limited
Maps and diagrams copyright © 1988 and © 1990 The Economist Publications Limited and Webster's Business Traveller's Guides Limited

British Library Cataloguing in Publication Data

China. - (The Economist guides)
1. China - Visitors' guides
951.05'8

ISBN 0-09-174340-0

Maps and diagrams by Oxford Illustrators, Oxford, England
Typeset by SB Datagraphics, Colchester, England
Printed in Italy by Arnoldo Mondadori, Verona

Contents

Glossary

ADB Asian Development Bank. Founded in 1966, it has 32 regional and 15 non-regional members.

ASEAN Association of South East Asian Nations, founded in 1967. Members are Brunei, Indonesia, Malaysia, Philippines, Singapore and Thailand.

BOC Bank of China (China's foreign exchange bank, not to be confused with the People's Bank of China, the central bank).

CAAC Civil Aviation Administration of China.

CCTV China Central Television.

CECF China Export Commodities Fair (Guangzhou/Canton).

CICT Consolidated Industrial and Commercial Tax (sometimes called Industrial and Commercial Consolidated Tax – ICCT).

CITIC China International Trust and Investment Corporation.

CITS China International Travel Service.

CJV Contractual Joint Venture.

COMECON Council for Mutual Economic Assistance (the Communist bloc economic and trade cooperation organization).

CTS China Travel Service.

dwt Deadweight tons.

ETDGs Economic and Technological Development Zones.

FEC Foreign Exchange Certificate.

FEITL Foreign Enterprise Income Tax Law.

FERT Foreign Economic Relations and Trade Commission.

FETAC Foreign Economic and Trade Arbitration Commission.

FTC Foreign Trade Corporation.

Ganbu Cadre.

GATT General Agreement on Tariffs and Trade, which came into force in 1948. It is the world's major forum for negotiating the reduction of tariffs and other barriers to trade.

GDP Gross Domestic Product. The best measure of a country's economic performance, GDP is the total value of a country's annual output of goods and services. It is normally valued at market prices; GDP can, however, be calculated at factor cost, by subtracting indirect taxes and adding subsidies. To eliminate the effect of inflation, GDP growth is usually expressed in constant prices.

GNP Gross National Product. A country's GDP plus residents' income from investments abroad minus income accruing to nonresidents from investments in the country.

Gongren Workers.

grt Gross registered tons.

IBRD International Bank for Reconstruction and Development (World Bank).

ICCT See CICT

IDA International Development Association (the "soft" loan arm of the World Bank).

IMF International Monetary Fund.

ITIC International Trust and Investment Corporation.

JV Joint venture.

Kongfuzi Confucius.

MOFERT Ministry of Foreign Economic Relations and Trade.

NPC National People's Congress (not to be confused with National Party Congress).

OECD Organisation for Economic Cooperation and Development.

OPEC Organization of Petroleum Exporting Countries.

PBOC People's Bank of China (the central bank).

Pinyin The system for transliterating Mandarin Chinese into the roman alphabet, officially adopted in 1958. It has gained wide acceptance as a replacement for the various systems formerly used in Western countries.

PLA People's Liberation Army.

PRC People's Republic of China.

RMB Renminbi (also called yuan).

SAFEX State General Administration for Foreign Exchange Control.

SEZ Special Economic Zone.

Waibin Foreign guests.

Waiguoren Foreigners.

Xinhua The national news agency: the New China News Agency.

¥ Yuan (also called renminbi).

Zeren zhidu Responsibility system.

Zhigong Staff.

Zhongshan Mao suit.

Using the guide

The Economist Guide to China is an encyclopedia of business and travel information. If in doubt about where to look for specific information, consult either the Contents list or the Index.

City guides

The city guide to Beijing, Guangzhou and Shanghai follow a standard format: information and advice on arriving, getting around, city areas, hotels, restaurants, bars, entertainment, shopping, sightseeing, sports and fitness, and a directory of local business and other facilities such as secretarial and translation agencies, couriers and hospitals. There is also a map of the city centre locating recommended hotels, restaurants and other important addresses.

Another 16 cities are covered in less detail, concentrating on arriving and getting around, hotels, restaurants, opportunities for relaxation and information sources.

Abbreviations

Credit and charge cards AE American Express; DC Diners Club; MC MasterCard (Access); V Visa.
Figures Millions are abbreviated to m; billions (meaning one thousand million) to bn.

Publisher's note

Although *The Economist Guide to China* is intended first and foremost to provide practical information for business people travelling *in* China, the general information will also be helpful to anyone doing business with China, wherever and however that business may be conducted.

Price bands

Price bands are denoted by symbols (see below). These correspond to the following actual prices at the time of going to press. (Although the actual prices will inevitably go up, the relative price category is likely to remain the same.)

Hotels
(one person occupying a standard room)

¥	up to ¥200
¥¥	¥200–250
¥¥¥	¥250–300
¥¥¥¥	¥300–350
¥¥¥¥¥	over ¥350

Restaurants
(a typical meal with wine and coffee)

¥	up to ¥50
¥¥	¥50–100
¥¥¥	¥100–150
¥¥¥¥	¥150–200
¥¥¥¥¥	over ¥200

INTRODUCTION

One billion Chinese are in the throes of a fateful experiment: that of leavening the Communist policies they have pursued for 40 years with the yeast of free enterprise, market economics and "open door" links with the capitalist world. The experiment was launched in the late 1970s by a veteran Communist leader, Deng Xiaoping, who recognized that collectivization and nationalization were barriers to economic growth. It is opposed by some Communist Party bureaucrats whose prestige and jobs are threatened and by others for ideological reasons. Hardliners supported the army's bloody suppression of pro-democracy demonstrators in June 1989. Purges and puritanical policies aimed to check the influx of Western culture followed. Deng, then 85 and in poor health, had retained ultimate control of the military despite his previous publicized resignation from other posts.

China has fallen back to the ranks of the very poor nations, yet for many centuries it led the world in wealth, art and technology. Even when Europe was in the ascendant, from the Middle Ages onwards, Chinese affluence and civilization continued to arouse the wonder of foreign travellers. But while the West surged ahead in the scientific and industrial revolutions of the past 200 years, China stood still. The 19th century found it impoverished, misgoverned and bewildered – an easy prey for Western imperialism.

The British first forced China out of its isolation by taking Hong Kong in 1842, after the Opium War, and compelling the Chinese government to allow foreign products to circulate. Other Europeans, closely followed by the Americans and the Japanese, nibbled at the edges of China right up to the 1930s.

In 1912, Chinese republicans toppled the effete Manchu imperial dynasty, but it was not until the 1950s that those republicans (by then Communist-led) re-established national unity after a debilitating civil war and Japanese aggression, and only in the 1980s that China began to climb the first rungs on the ladder of sustained economic advance.

Left behind

In the meantime, the prosperity gap between China and the West has become so wide that China's GNP per head is less than one-fiftieth that of the USA. All the infrastructure for development – roads, railways, ports, power supply, even education – remains lamentably weak.

The discipline of Communism might be thought to have benefited China's modernization. Unfortunately, Chairman Mao Zedong, the effective dictator of the Communist Party for much of the period between 1935 and 1976, launched wildly anarchic and ill-prepared movements such as the Great Leap Forward (1958–59) and the Cultural Revolution (1966–69), in a desperate attempt to accelerate his country's economic and political development. The Cultural Revolution, which robbed a generation of its academic training and killed a million people, has left deep wounds, losing for the Communist Party a great deal of the respect and legitimacy it had earlier won. Mistrust and cynicism make it hard for the reforms of Deng Xiaoping to take proper root and flourish. Yet a surprising amount of enterprise and resourcefulness has surfaced since those reforms were introduced. At the 1987 Communist Party Congress, the generation which had led the party since the days of the Long March stepped aside to make way for younger leaders.

Unity in diversity

China is more like a continent than a nation state of Europe. It is more than 40 times the size of Great Britain and 19 times the size of France. The population, more than four times bigger than that of the USA, represents one-fifth of the world's total. China's far north, on a latitude with Moscow, is chilled by Siberian snows. Yunnan and Hainan Island in the tropical south (level with Jamaica) are hot and humid.

Yet one ethnic group, the Han, predominates and the same written language (which is ideographic, expressing meaning and not sound) prevails across the whole country, lending unity to this huge segment of humankind. Furthermore, China's topography cut it off from the kind of continuous contact that existed between civilizations in western Asia and the Mediterranean. The Chinese perceived the people beyond their frontiers as, for the most part, "barbarians." They called their own country Zhongguo, which means "Middle Kingdom," and this assumption, that China is the centre of the world, still survives. Another distinguishing feature is the belittlement of individualism. Adherence to the group and deference to authority (whether the father of the family or the state) is a much stronger tradition than in Western societies.

The door is open

The Communism that China espoused after 1949 effectively insulated the country from Western ideas for three decades. Only after Mao's death did his successor, Deng Xiaoping, and other reformers put socialist distribution of wealth on the back burner in order to go all-out for bigger production. They dismantled the People's Communes, reverting to private family agriculture instead, reintroduced material incentives and released the energies of private enterprise.

The problems are immense, despite the doubling of GNP between 1979 and 1986 (from a low base, however). If Deng's reforms are to work, prices must be freed from government control; but that could unleash inflation, with its political repercussions. Many potential entrepreneurs are scared of being too forward in case the policy changes again and they are punished. However, the drive for modernization is already having considerable success. China is poised to "take off" and the market has opened up. Foreign exchange shortages hit contracts every few years, but the open door to the West is not going to slam shut again. For anyone with the means and persistence to play for the longer term, China will pay dividends.

The Political Scene

The Communist Party

Power in China resides with the Communist Party. Since coming to power in 1949 the Communists have ruled China as, in effect, a one-party state, although a few minor political parties are allowed token representation in the organs of public life. In the late 1980s, China has been attempting to distinguish between the Party, which formulates policies, and the government, which implements them. The Chinese Communist Party is the largest political party in the world, with 46m members. Mao dominated it as chairman for almost 40 years until his death, after which Deng became the single most powerful figure.

The Party was founded in 1921 as an indigenous initiative not dependent on the Soviet Union's support: many of its early leaders, including Deng Xiaoping, were converted to Marxism as students in France, although Deng did spend some months studying in Moscow on his way back from France.

Congress and Politburo

National Party Congress The fount of power is the National Party Congress, which is supposed to meet every five years to approve long-term policy and make necessary changes in the Party constitution. It last met in October 1987.

The Central Committee The National Party Congress also elects or re-elects a general secretary and a Central Committee of about 300 members, which acts as a permanent executive between Congresses.

There are two other important bodies under the Central Committee. One is the Party's Central Military Commission, through which the Party secures the support of the armed forces and maintains its control over them. The other is the Central Advisory Commission, a group of senior, often retired, politicians who have given up other powers.

Politburo The Central Committee in turn elects a Politburo, consisting of around 20 persons, to expedite its work. Within the Politburo a Standing Committee of only half a dozen or so leaders (the number can vary) supposedly controls day-to-day policy developments.

The Party is unaccountable The Party does not stick to its own rules, and is accountable to no one. Its organs do not necessarily meet regularly or as frequently as its regulations stipulate. The sources of real power are not always apparent from the formal structure, as Deng Xiaoping's influence illustrates.

Parallel structure

Below the central organs stands a network of provincial and local congresses and committees parallel with the structure of government. Only Party members can hold high government posts, so the structures overlap.

Internal problems

The major problem within the Party in the late 1980s was digesting Deng's economic reforms; these tend to reduce the Party's participation in economic and management decision-making, and confine its officials' role to purely political matters. Conservatives in the Party oppose this and they will put a brake on rapid reform. They may accept Western investment, but not political liberalization nor surrender of Party power – as was made clear by the events of June 1989.

The structure of government

The State Council under the premier conducts the government of the country through a large number of ministries and commissions. The state structure revolves around the National People's Congress, a kind of parliament which is formed by indirect election and elects the president of China, who is the head of state, but has no real power.

National People's Congress

Under the State Constitution of 1982 the National People's Congress (NPC) stands at the apex of state authority. Elected for a five-year term, it comprises some 3,000 deputies from all walks of life. They are indirectly elected by provincial people's congresses (which in turn are elected by county, commune, or equivalent local-level congresses). The People's Liberation Army also has seats in the NPC. The Communist Party effectively controls NPC membership, which often seems to be a reward for meritorious service to the Party or government.

The NPC examines and approves the budget and elects the president of the People's Republic and the premier (the latter on the nomination of the president) and several vice-premiers (on the premier's nomination). It is supposed to meet in annual session, to pass new acts of legislation and to decide on questions of war and peace. At times it has proved to be a mere rubber stamp, but in the mid-1980s it began to engage in lively debate, and even to use its powers to prevent bills from going through.

The State Council

The premier, assisted by a handful of vice-premiers, controls the government through the State Council, which is the executive organ of the NPC, acting as a kind of cabinet to its legislature. It formulates administrative measures (including the state economic plans and budgets), issues directives and supervises their execution. It also oversees the administration of the provinces, autonomous regions and large municipalities.

Ministries and commissions
There are more than 40 ministries and commissions and other bodies under the State Council, most of them dealing with some aspect of the economy.

Financial The group of bodies

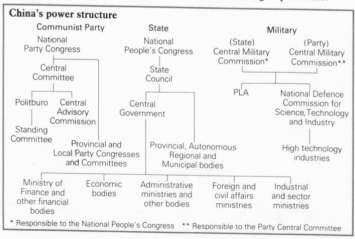

China's power structure

Communist Party	State	Military	
National Party Congress	National People's Congress	(State) Central Military Commission*	(Party) Central Military Commission**
Central Committee	State Council		
		PLA	National Defence Commission for Science, Technology and Industry
Politburo Central Advisory Commission	Central Government		
Standing Committee			
Provincial and Local Party Congresses and Committees	Provincial, Autonomous Regional and Municipal bodies		High technology industries
Ministry of Finance and other financial bodies	Economic bodies	Administrative ministries and other bodies	Foreign and civil affairs ministries	Industrial and sector ministries

* Responsible to the National People's Congress   ** Responsible to the Party Central Committee

dealing with the financial sector is headed by the Ministry of Finance, which has authority over the banking system. In this group are the various state banks, trust and investment corporations, insurance corporations and the State Audit Administration (see *The banks* and *Other financial institutions*).

Economic The State Planning Commission, the State Commission for Restructuring the Economy, and the Science and Technology Commission are all very influential and have various specialized ministries under their control.

Administration Bodies dealing with administrative matters include the State Family Planning Commission, State Nationality Affairs Commission, Overseas Chinese Affairs Office and Hong Kong and Macao Affairs Office. The last of these has become particularly important now that the countdown for resumption of sovereignty over Hong Kong, due in 1997 following an agreement signed with Britain in 1984, has begun. Bureaux for customs, meteorology and civil aviation are also in this group.

Foreign and civil affairs As well as the Ministry of Foreign Affairs there is the Ministry of Foreign Economic Relations and Trade (MOFERT), of particular relevance to foreign business visitors. A variety of other ministries deal with commerce, culture, education, justice, security, labour, health, agriculture, etc.

Industrial Finally there is a lengthening list of industrial ministries. Not only do many industries, such as chemicals, machinery and electronics, energy, railways and textiles, have their own ministries under the State Council; the crucial Ministry of Defence has some involvement, via the Central Military Commission, with a number of bodies handling high-technology industries of military or strategic significance. These include nuclear, space and some shipbuilding industries.

Leading Groups These are extremely important committees, formed in recent years to improve coordination between ministries. Their members are very high-ranking officials from two or more relevant ministries and are usually led by a vice-premier. Leading Groups make important policy decisions and some, such as the Leading Group for Investment, now sometimes hold meetings with foreign visitors.

People's Courts

The People's Courts, culminating in a Supreme People's Court, try cases, punish criminals and settle disputes within narrow, politically set limits. Only in the 1980s, with the open-door policy (which brought foreign investors requiring legal contracts), did a recognizable body of trained lawyers begin to appear – and it is still very small. Confucianism stresses conciliation more than adjudication of right and wrong, and so Chinese law has a different character from that of the West – more personalized and less consistent.

Civil service

Most civil servants are Party members working under the supervision of a Party branch secretary. The distinction between government and Party functionaries becomes more blurred the lower down one looks in the Chinese system. Since Deng's reforms began, the civil servants have supposedly surrendered some of their authority with farmers and factory managers taking more of the technical decisions about production.

Provinces, regions, municipalities

China is divided into 22 provinces (Taiwan still being counted officially as a province of China), five autonomous regions and numerous large municipalities. The three municipalities directly under the central government are Beijing, Shanghai and Tianjin.

The autonomous regions are Guangxi Zhuang (the mountainous area in the far south, on the Vietnam border), Nei Menggu (Inner Mongolia), Ningxia Hui (next door to Mongolia), Xizang (Tibet) and Xinjiang (the region on the Russian border which used to be known as Chinese Turkestan). Tibet attracts the most publicity abroad. Some Tibetans, together with a vocal refugee population across the border in India, back the Dalai Lama, the Tibetans' spiritual leader, and demand political independence.

Provinces Some of the provinces are bigger than France or Germany. All (except Taiwan) are under Communist Party control, and the natural leaders of provinces tend to establish themselves, even insincerely, in the provincial Communist Party, from which they can have a say not only in how the place is run but also in how far it responds to central directives.

Some provinces are traditionally less amenable to central command than others. Visitors who become accustomed to the heavily politicized style of life in Beijing are sometimes surprised at the forthright realism which they find in the provinces.

The wayward south Sichuan (Deng Xiaoping's home province) is renowned for its independence, and the southern provinces, with their different languages, character and terrain (especially Guangdong, Guangxi and Fujian), have always been considered difficult to keep in line. This is the area from which Sun Yat-sen and his Kuomintang (Nationalist) Party came, and which was the main focus of the Republican movement which toppled the Manchu dynasty in 1912.

More autonomy for some Some provinces and municipalities have been given a measure of autonomy in economic development and utilization of foreign exchange, and foreign business people may increasingly find it as valuable to cultivate those provincial leaders as the central ones. This is particularly true of the southern coastal provinces, and also of the immediate hinterland around Shanghai and Tianjin.

The reins of power

The power behind the scenes has been the reformist Deng Xiaoping, who emerged as the strong man of the Communist Party after Chairman Mao's death. At the 13th National Party Congress in late 1987 he succeeded in having a majority of like-minded reformists elected to the Politburo and "his" man, Zhao Ziyang, made Party general secretary. Although he himself stepped down from all but one of his official posts, he continued to wield enormous influence behind the scenes.

Deng Xiaoping

Deng became the central figure in China's leadership in 1978, two years after Mao's death. Mao was a rich peasant's son who educated himself into politics, but Deng, born in 1904, was a minor landlord's son who joined the Communists while studying in France after World War I.

In and out of power Deng had been Party general secretary during the Maoist era and had also deputized for premier Zhou Enlai during his foreign travels. Like many other Chinese leaders Deng was disgraced in the radical extremism of the Cultural Revolution of the late 1960s, and his own son was permanently crippled by the Red Guards. He was brought back to office in 1973 but after the death of Zhou in 1976 he lost power again until 1977. Nevertheless, by 1978 he had masterminded the downfall of the "Gang of Four" (the radical group led by Mao's widow who sought to sustain leftist policies after Mao's death) and had swung China round to a new pragmatic tack.

Behind the scenes Deng shrewdly promoted others into senior public office after 1978, while he remained the statesman behind the scenes. He put two trusted "youngsters" into the leadership of the Party and government respectively, Hu Yaobang and Zhao Ziyang (born 1915 and 1919). During 1987 Hu was forced to resign and Zhao took over as general secretary while temporarily retaining the premiership. The immediate cause of this downfall was his alleged inability to deal with the student demonstrations which had been taking place, but for some time he had been making other leaders nervous with his over-enthusiastic promotion of Deng's reforms. The fact that he was allowed to stay in the Politburo is a remarkable indication of China's altered political climate. Deng himself retained the chairmanship of the Party's Central Military Commission, from which vantage point he was able to secure the allegiance of the army.

Still powerful As expected, at the 13th Party Congress in late 1987, Deng retired from the Politburo and the Central Committee of the Party, and succeeded in taking with him the other octogenarians. He retained the important post of chairman of the Party's Central Military Commission, however, and continued to be an extremely powerful figure in Chinese politics.

Liberal Zhao Ziyang sacked

Zhao Ziyang, who was acting Party general secretary and Deng's long-time premier, was confirmed as general secretary at the 13th Party Congress. He was dismissed following the June 1989 suppression of student-led protests, which had built up after the death of the sacked reformer Hu Yaobang in April that year. Like Hu, Zhao was accused by hardliners of encouraging an intellectual and moral permissiveness. While many of his reformist supporters were sacked, other "liberals" have stayed.

General Secretary Jiang Zemin

Jiang Zemin replaced Zhao Ziyang as party general secretary in June 1989. Jiang was seen as a compromise candidate, but is no cipher. Acceptable to reformers for his efforts to invigorate sluggish Shanghai with foreign investment first as mayor then party boss, he impressed hardliners by muzzling the Shanghai media during the pro-democracy protests of April-May. Jiang, born in 1926, shares with Li Peng an engineering background and a Soviet education.

Premier Li Peng

A new generation is making its way to the top of the Party as the veteran leaders relax their hold on the reins of power. Foremost among these is the man who in 1987 took over from Zhao as premier, Li Peng. Li, born in 1928, is a Soviet-trained engineer who played a major role in China's nuclear power programme and is an adopted son of Zhou Enlai. He denies that his Soviet background has made him a devotee of rigid central planning, but he is known to favour a cautious approach to reform.

Groomed for power During 1987 he was groomed for the premiership: after being taken out of the Sino-Soviet border negotiations, he was given various high-profile tasks in which to demonstrate his leadership qualities. (His lack of success in one of these tasks – fighting forest fires – nearly ruined his reputation.)

Curbing the pace of reform Li's appointment was seen as a brake on Zhao's reforming zeal – the price exacted by the octogenarian conservatives for retiring from the Politburo Standing Committee.

A younger Politburo

China is still a gerontocracy, measured by the standards of Western countries. Nevertheless, the Politburo is now much younger than it was – even though it still has one or Politburo is now much younger than it was – even though it still has one or two aged members – and many of the new members have had considerable planning experience and are of a pragmatic bent.

New-look Standing Committee
When Deng stepped down from the Politburo Standing Committee, he forced two other veterans, Li Xiannian (who was replaced by Yang Shangkun as President of China in 1988) and Chen Yun, to follow him, making way for younger men. The old, sick and frail Chen Yun, formerly the Party's leading economic strategist, and a strong critic of Deng's reforms, has been "kicked upstairs" to head the Central Advisory Commission.

The six-man ruling team is now headed by Jiang Zemin, with Li Peng in second position. The other members are Song Ping, Qiao Shi, Li Ruihuan and Yao Yilin. The average age of the Standing Committee was 64 in late 1989. This is a great achievement on the part of Deng, who wishes to break with the Confucian tradition which awards power to the older generation and blocks the promotion of the young, thus retarding the country's modernization.

Decentralization
A degree of decentralization seems inevitable, and the authority of the central Party and government is likely to be weakened by provincial, regional and sectoral leaders wanting to go their own way. Decentralization will give rise to problems such as price rises and unplanned increases in industrial output; inevitably the government will claw back power from time to time.

The left wing
One unpredictable element is the rump left wing of the Communist Party which Mao championed. It suffers from being identified with the Cultural Revolution, for which

almost nobody has a good word any more. The 14m young people who were sent to the countryside during that disastrous upheaval are now the "missing generation" in China, and the memory of the million who were killed is still vivid. There is a deep distrust of anarchy.

Democracy demonstration
The Cultural Revolution activists may have become demoralised and apathetic, but their fervour and their aims (an end to corruption and nepotism) have been echoed by students, increasingly vociferous in the late 1980s.

Student protests, often limited to complaints about their meagre conditions, have turned to political and moral issues.

Following in the tradition of the great patriotic demonstrations of 4 May 1919, students in May 1989 called for another renewal in China, an end to corruption and nepotism, a more open government and a more liberal society.

They called for the resignations of Deng Xiaoping and Li Peng, but few spoke of democracy in terms of the overthrow of Party rule. Protesters, frequently singing the Communist anthem, the Internationale, looked for change from within the Party.

Intellectual support, initially confined to a handful of articulate dissidents, became widespread in the educational and cultural establishment. One million of Beijing's citizens also joined the demonstrations.

Hardliners reacted by crushing the demonstration in Tian'anmen Square on 4 June with troops and armour. Casualties among unarmed citizens were over one thousand. Justification for the army's violence was the humiliation of Beijing's symbolic central square - Tian'anmen - covered in ramshackle tents in defiance of martial law. Hardliners, subsequently denying any violence by the security forces, said they had prevented anarchy.

Defence and security

Because the Communists took power by armed rebellion ("through the barrel of a gun," as Mao used to put it), the armed forces (known collectively as the People's Liberation Army – PLA) have more political clout than might appear on the surface. Gradually a separate identity for the military has begun to be forged, and a sense of professionalism engendered. Badges of rank are being restored, for example, after years of egalitarian anonymity.

Military strength and weakness

The army comprises 3m men and women. The air force (about 500,000-strong) and navy (350,000-strong) are very poorly equipped – even more so than the army. There are about 130 submarines and 15 destroyers in the navy, and 600 bombers in the air force, mostly derived from obsolete Soviet models. The defence forces are deployed mainly along the Soviet border and their principal role is now that of defending the nation rather than controlling the population.

Defence cuts

Deng tried in the 1980s to reduce the strength and budget of the armed forces, with modest success. Defence spending has fallen as a proportion of the national budget since 1980, and stood at about 7% of GNP in 1987.

Army self-sufficiency

The armed forces, nostalgic for their heroic guerilla days, make themselves as economically self-sufficient as possible, operating farms and factories on a vast scale outside the scope of the civilian economy. Many ordnance factories have already been turned over to the production of civilian goods – anything from buttons to washing machines.

The Party cannot play down its military brass too much: it was they who saved the country from the anarchy of the first phase of the Cultural Revolution in the late 1960s. But the generals depend on the Party leaders for foreign exchange to buy military equipment and supplies from Japan and the West.

Under Party control

Deng kept the chairmanship of the Party's Central Military Commission (elected by the Party Central Committee every five years to decide commands and policy) after giving up other posts, a demonstration of the importance he attaches to reconciling the army to his economic and political reforms. The Party also seeks to control the army at lower levels through political commissars in every unit.

Two military commissions The formal structure of authority has two Central Military Commissions at its apex, one accountable to the National People's Congress, and the other accountable to the Party, through the Central Committee. Confusingly, they have the same title in Chinese, and membership overlaps to a great extent. Together they control the PLA General Staff.

Strategic industries The two Military Commissions also supervise the extremely important National Defence Commission for Science, Technology and Industry. This body in turn controls – with the assistance of the State Planning Commission under the State Council – a number of strategic industries including ordnance, nuclear power, electronics, aviation, space and shipbuilding.

The nuclear card

China vastly strengthened its international security by developing its own H-bomb capacity. This was built with Soviet aid at the outset but the project was completed by Chinese scientists, some US-trained.

International alignments

Pragmatism is the key to China's foreign policy, now that economic development has become the priority issue. The Chinese achieved their famous détente with the USA in 1971–72, and are today on reasonably good terms with all the powers, both capitalist and communist. However, the West reacted strongly to the June 1989 massacre: a range of sanctions was imposed and multi-lateral and soft loans were suspended. China was admitted to the UN in 1971, displacing Taiwan, and occupies one of the five permanent seats on the Security Council. It joined the IMF in April 1980 and the World Bank in May 1980.

At odds with the USSR

Relations between the respective Communist parties in Moscow and Beijing had been strained since the split in 1960, until Gorbachev's historic visit to China in 1989. State and government ties are reverting to normal and trade is increasing again.

The open door

Under the open-door policy of the 1980s China encourages investment and transfer of technology from all advanced nations, while reserving the right to keep out unwelcome influences defined broadly as "spiritual pollution" or "bourgeois liberalism."

American honeymoon China's honeymoon with the USA was begun under Mao and reinvigorated by Deng. By 1987 the Americans were supplying advanced technology and military equipment to China, exchanging visits of military personnel and accounting for one-tenth of China's foreign trade. The Chinese still complain, however, that advanced technology is being withheld.

Other problems are the USA's arms sales to Taiwan and its periodic protectionist moves which affect China's textile exports.

Return of Hong Kong and Macao Deng negotiated the retrocession of the two remaining European colonies – Hong Kong and Macao – by 1997 and 1999 respectively, clearing the ground for stronger links with Western Europe.

Recalcitrant Taiwan

The recalcitrant island-province of Taiwan for 40 years has been the last outpost of the Kuomintang (Nationalists). Taiwan calls itself the Republic of China, in opposition to the People's Republic, and still officially claims sovereignty of all the mainland. Deng's declared goal was to reunite Taiwan with the "motherland" by the end of the century. The *de facto* independence of Taiwan seems likely to persist, but the two sides are slowly relaxing their stances.

Japan is top supplier

Japan is China's biggest economic partner, and the Chinese greedily absorb all the new technology and capital they can get from it. Surviving rancour from wartime memories is still a major impediment to amicable relations, however, as is the huge trade deficit in Japan's favour, a source of great resentment.

Relations with ASEAN

China seeks to improve its relations with the ASEAN countries, though their governments are hostile to Communism, as are members of the Chinese business elite in South-East Asia. The latters' hostility may be gradually diluted by latent feelings for their original motherland. Meanwhile the mutual suspicion of Vietnamese territorial ambitions provides a bond with most ASEAN governments.

The Economic Scene

Natural resources

China's land area is 9.6m square km/3.7m square miles, of which 33% are mountains, 26% plateaux, 10% hills and only 31% basins or plains. Only one-tenth of the land is cultivated, mostly in the eastern half of the country. Forests extend over 120m ha/297m acres. Large-scale deforestation over the centuries has led to very serious problems of soil erosion. China's great rivers are prone to flooding but give the country enormous potential for hydroelectric power. The climate ranges from semi-tropical in the southwest to temperate, cold and dry in the northwest.

Minerals

Surveying of China's mineral and metal resources is not complete, but they are substantial and adequate for the country's industrialization, except for a few minor gaps. Iron and bauxite are available in good quantity but are so low grade as to need supplementing with imports. In the case of copper, about 60% of demand has to be bought in from abroad. Coal and petroleum are plentiful and earn valuable foreign exchange. Chrome, copper, nickel and zinc are present, but in small quantities.

Exports and imports Those minerals of which China has very large deposits, and which it can export, are antimony, asbestos, bauxite, bismuth, coal, fluorspar, magnesite, manganese, mercury, molybdenum, petroleum, salt, sulphur, talc, tin and tungsten.

Coal China is the world's second-largest coal producer (after the USA). Proven reserves are almost 780bn tonnes/860bn US tons, of which 90% is bituminous. Much of this coal is low grade, however, and inaccessible – more than half of it lying in the remote and undeveloped western interior, while most of the rest is concentrated in the northeast. Coal production in 1986 was 870m tonnes/960m US tons. This is to be increased by about 40% during the 1986–90 Five-Year Plan.

Oil fields Five major oil basins lie in the far northwest interior of China; others are in Sichuan, around Wuhan and in the northeast (Manchuria). More recently discovered are the offshore fields in the Bohai Gulf and those off the coasts of Jiangsu (in the Yellow Sea), Fujian and Guangdong (in the South China Sea). The Chinese also claim to have found a major oil field in the Pearl river delta. The four most important oil fields are at Daqing, Shengli and Dagang in the northeast and in Xinjiang in the northwest.

Foreign participation has been sought in offshore drilling, but the commercial discoveries up to 1987 were disappointing. Exploitation is hindered by the cost of laying pipelines from the fields. Substantial development of China's oil began only in the 1960s.

Oil reserves The figure for onshore oil reserves is disputed but probably lies between 4.6bn and 6bn tonnes/5bn and 6.6bn US tons. Offshore reserves may be slightly larger. All in all, China probably has almost 10% of the world's proven reserves.

Natural gas has so far been found in Sichuan province – where reserves are probably 700bn cubic metres/24,700bn cubic ft – and offshore in the South China Sea. A newly found gas field at Yinggehai, south of Hainan Island, is believed to have reserves of 90bn cubic metres/3,200bn cubic ft and is being developed with US partners.

Agriculture is the cornerstone

Agriculture accounts for only one-third of China's GNP. When the Communists took over the country in 1949 the proportion was double that, which demonstrates how much more development effort has been put into the factories than into the fields. But the agricultural areas contain and support three-quarters of the people, supplying industry with its raw materials and urban workers with their food, so this sector retains its primary importance in the national economy. China is largely self-sufficient in food, and imports of wheat are offset by exports of rice.

The major food crops With a shorter growing season and lower rainfall, the area north of the latitude of Shanghai is predominantly wheat-growing. The provinces to the south of this line enjoy year-round crops and abundant rain and are predominantly rice-growing. These two are the staple crops, but other grains – corn, barley, kaoliang (sorghum) and millet – are also important. State farms, averaging 2,000ha/4,940 acres, account for less than 5% of food production. Vegetables are also significant, though not on such an organized basis.

Cash crops China is a major producer of soyabeans, peanuts, cotton, rape seed and other oil seed. It also grows industrial oils such as tung oil and castor. Soya, the most important of these crops, is grown in the northeast, in what used to be called Manchuria. Cash crops, particularly those that are exported, such as cotton, compete with cereals for the limited land available for cultivation.

Livestock and fisheries are the two relatively neglected sectors of Chinese agriculture. However, decentralization policies in the 1980s have boosted livestock numbers. Pigs and poultry for city consumption are intensively reared on state farms. Live pigs are a sizable export – 3m of them in 1986.

Grains strategy The grain harvest has doubled over the past 30 years, because of what in other developing countries is called the Green Revolution, or modernizing the cultivator's techniques. However, grain harvests were failing to meet targets in the second half of the 1980s. Disastrous flooding and forest fires were partly to blame for the shortfall of about 15m tonnes/17m US tons in 1987, when the crop was about 385m tonnes/425m US tons. Since 1979 the government has shifted from the collectivism of the People's Commune in favour of the household contract system, giving families a greater incentive to produce more. The negative result of these changes has been that agricultural infrastructure, including roads and dykes, tends to be neglected because no one is responsible for its maintenance. The government is aiming at a cereal harvest of 500m tonnes/550m US tons by 1999.

Future harvest growth Future increases in the grain harvest must come from enlarging the units of private agriculture – to enable them to use modern farming methods efficiently – and from greater use of chemical fertilizer, specifically of phosphates and potash, since over-use of nitrogen is seriously damaging the soil.

Fertilizer shortage In 1986 less than 20m tons of chemical fertilizer was applied to the fields, and supplies are short. State-run industry fails to match demand, there is illegal hoarding by local officials and not enough foreign exchange is available for imports.

Farm price tangle A major problem, affecting in particular the feasibility of the grain targets, is that of farm prices. Farmers are now contracted to fulfil certain quotas of cereals and are free to sell the remainder of their crop on the free market. They have tended to use their new freedom to grow cash crops, including vegetables, rather than grain, which is less profitable.

Human resources

China has 22% of the world's population. At almost 1.1bn by at the end of 1987, the population is the largest in the world. China stands one-third higher than the runner-up in the numbers league, India, and is considerably more populous than the whole of Europe including the Soviet Union. This huge population is one of the major factors in China's economic backwardness.

Population growth

The numbers are still growing – by about 1.6% annually – adding 14m heads a year. In 1986 the birth rate appears to have jumped from 1.8% to 2.1%, while medical advances held down the death rate below 1%. The official aim is for a population of not more than 1.2bn by the end of this century but at the present growth rate it will reach nearly 1.5bn.

It is a young population. Two-thirds are under 30, and half are below 20 years of age. Stability of population will not come for at least another generation and possibly not until the middle of the next century.

Family planning In the 1970s the government and the Party tried to bring the birth rate down by tough birth control measures, placing intense pressure on couples to have only one child. It is questionable how successful this was in the rural areas, where sons (but not daughters) have the dual attraction of augmenting a family's earning power and preserving its name. Once Deng Xiaoping's economic reforms lifted Party controls off the countryside in the 1980s, the family planning campaign was one of the first to suffer. Females total 48.5% of the population.

The Han race predominates

The overwhelming majority of Chinese (94%) are Han, the mainstream Chinese family of races which share a common written (ideographic) language and culture. The remaining 6% are minority nationalities such as Tibetan, Mongolian, Uygur, Korean and Miao. They live on the northern, western and southern fringes of the central Chinese heartland, occupying vast areas of inaccessible land potentially rich in minerals, and traditionally have provided a buffer against external powers.

Mostly rural

More than 70% of Chinese people live in the countryside. The Communist government has limited the growth of its cities more effectively than other Asian governments. Most Chinese are peasant farmers, some of whom also work in rural industries. Increasing mechanization will eventually release millions from work on the land.

Population density

The overall population density, at about 109 people per square km, is not so high as, for example, that of Japan, Taiwan or Britain. However, the distribution is uneven and in some areas, such as Jiangsu and Shanghai, the density is very high, resulting in a severe shortage of agricultural land. There is some "colonization" of interior regions by Han settlers, even where, as in Tibet, it provokes local antagonism. The most populous provinces are the two rice "granaries," Sichuan (the size of France and with double its population at 109m) and Henan (81m). Of the cities, Shanghai municipality has 13m inhabitants, Beijing 10m.

Educational skills

A survey conducted in the mid-1980s classified 28% of the adult population as illiterate or semi-literate. Some 42% had completed primary school, but only 8% secondary (senior middle) school, and less than 1% had graduated from universities.

The nation's finances

The bulk of the central government's funds consists of funds transferred from the provinces, and the amounts are periodically renegotiated. Taxation is gradually replacing income from enterprises as the main source of revenue. In recent years the central government budget has produced a deficit; most of this is met by borrowing overseas.

Central government budget

Sources of revenue The main sources of revenue in the central budget are tax receipts, including customs duties, and profits of state enterprises. Salt tax, agricultural tax, industrial and commercial tax, and revenues of provincially controlled industry are collected by the provinces and shared by them with the central government. Profits of state industries used to be remitted to the centre, but now these are taxed instead, leaving only state-owned transport and energy utilities paying their net receipts directly to the treasury.

New income tax A new system of personal income taxation, aimed at smoothing out disparities of income, was introduced in 1987. But it is not conceived as a revenue-raiser and typically will affect only those earning more than five times the average income.

1987 Budget

Revenue	¥bn
Tax	219
State enterprise profits	18
Bond issues	6
Foreign borrowing	15
Total (including others)	238

Expenditure	¥bn
Capital construction	66
Culture and education	39
Price subsidies	34
Defence	20
Agriculture	12
Debt service	8
Total (including others)	246

Central government spending of ¥246bn in 1987 was to be met mostly from tax revenues, with a small amount of assistance from state energy and transport profits, bond issues and foreign loans, leaving a deficit of ¥8m, to be borrowed from overseas.

The deficit The central government traditionally pursues a goal of sound finance and a balanced budget but, in 1985, for the first time, there was a deficit, which grew to ¥7bn in 1986. This was attributed to lower world prices for oil and other primary export commodities, the devaluation that summer of the national currency – renminbi or yuan – a shortfall in customs duty receipts and excessive state investment in both fixed assets and consumption under the decentralization measures of the early 1980s. To hold down state investment, which is the only factor it can try to control, the government will have to increase its own role in financial decision-making.

A cut in price subsidies is the other obvious solution, but political opposition inhibits that. Such subsidies were actually 40% higher in the 1987 budget than in 1986.

Provincial budgets

Unlike the central budget, provincial budgets do not necessarily balance, reflecting a deliberate transfer of resources between provinces. Each province negotiates with the central government its annual spending figure and contribution to the central budget. The result is an element of subsidy for poor provinces, paid for by the richer ones. The municipality of Shanghai, for example, is a disproportionate source of government revenue.

Foreign debt burden

The burden of outstanding foreign debt probably trebled between 1983 and 1986, to reach the $26bn mark. The IMF has warned the Chinese government that its external debt is heavy, irrationally structured and poorly managed. Official Chinese figures for the end of 1985 show debts of $15.8bn or 6% of GDP. IMF and World Bank estimates were higher (about $20bn, or 7.5% of GDP). (See *Development planning and aid*.)

The portfolio The overall total of foreign debt does not alarm Western bankers, given China's size, economic potential and foreign exchange earning capacity. But about half of the portfolio is short-term debt, and this is considered unwise.

Balance of payments

Statistics for the balance of payments were published for the first time in 1985. They show that until that year there was normally a surplus on visible trade, with the services account more or less in balance, helped by transfers from overseas Chinese and tourism receipts in particular, as well as by interest earned on China's substantial foreign investments and by receipts from the export of labour. The capital account has tended to record a small surplus. In 1985 the current account swung round sharply into deficit, following a surge in imports, but in 1986 the deficit was reduced again, as a result of the government's efforts to boost exports and curb imports, devaluation of the renminbi, and growing tourism revenue.

Foreign reserves

Gross foreign exchange reserves, comprising those of the Bank of China and the state treasury, were over $10.8bn in March 1987, and gold reserves stood at $5.3bn.

The State General Administration for Foreign Exchange Control was incorporated within the People's Bank of China in 1982 to coordinate foreign loans. Foreign exchange has been made more difficult to obtain than it was in the early 1980s. Two provinces – Guangdong and Fujian – have some foreign exchange autonomy.

The currency

The unit of currency since 1955 has been the yuan, known as the renminbi (people's currency). Its exchange rate is fixed daily by the State General Administration for Foreign Exchange Control, calculated from a weighted basket of major convertible currencies. It was devalued by an effective 60% over the period 1980–86.

Inflation

Unknown in Mao's day, inflation has crept in with the economic reforms of his successors. The consumer price index rose by an estimated 6% in 1986 and was expected to have reached 10% in 1987, with a much higher figure for the cities.

Balance of payments ($bn)

	1984	1985	1986
Merchandise exports	23,905	25,108	25,756
Merchandise imports	−23,891	−38,231	−34,896
Trade balance	14	−13,123	−9,140
Exports of services	4,819	4,533	4,927
Imports of services	−2,766	−3,070	−3,200
Net transfers	442	243	379
Balance on current account	2,509	−11,417	−7,034

Source: IMF International Financial Statistics

International trade

China is large enough, and has the natural resources, to be potentially more self-sufficient than other countries. Its Communist government has generally pursued a goal of self-reliance. This explains why China's foreign trade represents only 1% of the world's trade volume (but a quarter of China's GNP). Despite China's enormous size, its foreign trade is on a level with Hong Kong's, at around $70bn in 1987 (although about 45% of Hong Kong's exports are re-exports). Taiwan and South Korea follow closely, though their populations are only 2% and 4% respectively of China's. China's trade used to balance in most years, but now it progresses in fits and starts instead of following a smooth line. It went into pronounced deficit – by more than $13bn in 1985, and by $9bn in 1986 – mainly because of the uncontrolled import of consumer goods. Total trade is also increasing rapidly, by an average of 15% a year over the decade to 1986.

Commodity pattern

China urgently needs modern machinery and technology from abroad for its industrial development, as well as certain raw materials (rubber, timber, copper), inputs for agriculture (chemical fertilizer) and supplementary food (grains, sugar) for the people. To pay for these, China has many traditional export items which command a good price in the West, from tea to duck feathers to silk. It can also offer many products of light industry, especially textiles and garments, consumer electronics, metalware, preserved and processed foodstuffs, and household goods. Certain Chinese primary commodities and raw materials – notably oil, rice, tin and coal – are also in sufficient surplus to allow exports.

Imports and exports

Imports are dominated by goods needed for the country's modernization programme and by cereals (mainly wheat). It is hoped that the latter will be steadily reduced, except when crop failures occur. The surge in imports of consumer durables in 1985 and 1986 was curtailed by government measures.

Industrial machinery was the main import by value in 1986, accounting for 17% of the import bill, followed closely by iron and steel (15.7%). Road vehicles and transport equipment represented 8.8%.

Crude oil and petroleum products are normally the largest single export, and accounted for 25% of total earnings in 1985. Falling oil prices and China's support for OPEC cut this share to 10.2% in 1986, when textiles became the top earner, with 13.7%, followed by garments (9.5%) and fruit and vegetables (3.5%). Cereals (mainly rice) had a 2.9% share.

View with caution Trade figures must be treated with care: the customs figures are bigger (by 24% in 1986) than those issued by the Ministry of Foreign Economic Relations and Trade (MOFERT). The former probably include countertrade or barter goods not involving foreign exchange payments and are the

External trade (¥bn)

	1983	1984	1985	1986
Exports	43.8	58.0	80.9	108.2
Imports	42.2	61.4	125.8	149.9
Balance	1.6	−3.4	−44.9	−41.7

Sources: IMF International Financial Statistics; China's Customs Statistics.

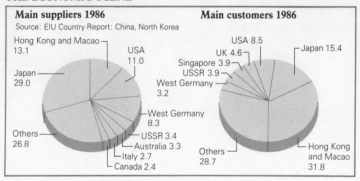

Main suppliers 1986

Source: EIU Country Report: China, North Korea

- Hong Kong and Macao 13.1
- USA 11.0
- Japan 29.0
- West Germany 8.3
- USSR 3.4
- Australia 3.3
- Italy 2.7
- Canada 2.4
- Others 26.8

Main customers 1986

- USA 8.5
- UK 4.6
- Singapore 3.9
- USSR 3.9
- West Germany 3.2
- Japan 15.4
- Hong Kong and Macao 31.8
- Others 28.7

China's main imports and exports by volume 1986

Imports	million tonnes *	Exports	million tonnes *
Grains	7.70	Grains	9.40
Sugar	1.20	Vegetables	0.64
Iron ore	13.70	Tea	0.17
Soda ash	1.20	Canned food	0.44
Chemical fertilizer	5.10	Cotton	0.56
Rolled steel	18.40	Coal	9.80
Copper	0.17	Crude oil	28.50
Aluminium	0.27	Petroleum products	5.50
TVs (m sets)	1.40	Cotton cloth (m metres)	2.05
Automobiles (m units)	0.15	Garments (bn pieces)	1.04

* 1 tonne = 1.1025 US tons

China's main imports and exports by value 1986 ($ bn)

Source: EIU Country Report: China, North Korea

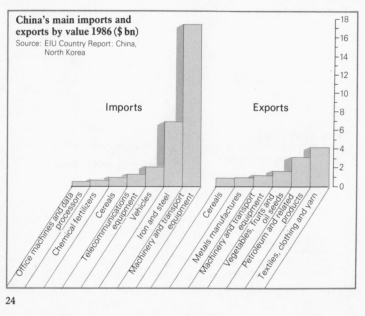

Imports

- Office machines and data processors
- Chemical fertilizers
- Cereals
- Telecommunications equipment
- Vehicles
- Iron and steel
- Machinery and transport equipment

Exports

- Cereals
- Metals manufactures
- Machinery and transport equipment
- Vegetables, fruits and oil seeds
- Petroleum and related products
- Textiles, clothing and yarn

sounder guide to the market, whereas MOFERT figures are a better indication of the foreign exchange needs. This book uses customs figures unless otherwise specified.

Trading partners

Japan was the dominant partner in 1986, followed by Hong Kong (including Macao), although Hong Kong was overtaking Japan for the top position during the early part of 1987. Together these two account for one-half of China's foreign trade. As customers, they were followed by the USA, the UK, Singapore, the USSR and West Germany; as suppliers, by the USA, West Germany and the Soviet Union. Other important suppliers are Australia, Canada (both of wheat) and Italy. Each of these three sold more than $1bn worth of goods to China in 1986.

The share of the Communist bloc countries in China's trade has fallen from about 70% in the 1950s to only about 15% today. However, with the easing of relations with the Soviet Union, trade with that country has picked up from its low point in the 1960s to reach an annual rate of $600m in the first quarter of 1987.

Singapore's position as fifth-best single export market in 1986 reflects the demand of overseas Chinese for Chinese foodstuffs and products.

Diversification Japan's pre-eminence in the Chinese market rests on equipment, of which it is the nearest and most competitive supplier. The Chinese are nervous about becoming too dependent on Japan, however. They are keen to lower their enormous trade deficit with that country and to spread their purchases of machinery more widely.

The US trade varies according to China's grain import needs. In 1987 China had its garment and textile exports sharply cut back by US import quota ceilings, and it complained bitterly about this move, which it said impeded its efforts to reduce its trade deficit with the USA of over $2bn in that year. The

Americans maintain that the deficit is much smaller, since the Chinese do not include in their total exports to the USA those goods sold through Hong Kong.

East Europe The Comecon countries of East Europe signed many new barter agreements with China in 1987 – generators for textiles, for example. Poland, Czechoslovakia and East Germany between them supplied almost 3% of China's total imports in that year.

Technology transfer Contracts to import technology are becoming increasingly important and eagerly sought after. In 1986 France led the list with $1.2bn worth, followed by Japan ($790m), the USA ($660m), the USSR ($510m) and the UK ($420m). The total contracts approved were for $4.5bn, half as much again as in the previous year – and half were with Western European countries. Many countries are nervous about the lack of copyright protection in China, however, and are reluctant to transfer technology. Eastern Europe has the kind of know-how – not too high-tech – that is particularly appropriate to China.

Tourism has become a valuable source of invisible earnings. In 1987, 22.8m visitors came – 28% more than in the previous year – bringing in $1.5bn. The number of actual tourists is much smaller, the majority of visitors being Chinese people from Hong Kong and elsewhere, visiting relatives, and business people. The government is keen to expand tourism, but the sector is woefully under-equipped to cope with the increasing numbers.

Joining the clubs

China has applied for GATT membership, and it collaborates with several important international trade organizations. It is a member of OPEC: oil exports were cut by 5% in volume in 1986 in support of OPEC policies.

Development planning and aid

China's GNP reached ¥938bn ($279bn) in 1986. Per head of population this represented only $263, placing China 95th in the world league – behind all the other Asian countries except India and some of its neighbours.

Economic development

In struggling to modernize its economy, China faces the problems of starting from a low base and of a huge and poorly educated population. Taking good years with the bad, it can hope to sustain an average growth of, say, 6% to 7% a year. Knock off 1.5 or a little more for population growth, and the optimum result is real growth per head of 5%, which, if pursued steadily, would lead to GNP per head of about $800 by the year 2000 – the level of Indonesia's in 1987. Little wonder that China's leaders have been driven to short cuts and crash campaigns to accelerate growth.

Slow start Very little economic development was carried out across the country as a whole in the first half of the 20th century, when China was ravaged by successive civil wars, Japanese invasion and greedy warlords. National economic planning began in earnest under the Communist government in 1952, and not surprisingly the Soviet model was invoked. The First Five-Year Plan (1952–57) aimed, with Russian advice, to build up heavy industry under centralized bureaucratic control. Agriculture, however, fell behind.

The Great Leap Mao Zedong therefore plunged into the hasty experiment of the Great Leap Forward (1958–59). The land was taken away from cooperatives and transferred to giant collectives called People's Communes. This reorganization maximized labour mobility, especially for large-scale projects such as irrigation and dams, but threw material incentives out of the window. Meanwhile, home-produced steel mills were improvised everywhere to ensure a decisive increase in industrial output. During 1952–59 average growth of 6.7% was achieved.

"Three bitter years" The Great Leap collapsed in 1959 in chaos and exhaustion, followed by three years of recession – which became known as "the three bitter years" – and exceptionally bad weather which caused famine conditions in some provinces in 1961. An estimated 16m people died of starvation in this period. The GNP fell by a quarter during the two years following the Leap.

Cultural Revolution Mao's more realistic colleagues, including Deng Xiaoping, sought to restore farm incentives in the early 1960s, but Mao made a second attempt to impose his radical politics on the country in the Cultural Revolution, the first and most extreme phase of which lasted from 1966 to 1969. Though not aimed at the economy, this violent struggle dislocated both industry and trade.

Deng's open door Only after Mao's death in 1976 did Deng emerge with his alternative platform of planned development on the basis of imports of Western technology (the "open door") and the de-collectivization of agriculture to win bigger harvests. It has produced some good results, although it began to run into problems and some political sniping in 1986–87. Average annual growth in 1973–86 was about 7%.

Planning

Planning is mandatory for the production and distribution of essential capital and consumer goods within the state-owned and collectively owned sectors, including such vital agricultural crops as grain, sugar and cotton. For another, middle layer of enterprises the state gives "guidance planning," using economic levers such as pricing policies, taxation and credit to persuade producers to make or grow what the state wants and in the quantities it requires.

More of the market At the lower end of the economy, small producers, whether farmers or independent urban artisans, are left broadly to the sway of market forces. The reformers would like to see more recourse to market forces and a further shift away from administrative to economic controls.

Seventh Plan State bureaucrats draft annual economic plans covering, especially, production, allocation of resources and wages. But the five-year plan is the main vehicle of China's economic development. The target of the Seventh Plan (1986–90) is to secure average annual growth in the national income of 6.7% (or 7.5% in GDP). Agriculture is intended to show 4% annual growth, industry more than 7%.

High priority is given in the Seventh Plan to energy, transport, communications and raw materials for industry, rather than to the expansion of industrial capacity *per se*, as in earlier plans.

Bunching The first two years of the Seventh Plan were set aside for "consolidation" after the over-heating of the preceding year or two. This meant that a 50% increase in state budget revenues and fixed assets investment would have to be achieved within the three years 1988–90.

Long-term planning In addition to the annual and five-year plans there is a long-term plan for the two decades 1981–2000, under which China would attain middle-income status in the world league with a GNP per head of $800. This would necessitate 5% annual economic growth over the 20 years, less than the actual average performance of 7% in 1979–86. The World Bank's opinion is that these goals are attainable, provided the rate of investment can be kept over 30% and the population increase below 1% a year.

Price fixing All these plans are formulated by the State Planning Commission under the State Council, and the premier takes a close interest in them. A key issue is prices, for which there is a cumbersome three-tier structure. Crucial commodities such as grain, steel and fertilizer have prices fixed by the state. For most other farm products and many light industrial manufactures, producers are free to set their own prices and follow market forces. In between is a range of industrial goods whose prices must keep within a given range.

Economic structure

The Chinese state owns and manages about 90,000 enterprises, including most large-scale plants. Starting at a very low level of ownership at the beginning of the People's Republic, the state's share reached a peak of over 80% of the national income in 1978. Then Deng's reforming zeal got to work, and many thousands of these outfits were subsequently either collectivized – put into the hands of the workers as a body – or privatized.

There were more than 300,000 collective (or cooperative) enterprises in 1985, mostly in the countryside. The collective share has consistently risen, but this disguises the fact that although farmlands are technically collectively-owned, in practice they are mostly worked by tenant-farmers on long-term leases – operating in every respect as independent or private cultivators.

The self-employed The private sector recognized in the official figures is composed of a large number of small service and repair enterprises, typically with no more than a dozen workers under a self-employed worker. There are more than 10m self-employed people in China.

Family farming The rural reforms

27

introduced by Deng Xiaoping from 1978 onwards created a system of household responsibility in which income varied with output. The People's Commune was disbanded and the household or family became the main unit of farm production. Cooperation between families for processing and marketing produce was encouraged. These measures were followed by an immediate and dramatic increase in harvests in the first years.

Urban reforms In 1984 Deng began to extend his reforms to the cities and towns. Urban enterprises were to be made responsible for their own profits and losses; managers were given more authority; the state relinquished its management role; pay was to vary according to the amount of work performed; subsidies were to be abolished; wages and prices were freed to find their own market level; and state enterprises were offered for sale to private entrepreneurs or collectives.

This marked a decisive break away from the old rigid centrally planned models towards an innovative – and slightly contradictory – mixed economy owing not so much to Soviet as to other Eastern European exemplars. Deng called it "socialism with Chinese characteristics" and his group in the leadership envisaged heavy and strategic industries and utilities remaining under state control, with the rest run privately or collectively under market forces.

Slow to change Implementation of the urban reforms has proved extremely difficult. There is a serious lack of trained managers; some members of the old bureaucracy are bent on obstructing the reforms; hiring and firing is problematical; and local leaders are reluctant to grasp the nettle of letting prices find their own market levels, fearing that consequent inflation would discredit the reforms and provoke a political backlash.

Polarization The main drawback of the reforms has been their tendency to increase discrepancies of wealth and development. Some lucky or energetic farmers have become very rich; others remain near subsistence level. Some provinces are able to gallop ahead of the others. Four of the 30 provinces, municipalities and autonomous regions – Jiangsu, Shandong, Liaoning and Shanghai, all on the coast – account for one-third of the nation's total output. The new system of taxing personal incomes is designed to tackle this polarization (see *The nation's finances*).

Overseas funding

By the end of 1986 China had borrowed for economic development, but not yet repaid, almost $21bn, according to official figures (IMF and World Bank estimates put the figure nearer to $25bn). This included $1bn of bonds, $3.6bn of inter-governmental loans, $1.2bn borrowed from banks and $6.4bn short-term borrowings below 12 months.

This total represented a trebling of external debt since 1982, but Chinese credit rating is good, foreign creditors were still eager to help finance Chinese economic development, and the Chinese showed every sign of continuing to borrow from abroad. The target during the Seventh Five-Year Plan (1986–90) was to borrow $25–30bn.

Soft loans The World Bank, which China joined in 1980, approved loans for 1986–87 totalling $1.4bn, of which $850m was to come from IBRD funds and $550 as IDA credits. Japan's Overseas Economic Cooperation Fund (OECF) lends about $1bn a year. The Export-Import Bank of Japan provided $4.4bn in low-interest credit in 1980–85. These were the three major sources of concessional finance.

China asked Japan to accelerate disbursements of the OECF for the rest of the 1980s and expressed hopes that the World Bank would double its lending to $2bn a year by 1989–90. The Asian Development Bank, a new source of funds for China, was expected to lend some $300m a year.

Private lending China has tapped private markets as well as official sources. Eighteen bonds and certificates of deposit worth over $84bn were floated, mostly in Japan, in 1985–86. Several large syndicated loans were arranged in 1986 for energy, property and transport projects. One was a $475m loan for the Pingshuo coal mine being jointly developed with Occidental Petroleum of the USA. Other examples were $215m and $397m for nuclear power stations in east China and at Shenzhen, near Hong Kong.

London and New York China may have overtaken South Korea in 1986 as the largest borrower in the East Asian region. The Bank of China raised a syndicated loan on the US capital market in 1987, and the green light for borrowing in London was given when China agreed in 1987 to extend £20m compensation to holders of dishonoured pre-1949 Chinese bonds.

Foreign funds are also solicited at the provincial and corporate levels. The provinces of Guangdong and Fujian are permitted to borrow in foreign currencies directly from abroad without prior reference to the centre, and so are two banks and two investment companies.

World Bank projects In the seven years of its membership of the World Bank from May 1980, China borrowed $4.7bn. The International Finance Corporation (an affiliate of the World Bank) masterminded the joint-venture Guangzhou Peugeot automobile plant. The biggest of the 438 World Bank loans approved since 1980 was for $300m, lent to the China Investment Bank to help improve its tapping of international capital markets, followed by $235m for railway capacity extension between Zhengzhou and Wuhan and $225m for a coal-fired power plant in Zhejiang province.

Some of the new projects which in 1987 the World Bank was considering helping were a mountain area development scheme, seed improvement schemes, a pharmaceutical project in Henan province and the modernization of the Heilongjiang Tools and Machine Tools plant.

Trends China is expected to depend on official aid sources for not more than a third of its financing needs. Larger private borrowings are envisaged after 1990, by which time total external debt may have reached 17% of GNP. Foreign investment constitutes a significant source of foreign funding. Between 1979 and 1986 a total of $7.4bn of direct foreign investment flowed into China.

World Bank loans to China approved 1986–87

IDA credits	$m	IBRD loans	$m
Agriculture and rural development		**Energy**	
Red soils area project	40.0	Shuikou hydroelectric scheme	140.0
Xinjiang agricultural project	70.0	Wujing thermal power project	190.0
Gansu Province project	150.5	**Industry**	
Urban development		Shanghai machine tools	100.0
Shanghai sewerage project scheme	100.0	Fertilizer rationalization	97.4
Transport		**Agriculture and rural development**	
Beijing-Tianjin-Tanggu exp/way	125.0	Gansu Province Project	20.0
		Urban development	
		Shanghai sewerage scheme	45.0
		Transport	
Source: World Bank Annual Report 1987		Beijing-Tianjin-Tanggu expressway	25.0

Communications infrastructure

China's economic development is hampered by poor infrastructure. Unlike India, whose development problems are not dissimilar, China lacks good roads and railways. Almost half of the country's goods traffic goes by water, and only 2.5% of it by the 700,000km/435,000 miles of metalled road. With one road vehicle per 500 people, and only limited telephone services, China has much ground to make up before being able to exploit its natural resources. Hence the priority being given in the late 1980s to the transport, communications and energy sectors.

Rail

Rail carries half of China's cargo and passenger traffic. Major cities are all connected to the rail network, only Tibet being excluded. There are about 52,000km/32,000 miles of track, and by 1990 an additional 3,000km/1,860 miles is to be built.

A major effort is being made to increase carrying capacity. Although double tracking and electrification can be undertaken with domestic resources, computer signalling and control and other methods of increasing traffic flow require foreign input. The World Bank is funding electrification and other improvements of lines carrying coal, which accounts for a third of all rail freight. Steam locomotives, which now pull 80% of trains, are gradually being replaced by electric and diesel engines.

Road

Plans mooted in the late 1970s for a national network of superhighways have been abandoned. The only high-speed roads under construction are the Beijing-Tianjin-Tanggu and the Guangzhou-Shenzhen-Hong Kong expressways, the latter a joint venture between the Guangdong provincial government and Hong Kong and Japanese construction companies.

The roads are unsuited to long-haul traffic. Bridges are designed for light trucks and highways are generally choked with bicycles, carts and other slow traffic. There is also a lack of fuelling and repair facilities.

Traffic congestion in major cities is notorious. Although Beijing and Tianjin have developed orbital roads and restricted traffic circulation, in many cases cities' plans have not substantially altered since 1949, despite a seventy-fold increase in motor vehicles to 3.6m. Most Chinese road users are somewhat lacking in traffic sense, and minor road accidents are frequent.

Shipping

Inland waterways are an important means of transport, especially in areas such as the Yangzi and Pearl river deltas, where the land is criss-crossed by rivers and canals. Ocean-going vessels can reach as far inland as Chongqing in Sichuan. The Grand Canal, dating from the 8th century, is still an important inland artery.

Neglect of inland waterways in the 1960s caused a decline in use; this trend was reversed in the 1970s.

Slow ports Turnaround time averages seven days, compared with half a day in Hong Kong. Expansion of facilities is planned or underway in most of China's ports and bulk-handling and other equipment is being imported.

Container terminals exist at Dalian, Tianjin, Qingdao, Shanghai and Guangzhou, but considerable cargo traffic passes through Hong Kong. Containers are not used to full effect, as there is no network of inland depots, and most containers are stuffed and stripped at the docks.

Shipping links There is competition between China's two shipping lines, the China Ocean Shipping Company (COSCO) and the

China National Foreign Trade Transportation Corporation (Sinotrans).

Air transport and aviation

Nearly all cities have their own airports, but most of these have only rudimentary flight and landing control systems and are suited only to fine-weather flying. Few new airports are being built, but those servicing foreign business people and tourists are being refurbished and equipped with modern control systems.

CAAC Until 1987 all civil aviation was controlled by the Civil Aviation Administration of China (CAAC), which acted as national airline, airports authority and regulatory authority. There have been moves towards dividing this lethargic giant into regional airlines. A small number of local airlines have already been set up in competition with CAAC, but they have to cope with severe disadvantages. Purchasing is the preserve of CAAC's subsidiary, the China Aviation Supplies Corporation.

Telecommunications

Telephone and telex capacity has lagged behind industrial and trade growth, and expansion of capacity has been uneven. Although international direct dialling is possible from Beijing and other major cities, taking a taxi ride across town is sometimes quicker than making a local telephone phone call.

The Ministry of Posts and Telecommunications plans and controls long-distance systems.

The telephone network The number of telephones (5m in 1985) is planned to reach 13m by 1990. However, burgeoning demand will continue to outstrip supply. China had an average of 5.3 telephones per thousand people in 1985 (compared with 550 in Western Europe).

Subscribers Most telephone subscribers are businesses or administrative organizations. Although there are a few private subscribers, most private calls are made through telephone bureaux. Public telephone booths are now being introduced.

Network development has concentrated on the south and east, connecting industrial centres. There has also been a development of satellite links to remote western regions. Communication between Hong Kong, Shenzhen and the rest of Guangdong has been improved with microwave links, which are replacing cable on key routes. Two 1,800-channel co-axial cables between Guangzhou and Beijing have relieved congestion. Some optical fibre links are being introduced.

Digital exchange equipment is being imported from Japan, Sweden, France and Belgium. There are difficulties in connecting digital equipment to the old analogue equipment. Additional problems have arisen because decentralized purchasing has led to provinces ordering incompatible systems.

Most foreign telecommunications manufacturers are discussing technology transfer. However, restrictions hamper the export to China of optical fibre, digital switching and other advanced technology; these are seen as having military applications by the Western nations' Coordinating Committee for Export Control (COCOM) which seeks to limit exports of sensitive technologies to communist countries.

Telex facilities exist in most large cities, supplemented by telegrams elsewhere. Being based on ideographic characters, Chinese is unsuited to telex and has to be translated into telegraphic code numbers for transmission as a telegram.

Fax Facsimile transmission is attractive because it can transmit Chinese characters without their having to be transcribed into roman letters or changed into numbers. However, the high-quality lines required for effective transmission are only now being developed.

The Industrial Scene

Government strategy

China's industrial development since 1949 has been impressive but uneven. Annual industrial growth averaging 9% in the mid-1950s gave way to negligible expansion during the early 1960s following the chaos of the Great Leap Forward. The Cultural Revolution likewise distracted plant managers and planners. The slogan of self-reliance (*zi li geng sheng*) meant that little new technology was introduced. The service sector (from banking to bars) was held to be unimportant, even unnecessary, in a supply economy, in which administrative rather than financial controls were the order of the day. Objective analysis of the economy and management skills took second place, with "politics in command."

Development trends

The strategy of spreading industry as widely as possible over the country has given way in the 1980s to a recognition that the coastal cities and provinces are the key to fast development.

Egalitarianism recedes Building up industries province by province coincided with Maoist egalitarian ideas and the ability to conduct a war of attrition against any invader; it also recognized the undeveloped infrastructure for trade between provinces. Although the problem of poor transport and communications remains, in the 1980s fears of invasion have receded, and the prevailing political philosophy tolerates some inequality of wealth, whether of individuals or of regions.

Heavy vs light industry

The first ten years of the People's Republic saw massive investment in heavy industry, with significant Soviet technical assistance. The political upheavals of the Cultural Revolution continued the bias against light industry and consumer goods. Only after Mao Zedong's death in 1976 did consumerism gain some political respectability and light industry catch up with heavy industrial growth.

Consumerism unleashed Deregulation and imports of televisions and other household appliances in 1984–85 have whetted consumer appetite. Deregulation of bicycle prices in 1986 has made Flying Pigeon and other high-quality bicycles more expensive; buying one now depends on the state of one's purse rather than on one's party status.

A socialist market economy

In the 1980s a more pragmatic leadership began to enliven a torpid economy by introducing a "responsibility system" (*zeren zhidu*), which gives rural producers and industry managers more independence. In agriculture, key decisions on what is grown and where it is sold are made by the peasant households.

The flight from collectivism has stimulated market gardening through the "free markets" (*ziyou shichang*), and sales have boomed. Grain production, which is less profitable, has tended to fall victim to the cash crop boom. The government is experimenting with incentive schemes to encourage the planting of grain crops.

Technology transfer

This has become the watchword of China's foreign trade policy. Whatever the product, project or service, the Chinese side will be looking for a boost to their own technical know-how. Training has become an essential part of any significant deal. In some cases, the Chinese are prepared to pay for a manufacturing licence in hard currency, but more often they will look for technology acquisition through joint ventures with foreigners, to minimize their own foreign exchange input. Ambitious plant managers lobby the Planning Commission and sponsoring departments to be included on the approved technology import list.

Ageing equipment A survey of 8,000 large plants in 1985 showed that 30% of their equipment dated from the 1950s and 1960s, 40% from the 1970s and 30% from the 1980s. In local and small enterprises, equipment is generally much older.

Indigenous technology

Technical competence varies enormously. Although 18% of spinning frames date from before 1949, in some fields China has technology and facilities to match any in the world. China's carrier rockets, which are now being backed by European and US agencies, are an entirely indigenous product. China is one of the five countries with developed nuclear weapons.

Research and development is usually funded and directed not by industry but by ministries or the Chinese Academy of Sciences under the overall supervision of the State Science and Technology Commission. Three-quarters of large plants have no R&D departments. Plans are underway to merge 80% of all research institutes with plants by 1990. There are incentive schemes to reward innovation.

Quality

Quality control has hitherto not been important to management or work force and output has been judged by quantity targets alone. It is not unusual for half of a factory's output to be defective; customers expect to give a brand-new car, bicycle or radio to a mechanic before it will work effectively. One vendor of transistor radios in Guangzhou enticed customers with what was apparently an unusual proposition: if a radio went wrong within a given period, it would be replaced.

Packaging and protection of products for distribution within China is often poor, although goods for export are generally well protected. Plants rarely give consideration to what happens to the product once it leaves the factory.

Export drive

China's sheer size means that most agricultural and industrial development remains focused on the domestic market. Although output of most products still falls short of domestic requirements, the government has been determined to maximize exports in order to pay for technology imports needed for development.

Incentives Large plants have been encouraged to export through incentive schemes which allow them to retain and use a proportion of the foreign exchange they earn. When the planners have their way, it is the exporting industries that are given hard currency to buy foreign equipment and technology.

Decentralization has given factories considerable choice in where their produce is sold, and those that have been allowed to keep only a small proportion of the foreign exchange they generate have been unwilling to export. It is far easier to sell to an uncompetitive and unsatisfied domestic market rather than to the competitive markets of South-East Asia and beyond.

The role of foreign investors Great expectations of the domestic market are the main lure for foreign investors in China. The Chinese government, on the other hand, has looked to foreign investors to regenerate Chinese export industries and to bring in technology.

Control of industry

"Once loosened there is chaos; once brought together there is paralysis." This Chinese proverb expresses the dilemma of maintaining central control while fostering local initiative.

Local autonomy Decentralization has encouraged local authorities to build up local industry faster than the central planners would like; investment funds and materials for projects with local and short-term benefits have grown much faster than funds for the major infrastructural and energy projects deemed by the central government to be vital to national development. Provincial loyalty and pride are strong.

Competition between provinces is also evident in technology import, with local authorities willing to buy foreign technology regardless of whether this leads to duplication on a national level. Uncoordinated imports of plastics machinery, for example, have resulted in severe over-capacity.

Ministry kingdoms Despite a degree of decentralization, the ministries in Beijing responsible for the major industrial sectors have fought to retain their power. The slogan of the anti-establishment youth rallies of the 1960s, calling the ministries "independent kingdoms," still has a certain amount of justification.

Too self-sufficient Each sectoral ministry (such as coal, textiles or agriculture) has under its ultimate control the main plants, research institutes and import-export corporations in its sector. The ministry systems have tended to be self-sufficient, with little interchange of equipment or technology. The Ministry of the Textiles Industry produces textiles machinery itself. Chinese factories usually manufacture their own components, with resulting inefficiencies.

One at a time The compartmentalized ministry structures make any deal involving more than one ministry virtually impossible. This generally rules out countertrade, even though it is superficially attractive to Chinese agencies short of foreign exchange.

Top body The only effective coordination of the activities of the ministerial "kingdoms" is at the top. The State Planning Commission draws up five- and ten-year plans in consultation with the ministries and oversees implementation of the plans on an annual basis. The support of the two commissions is essential for any major project.

Leading Groups Complementing the formal mechanisms of the commissions are the State Council Leading Groups, which exist for electronics, foreign investment, large projects and other key areas. They bring together the vice-ministers of the ministries concerned, usually under the chairmanship of a vice-premier.

Sectoral associations have been established to coordinate activities in particular industries. The Food Industry Association aims to avoid duplication in imported technology and other areas – a difficult task for an industry that is spread among three ministries (light industry, commerce and agriculture). Real conflicts can be resolved only by the Leading Groups.

Trading corporations The major trading corporations are closely identified with their sponsoring ministries, and there is a considerable overlap of personnel. The president of the Import/Export corporation may be the relevant minister or vice-minister. Although it may not always be apparent, the corporations have their own house styles and cultures, reinforced by the custom of working in the same organization for a lifetime.

Competitive selling Reforms since 1978 have increased the number of foreign trade bodies licensed by the Ministry of Foreign Economic Relations and Trade (MOFERT) from barely a dozen to over a thousand. Although most business is handled by the top dozen, the proliferation of trading organizations has added an element of competition. Branches of the corporations have disregarded the national interest, undercutting each other in foreign sales (especially of metals), depressing world prices and undermining the national effort.

State and township Of China's 460,000 industrial enterprises, 94,000 are owned by the state; the remainder are Sino-foreign ventures, or collectively or privately owned. State enterprises produced 70% of Chinese industrial output (by value) in 1986. While the state-owned share of output is falling, township and rural enterprises have grown fast in the 1980s. Locally run enterprises have proved flexible and effective in producing building materials and light industrial products for local consumption, as well as offering repairs, spares and servicing which the state-run plants ignore.

Management

Factory managers have gained increasing independence and responsibility in the 1980s. Under the totally planned system, raw materials and funds were allocated to an enterprise, and the factory's responsibility was to produce the quantity of goods specified. Sales of the factory's products were the responsibility of distributors under the Ministry of Commerce.

This uniform system gave way in the mid-1980s to a patchwork of different forms of deregulation affecting state-owned plants.

Free to decide By 1986 some 28,000 of the 54,000 larger state enterprises were run by managers who had signed fixed-term contracts which gave them the power to take management decisions, including the power to hire and fire, without having to seek prior permission from the bureaucracy, the Party or the unions. In return, the manager is responsible for achieving specific

output and profit targets within a specified period.

Many managers can exercise choice in the suppliers of their raw materials (40% of raw materials are no longer at prices fixed by the state), while the number of products distributed exclusively by the state commercial network had, by 1986, been reduced from 256 to 20.

Profit retention Factories have been permitted to retain up to 25% of net profits for reinvestment and other purposes, though what profit consists of is subject to negotiation.

Product update There is also scope for managers to redesign outmoded products to appeal to more discriminating consumers and to introduce new products outside the plan.

Back door The "back door" (*houmen*) method of cultivating contacts by giving lavish dinners and gifts, or arranging jobs for relatives, has been the only way for managers to bypass the inefficiencies of bureaucratic control of industry. Liberalizing factory management may reduce the need for such informal business arrangements, but having the right connections (*guanxi*) will remain essential as long as materials, power and transport are in short supply.

The Party's over Day-to-day control (but not ultimate authority) over business decisions has now been removed from Communist Party officials; party cadres still have offices in all but the smallest companies though their concerns, at least in theory, are restricted to social and moral issues. Ideology and management are supposedly separated. However, it is usual for a manager to show deference to those whose positions in the party give them seniority.

Educating managers has a high priority. A 1985 survey by the Office of the Industrial Census showed that only 11% of managers in China's 8,000 large enterprises had university or other degrees.

Manufacturing and processing

Chinese industry underwent major renovation during the 1950s under an extensive programme of technology transfer from the Soviet Union. Since the 1970s, China has turned to the West to remodernize its industries through the purchase of key equipment and know-how, and foreign investment, especially in joint ventures.

Household goods

The purchase of consumer goods has rocketed in the 1980s. Political restraints on individual ownership of the 1960s and 1970s have given way to gleeful materialism. Output of consumer goods has leapt up, but demand has become more sophisticated, as Chinese consumers look for a level of quality and design which is rare in the local product.

Bicycles China is famous for the number of its bicycles: there are over 250m of them. Despite production of 35m bicycles a year, many models are overstocked while Flying Pigeon and other superior brands are keenly sought. Light motorcycles have begun to replace the pedal cycle as an outlet for consumer spending and as a status symbol.

Foreign preferred A foreign name on a product increases its status value. Youths wearing foreign sunglasses prefer the manufacturer's label to be prominent. Brand-name video recorders and televisions are expected from relatives visiting from overseas. While demand for expensive Japanese watches remains strong, as many as 10m locally-produced watches remained unsold in 1987.

Ceramics China first taught Europe the finer ceramic arts. Porcelain and household pottery exports, worth $150m in 1986, are still important. Most export ware follows traditional styles and is often produced at large plants at centres with centuries of expertise, such as Jingdezhen in Jiangxi. In the 1980s, it has been necessary to import technology from the West.

Textiles

Although China is the world's largest producer and exporter of textiles, its potential in this industry is hampered by several factors. Output is restricted by the amount of raw material produced, necessitating imports, and increased exports are hampered by rising domestic demand and quota restrictions by major importers of Chinese textiles.

Cotton China is the world's largest producer of cotton, which accounts for 80% of its textile output. Cotton is grown throughout central China (the bulk of it being processed in Shanghai) but is supplemented with imports. The domestic demand for cotton clothes, although still not satisfied, is being undercut by the convenience of synthetic fibre. Cotton cloth is no longer rationed.

Silk Buoyant demand for silk in overseas markets keeps most of the annual silk output of 45,000 tonnes/49,600 US tons earmarked for export. China holds 90% of the world market for raw silk, and is attempting to undertake more processing itself to increase its 40% share of the finished silk market. Silk production is centred on Jiangsu, Zhejiang and Shanghai.

Wool, produced mainly in the herding lands of the northwest, has become increasingly important, especially for export. Spinning mills have been developed, not only in the major centres of Shanghai and Tianjin, but also inland, where the sheep are reared.

Synthetic fibre production is rising, although the need for imports remains. Production is based on both cellulose (from wood pulp and cotton waste) and polymers (from petroleum). Production capacity continues to increase.

Machinery import Although factories under the Ministry of the

Textiles Industry can produce spinning and other machinery for initial processing, there is a continuing demand for the import of more specialized finishing machines.

More finished products US and European restrictions on the quantity of textile imports mean that an increase in the value of Chinese textile exports depends largely on improving the quality and degree of processing of the product.

Design in the Chinese fabrics and clothing industry is rudimentary; few plants are prepared to alter the design and cut of garments at the speed required by the fashion industry.

Fashion shows and seminars by Western designers are fostering a more market-oriented design awareness in producing clothes for export. At the same time, the home market is changing, especially in style-conscious Shanghai. Standing out from the crowd was considered anti-social, even anti-socialist, during the Cultural Revolution. Now, dressmaking and fashion magazines feed the desire of young Chinese women to look distinctive. The faded blue cotton "Mao suit" (*zhongshan*) has given way, at least during the summer, to brightly patterned dresses, yellow polka dot skirts and synthetic-dye tops, even in some rural areas.

Jumping the quota

Decentralization in the export of textiles resulted in shipments in excess of the agreed quota arriving at US ports in 1987. Once quotas under bilateral treaties are agreed, it is the responsibility of MOFERT to allocate shipments to match the quota. Poor management was the reason behind some of the extra shipments, but a large number of forged papers were also in circulation. When US customs threatened to impound the extra goods, MOFERT, wary of losing its $2,600m textile market in the USA, announced it would impose tighter control on the issue of permits.

Vehicles

Demand for vehicles has rocketed with industrial growth and the influx of foreign tourists and business people. Shortfall in output from Chinese factories of 360,000 vehicles in 1986 was partially made up with the import of 150,000 vehicles.

Light trucks wanted The proliferation of new small businesses has played a major part in the rise in demand for light trucks. Chinese plants have been slow to respond to increased requirements.

Status While 300,000 vehicles are owned by individuals or private businesses, most belong to government organizations and state or collective enterprises. Having access to a car, especially a foreign model, is an important measure of status. Whereas Red Flag limousines have always been associated with the top leadership, the China International Trust and Investment Corporation (CITIC), China's equivalent of a merchant bank, boasts a fleet of Cadillacs.

Import boom Vehicles accounted for a substantial portion of the import boom which triggered a trade deficit, especially with Japan, in the mid-1980s. Since 1985, importing of vehicles has been restricted to a few licensed dealers.

Default on duty A leading part in the vehicles import boom was played by Hainan Island in the south. In 1984, it was granted the right to import trucks and other goods duty-free to accelerate development on the island. But organizations ranging from kindergartens to the local newspaper joined in a racket which imported 89,000 trucks and minibuses and 120,000 motorcycles. Over a period of 18 months the vehicles were sold to eager customers throughout China, netting the island a large profit until the central authorities stamped on this entrepreneurial initiative.

Foreign technology Joint ventures, together with technology imports, have been part of the government strategy to reduce the need for imports. Volkswagen's sedan venture in Shanghai, AMC's plant for jeep production in Beijing, and Peugeot's station wagons in Guangzhou are the main examples of joint ventures in the automotive industry.

For the home market Vehicles are produced mainly for the domestic market. Uneven quality makes the export of vehicles – like many other China-produced goods – difficult in a sophisticated and saturated world market.

Still on the road The automotive industry was established with Soviet assistance in the 1950s, and until the 1980s it produced versions of Soviet vehicles, themselves an echo of the standard American designs from the 1940s. The pastel-painted Shanghai sedan and bottle-green Liberation truck still provide adequate if unsophisticated service; they are cheaper to maintain and easier to repair than imported models.

Fragmented The industry is huge, employing more than a million people, and is also fragmented, with a total of 2,500 plants. Larger plants include the First Auto Works in Changchun (Jilin) and the Second Auto Works in Shiyan (Hubei).

Coordination of the industry has been a major concern. The China National Auto Industry Corporation (CNAIC) was established in 1982 to build up a coherent structure, at least for those parts of the industry under the sponsorship of the then Ministry of Machine Building. One of its most important functions was to examine technology-import requests to avoid duplication. The corporation was revamped as the China National Automotive Industry Federation (retaining the initials CNAIC) in 1987, and now also covers factories under local control.

Military output, civilian vehicles In the past few years military plants have turned to the lucrative civilian vehicle market. Harmonization of civilian and military vehicle production was the aim in the merger

of the Ministry of Machine Building and the Ministry of Ordnance to form in 1987 the State Commission for the Machine Building Industry (subsequently expanded to become the Ministry of Machinery and Electronics).

Aeolus The Aeolus Automotive Industry Import/Export Corporation, based on the Second Auto Works in Shiyan, is a new type of company in China: the conglomerate. The corporation, which produces one-fifth of China's vehicles, has been able to rationalize and specialize production in the 170 plants it controls, ending the inefficient practice of each plant making its own components.

Aircraft

The aerospace industry is extensive and has produced 10,000 aircraft over the last 30 years. Factories under the Ministry of Aviation and Space (MAS) have developed a range of military aircraft derived from Soviet originals, notably the J-8 Fighter, as well as smaller civilian aircraft.

Exports The 17-seat Y-12 transport, named the Turbo-Panda, became in 1986 the first Chinese aircraft to be sold abroad. While CAAC continues to buy most of its passenger aircraft from the USA and Europe, the ministry is looking to foreign companies to coproduce aircraft in the long term. In 1987 the CAAC took delivery of the first McDonnell-Douglas MD-82 airliner, produced from mainly imported parts.

Shipbuilding

Although shipyards in many countries are closing down, China's industry continues to expand. China was the third largest shipbuilder in 1986 (after Japan and South Korea). Major yards of the China State Shipbuilding Corporation (CSSC) are located in Shanghai, Dalian, Tianjin and Guangzhou.

Exported ships include bulk carriers, container and roll-on, roll-off (ro-ro) vessels and oil tankers.

Armaments

China has sold an estimated $1bn of arms abroad since ideology was relaxed in the late 1970s to permit sales of weapons with some independence from foreign policy. China ranked fifth in the arms export league table in 1987, after the USA, the Soviet Union, Britain and France.

Many of the weapons are sold to allies: Thailand has bought a large number of T-62 light tanks, Brazil several F7M fighters and Iran several batteries of surface-to-sea Silkworm missiles.

China is importing technology to upgrade weapons production, chiefly for export.

Food industry

With one-fifth of the world's population, China is fortunate to be largely self-sufficient in food. The food industry is expanding rapidly as living standards rise, and there is potential for increased food exports, which face few of the quotas which entangle exports.

Growing appetite With around 60% of average income spent on food, increased prosperity has stimulated demand for food products. Growth is especially fast in meat and eggs, children's food, beer and canned food.

Control The industry is spread among three ministries: those of light industry, commerce and agriculture. There is considerable overlap of products and competition to set up new projects, but the China National Food Industry Association, set up to coordinate activities, has yet to show that it can arbitrate between the giants.

In the can Spoilage of food is a major problem, so there is now heavy investment in processing and preserving. Processing and packaging equipment is being imported in large quantities to improve shelf-life of food and also to increase exports. In 1986, 450,000 tonnes/496,000 US tons of canned food were exported.

Joint ventures The food industry remains an attractive one for foreign involvement, since many of China's agricultural products have an export potential. Dynasty wine, produced by Rémy Martin in Tianjin, is perhaps the most famous Sino-foreign joint venture product in China; until recently the only significant dry table wine readily available, it has become a standard for Westerners in China.

Fast food has excited many Chinese city-dwellers, who see in the exotic hamburger a novelty lacking in the traditional street-corner dumpling stalls. Kentucky Fried Chicken, which now has an outlet in Beijing, McDonald's and Pizza Hut have been closely eyeing the trail set by Coca-Cola and Pepsi in their quest for the Chinese consumer.

Output of selected light industrial products (m units)

	1980	1981	1982	1983	1984	1985	1986
Bicycles	13.0	17.5	24.2	27.6	28.6	32.4	35.7
Sewing machines	7.7	10.4	12.7	10.8	9.3	9.9	9.9
Radios	30.0	40.6	17.2	20.0	21.9	15.7	–
Television sets	2.5	5.4	5.9	6.8	10.0	16.2	14.5
Wristwatches	22.2	29.1	33.0	34.7	36.4	41.7	64.5
Refrigerators	–	–	–	0.19	0.54	1.4	2.2
Washing machines	0.2	1.3	2.5	3.7	5.8	8.8	9.0
Cotton cloth (bn metres)	13.5	14.3	15.4	14.9	13.4	14.3	15.8

Source: State Statistical Bureau; Statistical Yearbook of China

Energy

Exploitation of energy resources is a high priority for the government and will remain so for the foreseeable future. A persistent shortfall in electricity generation disrupts and restrains development by making plants idle for up to two days a week.

Coal

Coal is still king in terms of both production and consumption of energy in China. It accounted for 73% of energy consumption in 1985. Oil is second, with 21%, followed by hydropower (5%). Most of China's energy production is for domestic use: only 1% of total production was exported in 1987. Inability to increase oil exports to finance development plans has reinforced the need to boost coal exports, which were projected to increase by 62% in 1987 (to 16m tonnes/17.6m US tons). The China National Coal Import/Export Corporation is the main vehicle for the export of Chinese coal.

Key areas In the northeast there are major mining areas in Heilongjiang, Inner Mongolia, Liaoning and Hebei; individual coalfields produce over 10m tonnes/11m US tons a year. The development of Huolinhe, an open-cast mine with a capacity of 20m tonnes/22m US tons, is being financed by West Germany. The Kailuan Mine, developed by British mining engineers in the 19th century, was China's major coal mining region until the earthquake at Tangshan in 1976 devasted the area. The other major mines are in Shandong, Jiangsu and Anhui, all in the east, and in Shanxi and Henan, in west-central China. Datong, in Shanxi, is the biggest producer, at about 28m tonnes/31m US tons a year.

Local mines have produced an increasing proportion of the coal mined since the early 1980s. These mines, which are run by local authorities, collectives or individuals, operate outside the state plan. From a production level of 350m tonnes/386m US tons of coal in 1983 they produced 440m tonnes/485m US tons in 1985 (more than half the national output). Although local initiative has boosted production, it has also led to waste, with up to 80% of recoverable coal lost at some mines. Some of the coal is sold through provincial import/export corporations, but the mines' small scale makes significant purchases of foreign equipment unlikely.

Development strategy China has looked to foreign investment to develop new mines. Occidental Petroleum Corporation of the USA agreed a $650m contract in 1985 to develop China's largest open-cast mine at Antaibao near Pingshuo, in Shanxi. Over 60% of the coal will be exported, but low world prices have reduced the attraction of foreign investment in coal. Japan is financing the development of seven mines to ensure adequate supplies for its own use. In 1985 the World Bank agreed loans totalling $126m for the development of fully mechanized pits.

Improvement of existing mines is the complementary strategy, along with improving transport facilities. It remains cheaper to ship coal to centres in the south such as Guangzhou than to develop mines in the southwest. The Chinese will continue to require foreign equipment to exploit steep and thin seams at existing fields.

Oil and gas

China has been disappointed that its hopes for rapid oil exploitation have not materialized. After it became self-sufficient in the 1960s and an exporter in 1974, its production subsequently stagnated. Foreign companies were invited in 1983 to explore offshore, but they had obtained few positive results by 1987, when they started to withdraw. Since oil accounts for 25% of China's foreign earnings, low world prices in the mid-1980s have dampened any hope of paying for a technology import boom with oil. Nevertheless China remains a major oil producer, ranking fifth in the world in 1986 with an output of 131m tonnes/144m US tons (averaging about 2.5m barrels a day).

The Songliao Basin in the northeast includes China's largest oilfield at Daqing in Heilongjiang province. Daqing's output in 1985 was 385m barrels (earning ¥3bn,. which made it China's most profitable state-owned enterprise). The basin stretches into Liaoning and Jilin provinces. The Liaohe field, in Liaoning, is being developed in a World Bank-financed heavy oil recovery project.

The North China Basin is centred on the Shengli field, China's second largest, with an output in 1986 of 206m barrels. Exploitation at the Renqiu field, in Hebei, began in 1976, but its potentially high output had not been achieved by 1987 because of extraction problems.

The northwest has major deposits in the Karamay and Tarim basins, in Xinjiang, and the Qaidam Basin, in Qinghai province. All three basins have great potential, but problems in transport from the landlocked northwest prevent increased exploitation. One solution would be a 2,000km/1,240-mile pipeline (probably funded by the World Bank) to take oil from Karamay eastwards to the coast.

Offshore In the initial round of offshore oil development in 1984, 20 contracts were signed with foreign operators; in the second round in 1987, only six. The geology of China's continental shelf has proved more complex than originally thought. The Chengbei field, in the Gulf of Bohai, is being jointly developed with a Japanese consortium. The East China Sea off Shanghai has shown some positive results from exploratory drilling; but a territorial dispute with Japan may delay exploitation. The South China Sea is the area most intensively explored by Western companies.

A major gas field has been discovered by Arco off Hainan Island (southwest of Hong Kong). It is planned to pipe the gas onshore and

The Chinese oil corporations
China National Offshore Oil Corporation (CNOOC) Responsible for all offshore oil and gas exploration and exploitation, under the Ministry of Energy.
Bohai Oil Corporation Subsidiary of CNOOC responsible for Bohai Gulf, centred on Tanggu, near Tianjin.
South Huanghai Oil Corporation (SHOC) Subsidiary of CNOOC responsible for the South Yellow Sea, centred on Shanghai.
Nanhai East Oil Corporation (NHEOC) Subsidiary of CNOOC responsible for South China Sea (Nanhai) east of Guangzhou.
Nanhai West Oil Corporation (NHWOC) Subsidiary of CNOOC responsible for South China Sea

west of Guangzhou.
China National Oil Joint Services Corporation (CNOJSC) A joint venture between CNOOC and Guangdong provincial government to provide supply and other services to the offshore operations through a number of subsidiaries.
China Offshore Gas Utilization Corporation (COGUC) Subsidiary of CNOOC.
China National Oil Development Corporation (CNODC) Responsible for onshore cooperation with foreign companies, under the Ministry of Energy.
China National Chemicals Import/Export Corporation (*Sinochem*) Responsible for most of China's oil exports.

to Guangzhou for power generation and domestic use and as feedstock.

Onshore Foreign operators' attention has moved to onshore exploration. Political considerations and patriotic pride have apparently prevented foreign access to the prime onshore sites; those on offer have complex geology or difficult access. In 1986 the Chinese opened ten southern provinces south of the Yangzi to foreign exploration, but Western oil companies, apprehensive of entrenched local interest, have been slow to make any commitment.

Sino-foreign joint ventures for onshore oil development are the responsibility of the China National Oil Development Corporation. In 1985, 19 oil companies were invited to survey for oil in the northwest and southwest. One onshore contract was awarded in 1985, when CSR Orient Oil took on an area on Hainan Island in the South China Sea.

Foreign technology needed Recovery rates, even at China's showplace field, Daqing in the northeast, have been inadequate, and foreign technology and assistance are needed to develop advanced recovery techniques for existing fields and to provide machinery (such as pumps and generators). Technical assistance and seismic and related equipment are required for further prospecting.

Electricity

Although China has the world's fifth-largest generating capacity (445bn kWh generated in 1986), it is not uncommon for Chinese enterprises to lose 20% of production time each year because of power shortages. The unreliability of supply disrupts industrial growth and deters foreign manufacturers from investing in China. Coal is the main source of electricity generation (accounting for 53%), followed by hydropower (31%) and small contributions from oil, gas and renewable sources. Industry takes 80% of the power generated, agriculture 15% and commercial and household users 5%.

Transmission lines needed Because substantial oil development offshore has not materialized, coal and hydropower will continue to be of prime importance. The distance of these resources from the industrial centres on the coast has made development of long-distance transmission lines a priority.

Small is wasteful Most power is distributed through 12 regional and local grids. Lack of interconnection between the grids and the existence of so many small ones mean that the power generated is not efficiently used. There is also a proliferation of small, relatively inefficient plants with a capacity of 50MW or less, which together account for 47% of all electricity generated.

Hydropower untapped Only 5% of a huge hydropower potential (estimated at 680GW) has been harnessed. Large projects have been undertaken at Gezhouba, on the upper Yangzi, on the upper reaches of the Yellow river and on the Hongshui river, in Guangxi. Although many projects are being undertaken without outside help – including the world's biggest dam, upstream from Gezhouba – some are receiving World Bank support and require foreign engineering input.

Nuclear Plans to commission six new nuclear plants in the 1980s have proved too ambitious and expensive, but there are two facilities in operation: at Daya Bay, in Guangdong province and at Qinshan, 80km/50 miles west of Shanghai. The latter is a largely home-produced installation, and China is negotiating sales of this size of reactor to developing countries. The Daya Bay facility, a joint venture between Hong Kong Light and Power and the Guangdong Nuclear Power Corporation, has a planned capacity of 1,800MW.

Renewable resources China is developing solar and wind-generated electricity, especially for remote areas such as Tibet. Small-scale tidal power units are already in use.

Metals and minerals

China has ample reserves of iron ore and most non-ferrous metals and minerals. It exports tungsten, antimony and tin, but a lack of processing facilities means it imports steel, aluminium and other metals.

Steel

Iron ore mining is spread across the country, and steel production is located in a number of centres. Iron and steel plants producing over 1m tonnes/1.1m US tons of crude steel annually include China's largest plant at Anshan (Liaoning).

Low-grade reserves China's extensive reserves of iron ore generally have a low iron content (25–35%). High-grade ore is imported to improve content and make up for production shortages. China imported 13.7m tonnes/15.1m US tons of ore in 1986, mostly from Australia and Brazil. To secure supplies of foreign ore, the China Metallurgical Import/Export Corporation (CMIEZ) took a 40% stake in a mine at Channar, in Western Australia and is buying all the mine's output (5m tonnes/5.5m US tons a year by 1990).

White elephant at work The Baoshan steelworks, 80km/50 miles from Shanghai, was conceived as a showpiece of technology in the late 1970s, but became a byword for an ill-conceived and grandiose project. Apart from the lack of infrastructure to support the plant, it relies almost entirely on imported ore.

Imports Although China is the fourth largest producer of steel (with an output of 53m tonnes/58m US tons in 1987), a construction boom and heady industrial growth necessitate the import of steel, mainly from Japan.

Plant upgrading Increasing efficiency in existing plants is the dominant government strategy. Foreign exchange is being allocated for revamping and expanding plants, and foreign investment is encouraged.

Non-ferrous metals

Exploitation of non-ferrous metals is growing rapidly. Output of a number of metals (including copper, tin, lead, zinc, aluminium, antimony and titanium) was expected to increase by 50% between 1985 and 1990. Export potential ensures allocation of foreign exchange to cover the import of technology and equipment. China has a 40% share of the world market for tungsten, which is found in the Lingnan mountains in the southwest. Recoverable deposits of rare earths, mostly located in Inner Mongolia, are the largest in the world.

The aluminium industry is growing fast. Annual production capacity is expected to double to 10.7m tonnes/11.8m US tons between 1985 and 1990 as some existing refineries are revamped and five new refineries are constructed.

Copper production similarly cannot keep pace with demand. Significant imports of copper are necessary, despite the existence of the world's largest copper ore deposits at Dexing, in Jiangxi.

Metals marketing

Until 1980, the China National Metals and Minerals Import/Export Corporation (Minmetals) handled all metal trading. The new policy of decentralization, adopted in 1980, allowed the Ministry of Metallurgical Industry to set up its own China Metallurgical Import/Export Corporation (CMIEC) to market iron and steel products. The China National Non-ferrous Import/Export Corporation (CNIEC) now markets non-ferrous metals.

Competition between the CNIEC, the CMIEC and provincial branches of corporations to sell tungsten overseas depressed world prices in 1986–87. The China Tungsten Ore and Products Export Association was formed in 1987 to coordinate export prices without re-creating a supply monopoly.

Chemicals

China is the world's largest importer of chemicals. Domestic production of fertilizers and key industrial chemicals cannot keep pace with industrial growth, despite continual increases in output. Western chemicals companies are reluctant to export chemical technology to China, where patent laws cover processes but not products, and pirating is a problem.

Industry profile

Output comes from a few large facilities and a huge number of small, often uneconomic plants. Major chemical industries exist in Shanghai, Tianjin, Dalian and Guangzhou. Petrochemical complexes have grown up on the major oil fields of the northeast (Daqing, Shengli, Dagang) and northwest (Lanzhou) and in the industrial centres of Beijing, Shanghai and Shenyang.

Petrochemicals Domestic oil production laid the basis for the development of a petrochemical industry in the 1960s. Complete plants for cracking and for olefin extraction, for plastics and synthetic fibre manufacture, and for other processes have been bought from the UK, West Germany, France, Japan and the USA. Foreign companies are involved in revamping and extending existing facilities.

Industrial chemicals are produced in large quantities, with annual output of 2.2m tonnes/2.4m US tons caustic soda, 2.5m tonnes/2.8m US tons soda ash and 8.2m tonnes/9m US tons sulphuric acid. However, demand far exceeds supply; soda ash, for example, will need to be imported into the 1990s.

Fertilizer production – at 15m tonnes/16.5m US tons a year, the third highest after the USA and the USSR – remains too low to fuel increasing crop production. China has reserves of phosphates and potassium but insufficient processing capacity.

Pharmaceuticals China is a major exporter of finished drugs to developing countries and of semi-finished drugs to Western companies. Exports reached $209m in 1986.

Control

The Ministry of the Chemicals Industry controls mining of chemical ores and most chemical production. The monopoly of the main trading body for chemicals, Sinochem, was ended in the 1980s with the creation of new corporations to control and market petrochemicals and pharmaceuticals.

Sinochem, the China National Chemicals Import/Export Corporation under the Ministry of Foreign Economic Relations and Trade, is China's oldest trading company, established in 1950, and it remains one of the largest with sales of $3.7bn in 1985. It markets China's oil as well as chemicals, and competes with Sinopec to sell petrochemicals.

Sinopec, the China National Petrochemical Corporation, controls most of the country's refineries and petrochemical plants. It reports directly to the State Council. Its wholly owned subsidiary, the China Petrochemical International Company, handles import and export of petrochemicals, plant and technology.

The China National Chemical Construction Corporation, under the Ministry of the Chemicals Industry, imports and exports equipment and technology for chemical plants.

The China National Medicine and Health Products Import Export Corporation (MEHECOS), set up in 1984, buys and sells pharmaceuticals. It answers to the state Pharmaceutical Bureau, a body directly under the State Council.

Service industries

The party's fixation on production statistics meant that until the 1980s tourism, advertising and other services were neglected, if not despised. Developing this area of the economy has now become a government priority, however.

Tourism

The Great Wall and the clay warriors of Xian have become standard attractions in the world's tourist brochures. Foreign exchange earnings of $1.5bn in 1986 from tourism have made the government take the industry seriously. A leading group on tourism has been set up under the State Council to plan tourist development.

Overseas Chinese In addition to the 1.5m foreign tourists who visited China in 1986, perhaps ten times that number of Chinese visitors arrived from Hong Kong and other Chinese centres abroad. Chinese tourists are usually visiting relatives, and bring with them household goods and hard currency as gifts.

Hotel construction has been rapid in the 1980s in response to the rise in business and tourist visitors. The major chains – including Hilton, Holiday Inn, Hyatt and Sheraton – have now moved into China. Built to accommodate guests paying hard currency, the joint-venture hotels have shown better potential for repatriating profit than have manufacturing ventures.

Special-interest groups and individual travellers are now allowed into China. Cycling and hiking tours are possible, and most of China's cities and towns are now open to foreigners. Only for a few towns must the time-consuming application for a special permit from the Public Security Bureau be made. Obtaining a tourist visa to enter the country has become a formality.

Tourist agencies Most tours are handled by the big national agencies (China Travel Service and China International Travel Service), but local and smaller agencies compete for business. Although the smaller agencies may be efficient in their own locality, they can be ineffective in making arrangements elsewhere.

Advertising

Roadside billboards, long confined to exhortations and worthy slogans ("Make Revolution, Increase Production!" "Long Live Mao Zedong Thought!") have been converted in the 1980s to promote cosmetics, watches and other consumer goods.

Growth in the advertising industry has been fast. Since it re-emerged in 1979, the industry has expanded by as much as 50% a year. Chinese companies spend a total of up to $200m a year on making their products known. Advertising has become essential as factories compete for customers.

Foreign products account for only 6% of advertising in China. Advertising successes include Seiko, which began to advertise its watches long before it was permitted to sell to Chinese customers.

Insurance

Insurance of business and personal property, halted during the Cultural Revolution, was permitted again in 1980. Since then the People's Insurance Company of China (PICC) has enjoyed fast growth in insurance policies for factories and peasant households – a trend encouraged by the government. Factories accounted for over 95% of the ¥250bn insurance provided in 1984, but by 1985 5m Chinese had taken out life insurance policies. PICC continues its main business of coverage for trade and joint ventures. It is linked to the international reinsurance network, contracting on its liabilities and taking on those of others.

The Business Scene

Official policies

The Chinese authorities are directing their efforts towards the overall goals of raising living standards and increasing efficiency. But holding on to socialist planning while trying to move towards a market economy has led to numerous problems, causing policies to alternate between promoting decentralization and reclaiming central control.

Reforming the system

Under the old system, enterprises leaned on the state for their livelihood and workers leaned on the enterprises which employed them. The state set production targets and provided raw materials, energy, working and capital funds, and interest-free loans. Morale of workers was low, products were of poor quality and growth rates minimal in sectors such as consumer goods and high technology.

The responsibility system, introduced in the rural sector in the early 1980s, was enough of a success to prompt the October 1984 Central Committee "Decision on Economic Reforms," which focused on the large state industrial enterprises.

Enterprise management Enterprises are required gradually to become independent economic entities. They can reserve and use part of their profits, which are now taxed instead of being handed over to the state.

Factory directors have gained a higher profile with the attempts to separate party activity and enterprise administration. State Council Directives published January 1987 defined the roles of factory directors, the party, and workers' congresses in state enterprises. The factory director is to take the lead and has the final decision over the management committee.

Less interference Government involvement in industry is now confined to planning at the macro level, leaving enterprises to pursue the micro level business of actual production.

Less planning The number of goods under "mandatory planning" has been reduced from 120 to 60. Many others are subject to "guidance planning." State resources are directed to supporting heavy industry, energy and raw materials, transport and communications; local funds go mostly into agriculture, textiles, light industry and commerce.

Price control presents an obstacle to overall reform. However, the October 1984 Decision began to chisel away at China's system of artificial prices and compensating subsidies, with a new three-tier price system: fixed state prices for priority products such as steel; free-floating prices for products in plentiful supply; and a system whereby prices are fixed up to a certain level of production, and the free market dictates the value of the surplus.

Obstacles and setbacks Price reform has proved difficult. Fears of inflation, popular opposition to rising living costs, ideological sensitivity, and recognition of the knock-on effects of decontrol have caused the more radical reforms to be postponed indefinitely. Nor have factory directors enjoyed as much autonomy as was envisaged.

Slowing the pace Disturbed by the symptoms in 1985–86 of an economy out of control, the state has slowed the pace of reform. In 1987 ¥12bn-worth of treasury bonds were issued to soak up extra-budgetary funds and bring investment back into line, and bank credit has been tightened. More emphasis is now placed on rational resource allocation and the use of feasibility studies. The 1986 bankruptcy law, which would have removed state support to ailing industries, has proved too radical and is unlikely to be exercised in the near future. Private businesses are hindered by a lack of legal protection, egalitarian ideology, bureaucratic interference and high taxes.

Foreign trade policies
In 1979 a retention system for foreign exchange was introduced, whereby the provincial authorities could retain a fixed percentage of foreign exchange earned by their exports. Using these funds to import outside the normal channels soon led to uncontrolled imports. Import and export licences were reintroduced in 1980, followed by a dual exchange rate system, which effectively subsidized exports and penalized imports. Further reforms in 1984 gave the end-user foreign trade enterprises more independence for import/export business, while requiring them to cover their own profits and losses.
Agents An agency system was also introduced, theoretically enabling every enterprise to trade through an agent. Direct control over foreign trade drained away from the Ministry of Foreign Economic Relations and Trade (MOFERT) and the other ministries to a multitude of new organizations.
Reverse gear The overvalued renminbi and high domestic prices led to a preference by enterprises for selling on the domestic market and an inflated import bill. In 1985 subsidies for foreign trade were reintroduced and centralization under MOFERT was strengthened via an expanded export/import licence system. The renminbi was devalued to help shrink the trade deficit and reduce the level of subsidies.
Recent changes In February 1987 MOFERT established a centralized quota system for all exports to Hong Kong and Macao, including those goods to be re-exported. Under this system all major export items would be subject to central control of prices and volumes. MOFERT again tightened its control over import/export corporations in 1989, in an attempt to bring trade back under central control and conserve foreign exchange.

Attitudes to technology
At least half of current plant and equipment dates from the 1950s. For years the Chinese merely copied whatever came their way; innovation was not part of the culture.
Technology transfer Cutbacks in 1981 led to a move away from expensive turnkey purchases of plant and equipment towards technology transfer as a means of raising China's indigenous production capacity. Problems of indiscriminate purchases, duplication and inability to integrate technology with existing production have led recently to greater selectivity – a focus on "key technologies" and the import of software and management skills in tandem with technology. It has, however, proved difficult to change the prevalent conception of technology as hardware and the emphasis on performance, which encourages short-termism rather than rational investment.

Foreign investment policy
The "open door" policies were instituted in 1979 as the best way to import foreign equipment and technology and at the same time save precious foreign exchange. However, only 50% of equity and contractual joint ventures and wholly foreign-owned enterprise projects approved by MOFERT in 1979–86 are in operation and most are in the light industrial or service sectors. Hong Kong and overseas Chinese account for around 60% of investments, and the average value of these investments is very low; Western and Japanese investors have not been very enthusiastic, despite the introduction of more incentives.

Power in business

Pinpointing where power lies in the Chinese business scene is like attempting to hit a moving target. Opaque and ambiguous, power relationships are founded on status and on command of strategic resources; personal wealth plays nowhere near the role it does in a non-socialist society. Power battles are fought between members of the bureaucracy, often behind closed doors. The puzzle is complicated further by the coexistence of power networks at national, provincial and local levels, and by the highly significant but barely discernible roles played by the Party and by ideology.

The ministries

Industrial ministries under the State Council dominate economic power. There are 20 of them. The most important are agriculture; animal husbandry and fishery; aviation and space industry; chemical industry; energy (which has replaced the separate ministries for the coal and petroleum industries); communications; foreign economic relations and trade (MOFERT); light industry; machinery and electronics;metallurgical industry; textiles; and posts and telecommunications.

The ministries have been confined more to planning and administrative duties in recent years, while the enterprises they oversee have been given more independence in daily production. Ministries are often split into departments, and sometimes into separate corporations, responsible for particular sectors of the industry – the Ministry of Light Industry, for example, has a separate corporation dealing with plastics production. A ministry will frequently be involved in negotiations on import or investment projects, and it or its subsidiary may take equity in a joint venture.

The commissions

Eight commissions also come under the State Council, the most powerful probably being that for restructuring the economic system, which is the initiator and final arbitrator on major economic policy changes. Also extremely powerful is the state planning commission, responsible for five-year and longer economic plans. The Scientific and Technological Commission has also been able to exert great influence on technology policy decisions.

Financial institutions

The financial lobby is another factor to consider, especially as the monopoly of the Bank of China is being broken by powerful new organizations such as China International Trust and Investment Corporation (CITIC). The bank's monopoly over import letters of credit has been broken recently by the Guangdong ITIC and SITCO (see *The banks* and *Other financial institutions*).

Provincial power

The network of local power is difficult to unravel. Central ministries have their provincial bureau counterparts, as do their foreign trade corporations, the MOFERT foreign trade corporations, provincial level planning and economic planning commissions and the financial organizations. In addition there are specifically provincial or local corporations, such as the Changjiang Corporation in Sichuan province, provincial or municipal international trust and investment corporations. The structure of provincial political power is also complex.

The provincial governor and the city mayors are powerful people, and in large cities there may be several deputy mayors responsible for particular sectors.

Some local autonomy The richer the province, the more powerful it is; and with greater resources and more foreign exchange retained from their greater exports, the coastal provinces carry greater weight than the hinterland. Similarly the major municipalities of Beijing, Tianjin and Shanghai have a great deal of autonomy and are able to approve projects involving foreign investment worth up to $30m; Dalian, Guangdong, Fujian and Liaoning have a ceiling of $10m. All provinces can approve projects up to $5m, but in practice the state will be involved in most decisions, especially those which affect strategic inputs or outputs.

Powerful giants Individual enterprises can also carry a lot of weight. Large strategic plants, such as the Anshan Iron and Steel Company, have a considerable degree of production and trade independence.

External trade corporations
Foreign trade is an important factor in the power game. The core of the

---

MOFERT's subsidiary corporations

The main MOFERT import/export corporations are:
Ceroils (China National Cereals, Oils and Foodstuffs Import/Export Corporation)
Chintuhsu (native produce and animal by-products)
Chinatex (textiles)
Light Industrial
Arts and Crafts
Sinochem (chemicals)
Minmetals (metals and minerals)
Machimpex (machinery)
Instrimpex (instruments)
Techimport (plant)
Sinopac (packaging)
Sinotrans (foreign trade transport)
Sinochart (chartering)

---

system is the Ministry of Foreign Economic Relations and Trade (MOFERT) and its subsidiary corporations. In addition there are the foreign trade corporations established by other ministries, such as the China State Shipbuilding Corporation, the China National Offshore Oil Corporation and the China Silk Corporation.

Power to approve projects
The approval process for projects is often the most tangible demonstration to the foreign investor of power relationships in China. According to project size, the State Planning Commission or the Provincial Planning Commission approves projects before serious negotiations begin. The approval of MOFERT's Foreign Investment Commission or the provincial Foreign Economic Relations and Trade Commission (FERTC) is also essential, and both of these bodies and the planning commissions review feasibility studies. MOFERT and the FERTC approve both the final contract and the joint venture's articles of association. They are also responsible for coordinating other bodies, such as the materials supply, labour, tax and customs authorities, and relevant industrial ministries and their corporations, all of which must approve the project. The difficulty of obtaining approvals from perhaps 30 different organizations is a striking demonstration of the negative effects of China's complex power structure.

Power relationships
The balance of power fluctuates according to policy trends and personalities. The military has been made leaner and fitter, but is still influential. With recent decentralization, economic organizations have proliferated, and it is exceedingly difficult to discover just who has the authority to make decisions. The power positions of individuals can also be disguised by their job-titles.

49

Employment

Founded upon an ideology that exalts labour, China is trying to escape from the low productivity which this view has led to. The current regime is attempting to avoid the rigid egalitarianism of the Mao years and yet preserve social equality. At the same time, its efforts to raise efficiency and increase the level of mechanization are hindered by the need to employ a huge and expanding population.

The work force

The working population in 1985 numbered 499m out of a total population of over 1bn. Of this, 62.5% were employed in agriculture and forestry; 16.7% in industry; 4.4% in construction and resources prospecting; 2.5% in transport, posts and telecommunications; 4.7% in commerce, catering, services, materials supply and marketing; 9.2% in other areas. Unemployment is known to be a problem, although figures are unobtainable. Underemployment is certainly rife.

Lack of skills Great efforts are now being made to train a skilled work force, but the virtual abolition of education during the Cultural Revolution and the drift of population from rural areas to the cities have led to a large floating population of unskilled labour.

Motivation needed Poor quality has characterized the work force. A long and sustained fall in real wages after 1964 and the abolition during the Cultural Revolution of incentive pay, labour management and supervision systems, led to a severe decline in motivation.

Jobs for life From cradle to grave, most factory workers in China look to the plant management for subsidized accommodation, medical treatment and childcare facilities. The life of an individual revolves around his or her unit (*danwei*).

When a man retires his job will usually pass to his son. Very often husband and wife work in the same plant. There is little job mobility. Some of the few job changes that do happen are achieved through handwritten notices pasted up near railway stations and other public places. Employees may transfer to a job elsewhere only with the permission of their unit. This has been a contentious issue in operating joint ventures, since Chinese enterprises are unwilling to permit able staff to leave.

No laying off It remains politically unacceptable for managers to dismiss staff to increase efficiency; reduction in manpower requirements is not a selling point in China. Factory and office workers expect a job for life, and competition, competence and efficiency are, to most Chinese people, new and foreign ideas. However, an increasing number of workers are now being hired on fixed contracts, renewable only after assessment of performance work.

Reforms Wage increases and links between pay and performance were restored post-Mao, and after 1979 larger enterprises were allowed to retain a percentage of their above-target profits for a wage-bonus fund. Absenteeism, theft and other symptoms of low morale have diminished, but productivity has been slow to improve.

Wage demands Disputes over wages have increased as living standards and the appetite for consumer goods have risen. Chinese enterprises still play a role as providers of social services and pressure on managers in enterprises to give bonuses has resulted in a large slice of post-target profits being allocated to such demands, rather than to investment in productive assets.

Despite the recent reforms, the authorities have little experience in handling labour relations.

Wages and conditions

The wage system divides into three parts: generally 70% is in the form of basic wages, 15% in bonuses, 15% in subsidies. State-owned enterprises also pay for labour insurance and welfare benefits, and the state subsidizes living costs by charging under cost price for some foods, housing and services.

The average annual wage in state enterprises in 1985 was ¥1,166, with an average annual increase in real wages between 1979 and 1984 of 8.2%. Urban wages have risen much faster than those in rural areas. The system distinguishes between workers (*gongren*) and staff (*zhigong*). A structural wage system is gradually being introduced, whereby wages are divided into basic pay, occupational pay and variable allowances. Piece rates are also becoming more common, as is the system of floating wages, whereby a given percentage of wages may vary with profits, output or other economic indices.

The working week is generally six days, 7–8 hours a day for blue collar workers and five and a half days for office staff. Sundays are free, and there are seven statutory holidays – January 1, three days at Spring Festival (late January or February), May 1 (Labour Day), and October 1–2 (National Day).

Labour unions

The main concern of trade unions in China is social welfare. It has been rare for workers in China to strike, although there have been some examples in Sino-foreign joint ventures. Key figures in unions and management meet on the ultimate decision-making panel, the Party committee. A single union exists in each factory or institution. The union organizes sick leave, retirement pensions and other benefits, as well as acting as marriage guidance counsellor. The union also arranges the sale of scarce commodities, from refrigerators to fresh vegetables at the work-place.

Points for the foreign investor

Foreign investors should in theory find cheap labour an incentive to invest in China. In practice, however, inflated wages and low productivity militate against this.

Cost of labour Chinese workers in joint ventures legally receive 120–150% of the average salaries state employees earn for the same job in the same locality. Bonuses, welfare and other additional payments are made out of the relevant funds remaining from post-tax profits. Joint ventures also pay for social insurance and other state subsidies at a higher rate than state enterprises, and may also be subject to local charges.

Chinese management is awarded the same, or nearly the same, level of salary as expatriate management. This has caused much grievance among investors, since the Chinese side is often less experienced and skilled. There are signs that some areas in China may now be making concessions on this subject.

Outside interference Joint ventures can in theory hire and fire, but in practice are often forced to go through the local labour bureau, which can lead either to shortages of skilled labour or to overstaffing and higher costs. The venture cannot always pay employees directly, which makes it difficult to establish an incentive structure. Another serious problem is the arbitrary transfer of trained employees away from the venture. The Party appears to play a backstage role in joint ventures, but the trade unions, which a joint venture must allow to be established and with which it signs its labour contract, have a higher profile, with the right to participate in board meetings on relevant matters.

Foreign investment

Domestic legislation does not, on the whole, affect the foreign business person, who should nevertheless beware of the tendency of the Chinese opposite number to cite "internal," protected and hence unavailable, regulations when this is to his advantage. Foreign business legislation has existed only since 1979. It covers three major categories: equity joint ventures, contractual or cooperative joint ventures, and wholly owned foreign enterprises. Many laws have been drafted during the 1980s, and although creditable, the rapidity has often led to vagueness and ambiguity. Strict attention should, however, be paid to the relevant legislation, especially the implementing regulations issued pursuant to "laws." The services of a good foreign law firm are indispensable – and expensive.

Scope of legislation

The patchy legislative environment is due to improve as company law, foreign trade law, banking law and others in the pipeline are promulgated. Already major legislation covers many areas, including patents, trademarks, contract law, taxation, export and import duties, technology import, environmental protection, exchange control, import and export licences and representative offices. There are also many local regulations, including those for the Special Economic Zones (SEZs) and the Economic and Technological Development Zones of the coastal cities.

Foreign investment climate

The opening of the Chinese door to foreign investment was marked by the watershed 1979 Joint Venture Law. The initial response from foreign companies was enthusiastic, but in the intervening years problems have surfaced.

Slow to change The Chinese view foreign investment as a means of absorbing foreign equipment and technology at minimum foreign exchange cost, and only lately have they begun to pay attention to the need for investments to be profitable. They have been slow to accept foreign business practices, and a lack of infrastructural support has been a hindrance. The most serious problem has been the shortage of foreign exchange.

The authorities are, however, now trying hard to address these problems, and in the medium term the situation is likely to improve.

The investment options

Foreign investment is welcome only in priority sectors, such as energy, transport, chemicals and food processing. The scale of the project should be within the scope of Chinese reality: the larger the project, the less chance of success.

The investment should be sited where raw materials are plentiful and easily shipped in, where power and other utilities supplies are reliable, where product distribution facilities are adequate and, above all, where the regulatory environment is conducive to business enterprise and the authorities relatively helpful.

Local rules Different localities in China have their own set of investment incentives in addition to those applying nationwide. Since late 1986 local regulations allowing favourable tax treatment, reduced land-use fees and other advantages have proliferated. These are available in translation from various sources such as banks, lawyers and trade promotion organizations and should be consulted before an investment decision is made.

Local reputations Similarly the

record of the local authority should be examined. Has it a reputation for being excessively difficult to negotiate with? Does it arbitrarily raise costs or breach contracts? Has it proved reasonably sympathetic?

Equity joint ventures

The equity joint venture (JV) is a limited liability enterprise with the status of a legal person under Chinese law, jointly invested in and managed by a foreign firm and a Chinese partner. The latter must be a registered corporation, not an individual or private enterprise or government agency. The two partners share profits, risks and losses on the basis of equity shares. The total investment refers to the sum of capital plus construction and working capital funds as stipulated in the contract, and the share of the foreign partner is not less than 25%. Registered capital may not be reduced during the term of the JV.

Who contributes what The Chinese partner usually contributes the site, factory buildings and raw materials; the foreign partner provides advanced equipment and technology and foreign exchange in cash.

Land The JV itself cannot own land; instead, land-use fees are paid to the local authorities.

Investment certificates Cash contributions are made according to the stipulated schedule and deposited with the Bank of China (BOC). On verification of this and other contributions an investment certificate can be issued to each party; this takes the place of stock in the JV.

Capitalization of technology is discouraged, the authorities being concerned about the underfinancing of some joint ventures. In Shenzhen SEZ it is restricted to 20% of registered capital; in Guangzhou Economic and Technological Development Zone, to 30% for "advanced technology." The Chinese

require any foreign company capitalizing technology also to contribute cash or goods worth not less than the value of that technology.

Gearing is governed by regulations of March 1987. JVs with a total investment of: $1–3m are permitted 30% debt (70% equity); $3–10m, 50% debt (down to a minimum registered capital of $2.1m); $10–30m, 60% debt (down to a minimum capital of $5m where total investment is less than $12.5m); $30m and over, 70% debt (down to a minimum capital of $12m where total investment is less than $36m).

Who approves? Ultimate approval for JVs lies with MOFERT. Since 1985 more autonomy has been granted to localities. Beijing, Tianjin and Shanghai can approve projects with a total investment of up to $30m; Guangdong, Fujian, Liaoning and Dalian, up to $10m; and other areas, up to $5m. In practice MOFERT will intervene, especially where important materials, communications and power supplies are utilized.

Duration The JV Law Implementing Regulations stipulated a term of 10–30 years with 30 years-plus for large investments, long construction periods and low profit margins. This was amended in January 1986 to a maximum term of 50 years for the special cases and for JVs where advanced technology is contributed. This limited duration has irked many foreign companies.

Setting up

Negotiations proceed in stages, often beginning with a letter of intent and proceeding with protocols and memoranda. These are not contracts and have no binding force, but are nonetheless useful in gaining approvals. Although they are usually worded very generally, the Chinese do not welcome any attempts to change commitments made at the outset.

Studies Prefeasibility and joint feasibility studies must be approved by the state and local economic commissions and by MOFERT or its local commission.

Establishment After the contract is signed, it and all other relevant documents, such as the articles of association, list of board members and statements by the local administration, must be submitted to the department in charge of the JV and then to MOFERT for final examination and ratification. Within one month of ratification, the JV should apply for registration with the provincial or municipal administration for industry and commerce. The date of licence issue is the date of formal establishment.

The contract is a binding statement of rights and obligations of particular importance in the context of a relatively underdeveloped legal framework. It is important to provide for all eventualities in it. Contracts are governed by the Foreign Economic Contract Law, which provides that new laws need not be retroactive and also that in matters for which Chinese law does not provide, international law will apply.

Arbitration Friendly consultation is preferred, but the judiciary of a third country can be used if stipulated in the contract. However, the Chinese prefer to use their own organization, Foreign and Economic Trade Arbitration Commission (FETAC).

Directors There must be a minimum of three directors. The chairman and vice-chairman are usually nominated by the Chinese and foreign parties respectively. The general manager, effectively the chief executive officer, is generally foreign. In the start-up years the board of directors is split according to equity shares. The board appoints management, and its unanimous approval is required for major decisions such as alteration of the articles and termination. It must meet at least once a year in China.

Labour Employment of labour is governed by the 1980 Provisions of the PRC for Labour Management in

Joint Ventures using Chinese and Foreign Investment and their 1984 Implementing Regulations. In theory JVs can hire and fire, but in practice neither has proved easy. The JV labour plans must be submitted to the department in charge of the JV and to the local labour and personnel department. Labour and staff are employed on a contract basis either individually, or through the local labour service company. A contract is signed with the trade union, which should be consulted on relevant matters.

Accounting The JV must register its accounting system (which must be double entry and accruals-based, on a calendar year) with the local tax authority. It can appoint a foreign chief accountant and extra foreign auditors, but auditing by Chinese auditors is mandatory. The certificates of investment issued to the JV partners and the annual reports must be verified by a Chinese-registered accountant.

Remittance of profits The JV must open renminbi and foreign currency accounts with the BOC, and it may open accounts with additional banks in China and abroad. Approval must be obtained from the State General Administration for Foreign Exchange Control for remittances to be made from these accounts. The JV must deduct reserve, welfare and development funds from post-tax profits, with the remainder available for distribution, after past losses have been made up.

Foreign exchange

The foreign exchange balance of JVs has been a major concern. The JV Law Implementing Regulations encourage JVs to sell products on the international market and stipulate that they should keep a balance between foreign exchange income and expenditure. Since the renminbi is nonconvertible, most JVs are forced to export. In this case the quantities of products to be exported in specific years, marketing channels and liabilities of each party should be addressed in the contract. In theory the JV can fix its own export prices, but export licences, where required, should be applied for every six months.

Local sources of foreign exchange Sales in the domestic market are in theory possible where the products concerned are in short supply, or are import substitutes, or are manufactured with advanced technology. Sales channels are complicated – the products must be listed in the distribution plans of the materials control department and then sold to end-users. Any surplus can be sold for renminbi or foreign exchange. Price guidelines are ambiguous, but international market prices are used as a benchmark. Any resulting foreign exchange imbalance can be rectified in various ways: where the products are included in the local plan, the local government should provide foreign exchange, and where the JV is under the charge of a ministry or state council bureau, the latter is responsible. If the JV's applications to these bodies fail, the JV can apply to MOFERT.

Adjusting the imbalance Subsequent legislation has provided further methods for rectifying foreign exchange problems – such as using renminbi revenues to purchase local products for export in order to earn additional foreign exchange – but most methods have proved difficult in practice. Foreign currency adjustment centres have been established (see *The banks* and *Other financial institutions*).

Other types of foreign investment
Contractual joint ventures (CJVs) Once much more popular than the equity type, the CJVs are now less so. Since October 1986, they have been covered by some of the same legislation as equity JVs. They are, however, different in many respects, and a law on CJVs was promulgated in April 1988. In a CJV no legal entity is

formed by the partners, who instead agree in their contract to undertake a particular type of joint activity. They share profits and control according to negotiation. Many foreign companies have preferred the less regulated environment of the CJV, but have come under increasing pressure from the Chinese to make an equity commitment.

Wholly-owned foreign enterprises These are far fewer than other types of investment, and until basic legislation covering them emerged in April 1986, they were permitted only in the SEZs and the coastal cities. The law governing them is very similar to the equity JV law, but is vague in some areas, such as the definition of the scope of their operations, their legal nature and organizational structure, and their duration. Taxes and other matters are mostly covered by the relevant JV legislation. Despite the apparent freedom of this type of investment, most foreign companies have preferred to work with a Chinese partner, without whom the foreigner may have little bargaining power with the authorities.

Taxation
Where the foreign party has an "establishment" in China, the Foreign Enterprise Income Tax Law (FEITL) applies; where not, withholding tax is levied on gross income, but this is often reduced to 10%, especially if a double taxation agreement exists between China and the relevant foreign country. Other taxes that may apply include withholding tax on interest and royalties, consolidated industrial and commercial tax (CICT – a type of turnover tax), import and export taxes, and personal income tax.

Get it in writing Professional advice should be sought on tax matters. In negotiations, it is wise to obtain a written ruling on the tax consequences of any agreement and have this appended to the contract, but in practice most Chinese tax authorities refuse to make a ruling until after the contract is signed. Alternatively the foreign party can outline the expected treatment in the contract and make the Chinese party responsible for best efforts regarding its implementation, with the contract rendered ineffective if the outcome is adverse.

Taxation of joint ventures The JV Income Tax Law levies a basic tax of 33% on net income, including a 10% local surcharge. Exemption is granted for the first two profit-making years, plus a 50% reduction for the next three years if the JV term exceeds 10 years. A 40% refund is given for profits reinvested for a minimum of five years. A 10% withholding tax is also levied on profits, and may apply to any interest, rentals and technology fees.

Imported materials and equipment are subject to CICT (3–70%) and to customs duty, although there are exemptions available for initial imports and for JVs that are technically advanced or export-oriented.

Urban real estate tax varies with the locality. It is levied on the appraised value of buildings contributed to the JV and may be paid by the JV or by the Chinese partner. When registering with the tax authorities it is important to state the type of JV and to define taxable income.

Contractual joint venture taxation is covered by the FEITL. Tax is levied on earned income and is progressive, ranging from 30–50% including a 10% local surcharge. Other taxes apply or are waived in accordance with the available legislation and the October 1986 provisions.

The October 1986 incentives
In October 1986 new Provisions for the Encouragement of Foreign Investment were introduced. For the first time the incentives applied not just to equity JVs but also to contractual JVs and wholly owned foreign ventures, and in particular to certified export-oriented and technically advanced enterprises.

Certified enterprises have priority in provision of water, power, transport and other utilities and are charged at the same rate as state enterprises. Raw materials are not normally covered. Domestic prices apply for all but a few raw materials such as strategic metals which are priced at international market levels. The provisions also extend available tax breaks for such certified enterprises, abolishing withholding tax on remitted profits and giving an extra three years of the 50% reduction in the income tax rate.

Local borrowing Chinese banks give JVs priority for loans in both renminbi and foreign exchange. Instead of selling foreign exchange to buy renminbi to pay local costs, the venture can now collateralize foreign exchange and borrow renminbi, hence increasing its security.

Further help CICT and customs duty have been waived on imports used to manufacture export products; land-use fees have been reduced; and protection is given against any extra labour charges other than wages, insurance, welfare and housing subsidies. The JV's rights to hire and fire and to manage its own affairs are reconfirmed, and in problem situations rights of appeal to the state or local economic commission are granted.

Implementation The October 1986 provisions have been rapidly followed by various implementing regulations, including those on preferential tax treatment, on renminbi loans mortgaged with foreign exchange, on import/export licences and on the purchase and export of domestic products.

The Special Economic Zones

Handicapped by underdeveloped infrastructure and inadequate planning, the Special Economic Zones (SEZs) have experienced weak growth. Furthermore, they have had to compete with newer development zones for domestic funds and foreign investment, such as those being set up in the 14 coastal cities.

The four SEZs

There are four SEZs: Xiamen, in Fujian province; Shantou, Shenzhen and Zhuhai in Guangdong province. Shenzhen, bordering Hong Kong's New Territories, is the largest and best known. All four were set up in 1979 as export zones, and aimed to attract foreign investors by more liberal policies, and tax and other incentives. The SEZs were experiments for new economic policies which, if they succeeded, might be extended; if they failed, the SEZs were too isolated from the rest of the economy to cause much harm.

Shenzhen disappoints This isolation has not helped. The SEZs' growth rates have lagged behind those of many other areas in China. From being a paradigm of progress, Shenzhen became, in Deng Xiaoping's words, an experiment that "could fail," criticized for its low levels of output, productivity and exports, its failure to attract foreign investment in quality export-oriented manufacturing, its over-reliance on property development and its role in major scandals involving corruption, smuggling and black-marketeering.

Successes elsewhere The other zones have been hit less hard. Xiamen has some sizable and successful foreign investments. Shekou, an "industrial zone" in Shenzhen (but physically distant from the city), has proved more successful than the actual Shenzhen SEZ. Run by the Hong Kong-based China Merchants Steam Navigation Company, it has a reputation for efficiency and competitiveness.

Slow recovery likely The SEZs are likely to recover slowly from their problems, although they may not catch up with other areas. The

potential foreign investor should be aware that there exists a large body of legislation on the SEZs, covering areas such as labour, land use and technology import.

Overtaking the SEZs As well as the SEZs, other areas are introducing their own regulations to attract foreign capital and technology. Hong Kong companies have set up small-scale light industries in Guangdong province mainly on a co-production or contractual basis, in preference to equity joint ventures (see *Foreign investment*). Negotiating locally, they can obtain terms as good as, or better than, those offered by the SEZs.

Politically useful Perhaps the main *raison d'être* of the SEZs is political – Xiamen lies opposite Taiwan, Zhuhai faces Macao, Shantou is the family home of many overseas Chinese, and Shenzhen borders Hong Kong. A second border crossing between Shenzhen and the rest of China has been opened. Traffic through the crossing into Hong Kong has been made easier by the introduction of special entry regulations and new road and rail links with Hong Kong will accelerate the process of integration.

Economic and Technological Development Zones

These were launched in 1984 in 14 coastal cities, and designed to house new light industrial and high-tech ventures. Although the central government withdrew financial support soon afterwards, they have developed slowly on their own. Most offer special incentives which are almost as beneficial to the foreign investor as those available in the SEZs. Shanghai has three special development areas.

Selling to China

There are many ways of exporting technology and equipment to China, including straight sales, licensing and leasing agreements. China has the reputation, however, of being a difficult market to penetrate. Foreign exchange is in short supply, approvals and other procedures are complicated, and negotiations are extremely tough and time consuming. Even if success is achieved, constant attention is required to stay in the market. Relationships must be nurtured, visits made, perhaps a representative office established. None of this is easy or cheap. Neither do practical considerations cease when an order is placed by either side. Questions of shipping, insurance and payment arise. Profitability must be measured against all these factors.

Market entry

The "open door" As far as imports are concerned, the open door in China tends to swing with the economic wind. The first thing the foreign exporter must realize is that there is no point in trying to sell the Chinese anything they do not need. Over-enthusiastic importing of some items, particularly consumer goods and their production equipment, has led to restrictions on such imports. The lists of banned products and of items requiring import or export licences are subject to arbitrary revision and should be checked regularly.

Priority imports are dictated by China's economic priorities and thus include energy development, transport equipment, iron and steel, non-ferrous metals, building materials, chemicals, food processing and textiles. Only when the need is pressing will finished products be imported. The Chinese much prefer the equipment and/or knock-down kits to make into the finished product themselves. Always an element of technology transfer is desired, so foreign exporters would be wise not to sell their very latest designs if they want repeat orders.

Aid-funded projects There is scope for supplying goods and services to projects that are funded by multilateral bodies, such as the World Bank, various UN agencies, the European Development Fund and, lately, ADB. There is likely to be an increasing number of aid-funded infrastructural projects in which foreign investment is simply not economic. Many of these projects are concerned with port, road and rail modernization and with human resources development such as education. All involve a significant degree of local participation, but are open to international tender through normal channels.

Constraints on Chinese imports

Foreign exchange availability A Chinese enterprise has three main sources of foreign exchange. It can retain foreign exchange from its own exports, but this amount is generally limited – 25–40% of the total – the remainder being submitted to Beijing for redistribution from the central coffers. The inland provinces, which export less than those on the coast, thus tend to have much less to spend on imports than do central organizations. Some inland provinces are, however, establishing their own trading companies in coastal cities.

Importing enterprises can be allocated funds by the central or regional government, but these funds are limited in amount and strictly controlled. Importing corporations or enterprises can also borrow from Chinese or foreign banks, but again credit is tightly controlled. Few organizations can borrow directly from foreign banks, and guarantees are hard to obtain.

Import plans must be submitted for

approval by the enterprise to its supervising organization (usually an industrial ministry or provincial industrial bureau), the local or state planning commission and the State General Administration for Foreign Exchange Control.

Importing a specific item requires the enterprise to gain the approval not only of the above bodies, but also of the local foreign economic relations and trade commission and the foreign trade corporation (FTC) concerned.

Import prohibitions applied to more than 80 items as of June 1987; these included cars, air conditioners, washing machines, other consumer electronics and their assembly lines, steel, synthetic fibres, rubber, timber; certain herbs, and all other strategic materials or items that the Chinese wish to manufacture domestically.

The foreign trade corporations

The FTCs play a pivotal role: together with the end-user they negotiate and sign the purchase contract with the foreign party, and they actually import the goods, usually charging a small commission to the end-user. On occasions the FTC may allocate part of its own foreign exchange quota to an enterprise short of funds, as long as the other necessary approvals are obtained.

There are 18 FTCs, each dealing with a specific commodity, under the Ministry of Foreign Economic Relations and Trade (MOFERT). Other ministries have recently set up their own FTCs, in competition with the MOFERT FTCs.

Tariffs

A two-tier tariff system is in operation – the "minimum" rate applying to Hong Kong, Macao and countries with reciprocal commercial agreements with China, and a "general" tariff applying to all others. Tariffs are very low on priority items but high on, for instance, consumer goods. These, plus additional surcharges such as local import taxes, can add up to more than 200% of the product's ex-factory price, as many expatriates importing cars for their own use have discovered.

Tariff exemptions are given to imports of materials and equipment for foreign operations that manufacture products using advanced technology or products for export. Exemptions are also given for office equipment imported to establish a representative office in China, although subsequent imports are taxed. Goods sold into the Special Economic Zones (SEZs) are also given a 50% reduction if they are to be used or sold in the SEZ, and full exemptions have been granted in Xiamen SEZ since late 1986.

Payment methods

Letters of Credit (LCs) are used for payments up to very large amounts. Until mid-1987 only the Bank of China (BOC) could open an LC for imports, but its monopoly has recently been broken by the international trust and investment corporations in Shanghai and Guangdong. China International Trust and Investment Corporation (CITIC) has a banking licence but so far has conducted only limited trade finance business.

China is not a member of the International Chamber of Commerce. In the past foreign banks would often deal with Chinese LCs only on a collection basis, but in May 1987 this situation changed when the BOC began adding the phrase "subject to UCP No. 400" to its LCs. BOC LCs are payable only at the branch that opened the credit, and therefore all documents must be mailed by the seller's bank to that particular branch before payment is made. Payment by telegraphic transfer should be stipulated to avoid delays.

Credit is generally taken only for major purchases, and a debt-service ratio that rose to 15–20% in 1987 is causing the Chinese to keep strict control over debt.

Guarantors Organizations able to

guarantee Chinese debts to foreign banks fall into two categories. Financial institutions (which include BOC branches, some other Chinese banks, CITIC and various ITICs) can issue guarantees amounting to 20 times the sum of their foreign exchange reserves. By contrast, non-financial institutions with foreign exchange reserves (for example some trading corporations) can issue guarantees only up to the sum of their foreign exchange reserves. Debtors and guarantors should in theory be able to provide foreign creditors with information on their financial status, but in practice this information is frequently difficult to obtain and may not even exist in sufficient detail.

A 100% guarantee is extremely rare: 60–70% is the norm, and the BOC has recently been guaranteeing only major projects. It is becoming more usual for major borrowers not to offer guarantees at all, alternative forms of comfort being offered instead. Foreign export credit agencies, however, generally insist on a BOC or CITIC guarantee.

Saving foreign exchange
Barter trade, whereby no funds, only goods, change hands, is generally conducted on a government-to-government basis between China and other countries with planned economies.
Offset agreements are becoming more common, especially in the aviation, defence and machine-building industries.
Compensation trade agreements In these, the foreign exporters of plant or equipment receive all or part of their payment in the form of product manufactured with the plant or equipment. It is normal to open separate LCs for the transactions in either direction.
Countertrade involves payment for imports with unrelated products, both parties being invoiced in the same currency. In 1985 MOFERT set up a small countertrade department.

This will not act as a principal or arrange deals, however, but will help to implement those already set up. Countertrade is possible only where Chinese organizations within the same province and of the same level of bureaucracy are involved, and the Chinese are interested in countertrading mainly goods that they otherwise find difficult to export.

The major problem of countertrade is finding marketable products to export, and then there are problems of adequate supplies, export licences, pricing and shipping, inter-province and bureaucratic rivalry, quality control and cash flow for the foreign firm. Chinese demands for additionality are another problem, and the premium demanded by a countertrader can be high. Countertrade is, however, growing in importance in larger deals such as those concerning the importation of power stations, and is likely to increase in the future.

Leasing
Fashionable in China as a way of importing outside the normal channels, leasing grew to an estimated $1.5bn market in 1985. With the general clampdown in credit since then, and the drafting of leasing regulations, it has tailed off slightly at the smaller end. On the other hand, big ticket leasing – for example of airplanes – is expanding. Lease periods are generally short – three to five years.
Three types of leasing With direct leasing the foreign supplier sells capital goods to a leasing company (lessor), which then leases them to a Chinese end-user (lessee). Most leasing companies involved in importing into China are Sino-foreign joint ventures, usually between foreign banks and Chinese banks or ITICs which are able to provide adequate guarantees of repayment. Cross-border sub-leasing involves the foreign supplier leasing the goods to the lessor, who then

leases them to the Chinese lessee, but is less common than direct leasing. Tax-based leveraged leasing is generally used for large items such as aircraft.

Financial leasing is more common than operative leasing; the latter, involving the return of the goods after a period, is not really feasible in China, because the socialist system prevents the foreign party from taking a charge on assets on Chinese soil. The Chinese also prefer the instalment payment nature of financial leasing, whereby title passes at the time of final payment.

Benefits The advantages of leasing to the Chinese party include the avoidance of large up-front payments of foreign exchange, the comparative ease of getting approvals to import and the fact that leasing can be conducted off-balance sheet. Withholding and income taxes, customs duties and CICT may also be reduced or abrogated. Leasing can also be combined with export credits on larger items.

Licensing

Licensing contracts are approved by MOFERT's Technology Import-Export Bureau. They are covered by the Regulations of the PRC on the Administration of Contracts for the Import of Technology and Measures for the Examination and Approval of Technology Import Controls except where superseded by local regulations or where technology is capitalized as part of a joint venture.

Read carefully The Regulations should be well examined. Although comforting in some ways – for example, they afford protection against the spread of proprietary technology to third parties – they impose restrictions in various areas such as tie-ins for supplies of materials and spare parts; they prevent the foreign party from defining permissible export markets; and they impose an extensive burden on the foreign party in terms of product-quality guarantees. They also

provide that the licensee may not be restricted from acquiring similar technology from other sources. In practice, however, it is possible to compromise on most of these matters.

Duration The Regulations effectively make a licence contract into an instalment sale by prohibiting the restriction of the licensee's continued use of the technology following expiry of the contract. Contract length is generally limited to ten years. Licensors can protect themselves by registering patents or trademarks, but these are lengthy and complicated processes.

Training Obligatory training is provided for by the Regulations. This can be either in China or abroad, but is best *in situ*. The contract should provide for reimbursement of costs incurred.

Payment is generally by letter of credit and can be by lump sum and/or royalties. A lump sum payment can be made in instalments. The Chinese try to base royalties – usually 2–5% – on the net sales value of the goods produced, that is the gross sales revenue, minus all costs involved in marketing and selling, including sales tax. It is a matter of negotiation whether the definition of gross sales revenue is based on the Chinese domestic price or the licensor's own export price, or somewhere in between.

Approvals for licence contracts depend upon the contract being submitted within 30 days of signature. If there is no action by the authorities within 60 days, the contract is deemed approved, but in practice the foreign party should demand an approval certificate, which in any case is needed for tax and other purposes.

Agents, consultants and contacts

There are sole operators and specialist companies in most countries who will act on behalf of principals, seeking opportunities and participating in the early stages of negotiations, but the most common source of agents is Hong Kong.

The Hong Kong/China relationship Many Hong Kong Chinese have excellent family, business and political ties with the mainland and speak not only Mandarin Chinese but also the other Chinese dialects. Hong Kong business people are well placed to arrange buy-backs and other forms of countertrade, and they form a useful interface with countries with which China has no diplomatic relations.

Hong Kong-based agents There are many agents in Hong Kong, from one-man bands to major consultancies such as Mark Wong and Company, to Hong Kong-based organizations such as Jardine Matheson, or the Hong Kong offices of foreign companies such as Wogen Technology in the UK. Most of these larger firms are well represented on a permanent basis in major cities in China.

Chinese corporations Between 300 and 500 Chinese corporations have offices in Hong Kong. Many of them act as trading agents for their parent organizations, such as the China National Foreign Trade Transportation Corporation, or for their province or city, either selling their products or obtaining technology, equipment, materials and funds for them. Hence foreign business people can either source Chinese goods in Hong Kong or initiate import deals there. Of particular importance to the foreign importer of goods from China, is the fact that the Hong Kong-based subsidiary of a central import/export corporation holding company can, in many cases, handle all negotiations and sign contracts.

Chinese consulting firms on the mainland have also multiplied in recent years. The best known are those attached to Chinese ministries and other major central organizations, such as China International Economic Consultants (CIEC) for CITIC, Consultech for

MOFERT, Ecotech for the China Council for the Promotion of International Trade (CCPIT), and the Bank of China Trust and Consultancy Company. They all claim to be able to conduct market surveys and act generally as representatives for foreign principals. How far they are able to act independently in the sense of employing Western concepts and logic is a matter of argument, but the *guanxi* (connections) obtained can often be worthwhile.

China's provinces have also established offices in Beijing and other major cities, as well as in Hong Kong, to liaise with other Chinese organizations and provinces, but since 1984 they have been allowed to deal with foreign firms. They can provide useful information and contacts, but most are not entitled to sign contracts.

Opening a representative office

For the company that has a significant turnover of business with China, or that liaises with a broad spectrum of Chinese organizations, opening a representative office can be well worthwhile. The Chinese certainly appreciate the gesture. There is no real substitute for an on-the-spot presence.

Hundreds have done it By late-1986 more than 1,700 foreign, overseas Chinese, Hong Kong and Macao firms had established offices in China. More than half of these were in Beijing, the remainder mostly in Shanghai and Guangzhou. Japan accounts for the majority, followed by Hong Kong and Macao and the USA. Two-thirds were involved in trade, while the most rapid growth has been in financial services. However, opening an office is fraught with difficulties.

It takes time Establishment procedures are complex and time consuming. Approval from the relevant Chinese organization must be obtained in advance – for example from the People's Bank of China for a bank representative office, from Minmetals for a metals trading firm – and this can take several months. Various documents must be submitted and, registration made with the tax bureau, customs, Public Security Bureau and the State Administration for Industry and Commerce; bank accounts must be opened and office staff employed. Variations in procedure from city to city have to be taken into account.

It's expensive Beijing is estimated to be the sixth most expensive city in the world, considerably more expensive than Hong Kong. Accommodation in China has been scarce and costly, particularly in Beijing. Most foreign companies are forced to maintain offices and staff residences in hotels. Until recently, discounts for long-staying guests were rare, and steep price rises common. With the increase in hotel rooms in the major cities the situation is easing, and now concessions are granted and apartments are available. Nevertheless facilities are poor – there are long waiting lists for telex and telephone facilities, which are expensive for foreigners; imported office equipment is taxed; and imported food and other items are tariff-ridden.

Staffing Foreign companies must contract their Chinese office staff from local service bureaux, which charge high rates. There is a shortage of well-trained staff.

Tax liability It is important for the foreign representative office to be "non-profit-making;" otherwise it will be subject to the Foreign Enterprise Income Tax Law (FEITL) on revenue accrued or on a deemed liability.

Lack of facilities The poor facilities for recreation and for education are additional factors that dissuade many companies from setting up office in China and opting instead to do business out of Hong Kong.

Insurance

Imports and exports insurance is the monopoly of the People's Insurance Company of China (PICC). It gives cover equivalent to that generally available. If the policy is considered insufficient – for instance the Chinese do not acknowledge the risk of strikes – the foreign party can top up the policy by, for example, purchasing a difference in conditions cargo policy from a foreign non-admitted carrier.

Export credit agencies Most of the major export credit agencies limit cover to around 90% of the contract amount, the remaining percentage, according to the type of risk, to be borne by the exporter. There are many different types of policy available, according to the business involved, length of cover and so on, all of which command a premium based on the degree of risk.

Subsidized credit is also available under Organisation for Economic Cooperation and Development (OECD) rules. In some cases it is tied to export credit insurance, in others it is not. OECD rules limit the provision of this credit to 85% of the contract amount, the rest to be paid in cash or obtained from commercial sources. China, since it is classed as a low per capita income country, is eligible for the lowest interest rate credit under this scheme, the difference between this and the cost of the finance, plus a margin, being made up by the lending banks.

Guarantees are required to back a Chinese borrower – most Western agencies accept either the Bank of China or CITIC as a guarantor, and some accept the provincial or local International Trust and Investment Corporations.

Trade fairs and exhibitions

Hundreds of exhibitions and trade fairs have been held in recent years. Some are sponsored by major companies such as Adsale or Cahners – often located in Hong Kong – and some by local Chinese organizations. The main Chinese sponsor is CCPIT (or its sub-councils in local areas), but the Chinese ministry concerned will also usually be involved.

The problem for the foreign business person is choosing which trade fair or exhibition to attend, because although they provide valuable contacts, standards of organization vary considerably. In addition the cost of participation, shipping equipment and so on can be high – reportedly as much as $40,000. There is always the possibility of selling equipment on the spot, but if too many exhibitions of one type are held close together this becomes less likely. The trend now is towards holding one major exhibition a year for a particular sector, instead of several smaller ones.

Checking credentials The potential exhibitor should examine the credentials of organizers and seek the opinion of others in his or her particular industry. The status of the Chinese sponsor is also vital and a clue to whether or not money will be spent at the exhibition. Apart from a few major events, the audience at exhibitions tends to be limited to people from the surrounding area.

Invitations Even though most exhibition organizers claim to have invited a wide audience, the exhibitor is also wise to send out his or her own invitations to potential customers and to prepare the maximum quantity of company literature – in Chinese – likely to be needed.

Seminars It may be possible to hold technical seminars, which appeal to the Chinese. Audiovisual material may also be needed for seminars, and this can often be prepared more cheaply in Hong Kong.

Sponsorship Some foreign government trade departments sponsor attendance at exhibitions – this should be investigated.

The Chinese Export Commodities Fair (CECF)

in Guangzhou, held every spring and autumn since the mid-1950s, is attended by export corporations from all over China and from every industrial and agricultural sector. Its importance as a venue for buying and selling has declined under the "open door" policy. Direct contacts between foreign traders and Chinese organizations have grown, while the proportion of exports handled by the Fair has fallen to around 20%.

Specialist fairs The specialist buyer should also watch out for notices of the specialist product fairs and local fairs now being held.

Overseas fairs There is also a growing trend for export fairs to be held abroad – in particular in the USA, Japan and Western Europe.

Buying from China

Importing from China has its problems. Chinese exports are subject to licences and quota restrictions, and supplies cannot always be relied upon. Many products are sold forward at the twice-yearly China Export Commodities Fair (CECF) in Guangzhou, better known as the Canton Trade Fair (see above), and at a few other fairs. Even after orders are placed, however, problems of late delivery and non-delivery are not uncommon. Decentralization in the 1980s has given corporation employers greater independence in decision making but most of them are very inexperienced in this role. This has tended to exacerbate the problems. It is sensible for foreign importers to maintain good relations with the representative office in their country of the Chinese corporations they are dealing with, in order for contacts to be made.

Advertising and public relations

Until the late 1970s there were few opportunities for corporate and product promotion other than personally meeting end-users. The direct approach is still important, and agents can be useful in this respect, but the recent growth and internationalization of the Chinese media means that there are now cheaper and easier ways of reaching customers.

Advertising

The choice of medium employed depends upon the market strategy of the foreign company: mass media, such as newspapers, radio and TV and billboards, for consumer products (although few of these are imported) or for promoting a name; local papers or technical magazines for products aimed at narrower customer groups.

The main Chinese corporations are: the China United Advertising Corporation, established in 1981 by the State Administration for Industry and Commerce; and the China National Foreign Trade Advertising Corporation and the China International Advertising Corporation set up in 1981 and 1985 respectively by MOFERT. All three liaise with local advertising corporations. They also coordinate Chinese advertising abroad. Chinese foreign trade corporations have been instructed to spend about 1% of their foreign exchange earnings on product promotion.

Chinese advertising abroad is becoming more sophisticated, but ignorance of Western media still restricts its development and impact.

Foreign agencies Various foreign advertising agencies have been involved, particularly Hong Kong-based firms, such as Interpublic Jardine and Ogilvy and Mather.

Technical magazines are probably the most widely used advertising media. In addition to Chinese-language journals, such as *China Textile* and *Automotive Engineering*, Chinese editions of Western magazines, including *Scientific American*, are now available, while various Western publishing firms, such as McGraw-Hill, are producing specialist magazines for, among others, the Chinese computer industry.

Television advertising reaches the widest audience, as many urban Chinese homes now have a television. Both China Central Television (CCTV) and local stations have signed deals with foreign television stations and media companies to sell advertising time. Rates are about $4,000 for a 30-second slot on CCTV, estimated to reach 300m viewers. Local stations usually charge less – about $600–1,000 for the same time.

Public relations

Promoting corporate image by press coverage, cultural and sporting sponsorship, media "events" and so on is also emerging in China. One of the first major developments in this field was an agreement in 1985 between China Global Public Relations, a Xinhua News Agency subsidiary, and the international PR company Burson-Marsteller providing for China Global to use the Xinhua network to provide services for Burson clients.

Careful handling Care is needed in the presentation of material. Translation must be handled very carefully to avoid mistakes in technical terms; simplified characters should be used and company names in Chinese should be chosen to convey an image rather than to provide a strict translation. Advice should be taken on humour and other cultural idiosyncrasies. Sex and politics should be avoided. It is inadvisable to use maps in advertising material; a misplaced border could cause offence. Similarly, Hong Kong should not be referred to as a separate country.

Shipping

China enjoys a comparative advantage in both import and export shipping. Chinese companies generally prefer to import on an fob basis and export cif, which allows them to arrange transport in both cases.

Chinese transport companies

Chinese trade is dominated by two state-controlled transport companies: the China Ocean Shipping Company (COSCO) and the China National Foreign Trade Transportation Corporation (Sinotrans). COSCO has a fleet of about 600 vessels, with a total capacity of about 14m dwt. It serves more than 430 ports and harbours in more than 100 countries and has more than 50 agency relationships in 35 countries around the world. Sinotrans is the state freight forwarding agency, responsible for booking all shipping services and has various offices abroad.

Criticism of COSCO and Sinotrans is common. Complaints centre on delays in shipment and in documentation, inadequate dockside handling and packing facilities, lack of motivation of management, and inexperience of crews. Whether or not these criticisms are valid, a real problem has been the lack of container-handling facilities at Chinese ports and general congestion. COSCO's ability to deliver to Chinese ports on time was not helped by the system of dispatch agreements; these were payments by shippers to the harbour administration to assure priority berthing. If COSCO ships were unable to pay in foreign exchange, they were not awarded priority.

New competition In recent years the COSCO-Sinotrans monopoly has been broken by competition from joint ventures, especially between Hong Kong companies and local authorities – such as the Jardine-Matheson venture, Tianjin Marine Shipping Company – and smaller provincial and regional lines. Even COSCO's bureaux in China's major ports, such as Tianjin, Guangzhou and Shanghai, are significantly independent of COSCO Beijing. This has meant that Chinese trading organizations have been freed of their dependence upon COSCO, although in theory rates are still set by Sinotrans and COSCO Beijing.

Routing through Hong Kong

Given the expense – Chinese port fees are reputedly among the highest in the world – and problems of shipping into China, and the limited number of ports able to take large ships, many foreign lines have abandoned direct services in favour of collecting and discharging in Hong Kong and using Chinese feeder ships for the remainder of the journey. The feeder link is claimed by China as exclusively Chinese on the grounds that it is a domestic route; Hong Kong is seen in this context as Chinese. Sometimes goods, especially those from southern China, are sent by road or rail to Hong Kong where transport is arranged, usually by Chinese forwarding agents there.

Freight forwarding

Freight forwarding within China is out of bounds to foreign companies. Even if they ship direct to China, they cannot control the movement of goods thereafter. Various means have been sought to get around these restrictions. The US-based Schenkers International Forwarders Incorporated has a joint venture with Sinotrans land transport department which subcontracts to Chinese entities various stages between arrival in China and final destination. Other foreign shipping companies have established overland services between Europe and China, via the USSR. A few have agency agreements with Sinotrans sea transport department to develop freight forwarding and improve cargo delivery services.

Problems

The billion-toothbrush market is unfortunately only a figment of an optimistic exporter's imagination. The potential for selling finished products, especially consumer goods, is very low and access to the market for any product or service is highly restricted. The suddenness with which new regulations are imposed, rents raised, telex charges increased, discounts demanded and projects cancelled also make doing business very difficult. Experiences do vary, however, and further advice should be sought from those already experienced in the field.

Data difficulties

Little market information is available. This is hardly surprising because statistics, as a discipline, disappeared during the Cultural Revolution and has only recently been revived. Gathering reliable data on resources, production and consumption from far-flung provinces presents enormous problems, as does verification of the figures, which may have been "improved" by local officials for one reason or another, or simply be inaccurate. This makes planning a market strategy or conducting a feasibility study extremely difficult. Market research has only just begun in China but there are one or two Chinese agencies that claim to be able to do it.

Getting a response

After years of Cultural Revolution intimidation, many Chinese are unwilling to volunteer information or show initiative. The inability to respond or to make a decision persists beyond contract signature. Many Sino-foreign joint ventures have had difficulties in finding someone with sufficient authority to deal with their problems.
Tangled web The vertical and lateral lines of authority – between cities and provincial capitals, provinces, municipalities and Beijing, between production units and industrial bureaux, import/export corporations and ministries – form an intricate mesh which utterly confuses the foreigner. Added to this are the personal dimension of power politics and the fact that so much in Chinese politics and policy-making remains invisible to the Western eye (see *Power in business*).

Costs

Operating costs for projects in hand often turn out to be much higher than expected. Delays are endemic, and although wages and social insurance costs, for example, can be predicted, other labour-related expenses, such as housing costs and salaries for expatriate staff retained for longer than expected, can far exceed expectations. Hospitality, telecommunications and similar facilities, and duty on cars imported for staff, must all be allowed for.
Hidden costs The business person visiting China on a reconnaissance trip or taking part in an exhibition should carry extra cash to cover costs such as higher-than-expected hotel fees or air fares. Particularly when a Chinese sponsor is involved, it is not unusual for costs of transport and interpreting and so on, to be levied on the foreigner's account, even without prior agreement.

Supply failure

Most damaging to projects is the need to import equipment or raw materials that should have been made available in China but have not been forthcoming. Having to spend precious foreign exchange in place of local currency can completely upset the profitability of a project. The lack of competition among Chinese organizations to supply goods and services tends to result in high prices and poor service.

The banks

The financial scene has undergone great changes in recent years and is still being reformed. In the 1950s and 1960s, Chinese banks were just the means whereby funds were allocated by the state to end-users in fulfilment of successive economic plans. But as China's economy has become more flexible and decentralized, the financial sector has had to modernize to provide more fund-raising channels and banking services.

Central and commercial banks

China's banking structure is dominated by a central bank, the People's Bank of China, which supervises a range of specialized banks. Until recently, Chinese regional banks could lend only up to the limit of cash reserves allocated by the central government. Now only loan targets are set (although there is a reserve/asset ratio system in operation). The banks are left to compete for deposits and to offer a wider range of credit instruments, although interest rates are strictly controlled. This system is intended to streamline control, creating a pyramid structure running from the People's Bank of China at the apex down through the specialized banks to the many international trust and investment corporations and similar bodies. Banks will eventually have more responsibility for their own profits and losses.

The People's Bank of China

(*PBOC*) In 1978 the PBOC became a central bank, a direct adjunct of the State Council, China's ruling body. In 1983 it lost its remaining commercial functions and became free, in theory, to formulate policy, no longer subordinate to government fiscal policy, and to manage the economy via monetary levers. It now controls the money supply and circulation, issues the national currency, supervises credit funds, sets interest and exchange rates, and controls the national foreign exchange and gold reserves. Its foreign bureau represents China in international institutions and controls foreign bond issues. The PBOC "guides" the specialized banks and insurance companies. The former remit a fixed proportion of their deposits to the PBOC, which redistributes them according to budget policy. The PBOC also vets the establishment of financial institutions, coordinates their activities and inspects their accounts.

The Industrial and Commercial Bank of China (*ICBC*)

It took over the PBOC's commercial functions, when they were spun off in 1983. It is the main source of capital for the urban economy and provides most of its short- and medium-term technical renovation loans. In addition to its normal deposit and loan business it handles commission, agency, leasing, consultancy and trust work, and has launched new services, such as housing loans, and also some foreign exchange business in the Shenzhen, Xiamen and Zhuhai SEZs. The bank has about 20,000 branches within the country and has set up correspondent relationships with major international banks.

The Agricultural Bank of China (*ABC*)

Founded in the 1950s, then abolished before the Cultural Revolution, the ABC was reincarnated in 1979, when it took over the rural branches of the PBOC. It now has 84,000 offices, including branches of the rural credit cooperatives. When the "responsibility system" was introduced in the countryside in 1983, the ABC announced that it would lend to individuals as well as to collectives, thus aiding the recent rapid growth of rural industry. Of its overall financial resources available for lending, 60% now derive from rural deposits and the remainder from fiscal allocations from the state. Eight branches can now handle foreign exchange business. A joint-venture agricultural development bank has been established in Xiamen between the ABC and various international organizations and foreign banks. It will act as a rural counterpart to the China Investment Bank, channelling multilateral aid funds to small and medium-sized rural projects.

The Construction Bank of China (CBOC) China's investment bank, the CBOC was founded in 1954 as the conduit for budgetary grants for capital construction and resource exploitation by the Ministry of Finance. Now it grants loans on the basis of credit-worthiness, supervised by the State Planning Commission. Its major role is in the planning of investment and the supervision of funds application. It has formed its own Trust and Investment Corporation and has taken a major international syndicated loan for a construction project in Beijing.

The Bank of China (BOC) Originally established as China's issuing bank, the BOC became China's foreign exchange bank in 1978 when the PBOC became the central bank. With China's open door policies its role has expanded: it finances foreign trade by acting as a correspondent bank with foreign banks and by granting loans to exporting enterprises and to other enterprises, including Sino-foreign joint ventures, for the import of goods and equipment. It is the bank in which Chinese enterprises and joint ventures must deposit their foreign exchange funds, and through which remittances in and out of China must be made. It also deals in foreign currencies and gold. Its monopoly on foreign exchange loan and guarantee business has been breached by CITIC and some other organs. The BOC is very active outside China: its 260-odd domestic branches are outnumbered by those abroad, and the latter can conduct a wider range of banking activities. It has made several bond issues abroad, participated in international syndicated loans for projects in China and Hong Kong, and financed Chinese investment overseas. The BOC is soon to expand its trade finance activities, and to handle forward foreign exchange business. It has issued renminbi-denominated "Great Wall" debit cards for use by foreigners in China. The bank plans to grant more freedom to six coastal branches – Dalian, Shanghai, Tianjin, Guangzhou, Zhejiang and Fuzhou – to handle foreign exchange, to open accounts in overseas BOC branches and to trade in foreign exchange and raise loans abroad.

Foreign banks
There are about 200 representative offices of foreign banks in China, mostly in the major cities such as Beijing and Shanghai. However, with the exception of the four foreign bank branches in Shanghai (Hongkong and Shanghai Banking Corporation, Standard Chartered, Bank of East Asia and the Oversea-Chinese Banking Corporation), branches are allowed only in China's SEZs. There are only a handful of these, mostly in Shenzhen because of its proximity to Hong Kong and its consequent entrepôt role. The representative offices are limited mainly to liaison work and conduct no banking activities, and even those fortunate enough to have branches cannot open letters of credit for Chinese imports, and they cannot finance in renminbi. They can, however, lend foreign exchange to Chinese organizations and to joint ventures, handle remittances, and advise and negotiate letters of credit for Chinese beneficiaries exporting from China. In this last area they are providing a service very competitive with that of the BOC.

Other financial institutions

Financial institutions of many types have proliferated in the past few years, at national, provincial and municipal levels. Those described below represent only a selection, and the situation is constantly changing.

China International Trust and Investment Corporation (*CITIC*)

In 1979 CITIC was formed as a quasi-merchant bank, not conducting commercial banking, but encouraging foreign investment in China and itself investing in both domestic projects and Sino-foreign joint ventures. It answers directly to the State Council and has considerable autonomy. In 1984 it was given a full banking licence, in theory allowing it to compete with the BOC for domestic foreign exchange deposits and for trade finance (letters of credit) business. Since then CITIC has developed its banking department into the CITIC Industrial Bank. Its other offshoots include a real estate corporation and a trading arm. Apart from the Bank of China, CITIC is the one organization in China acceptable to most export credit agencies as a guarantor. It has made several bond issues abroad, and has taken the lead in Chinese investment overseas. CITIC is a partner in China Investment Finance Corporation with the Royal Bank of Canada, a deposit-taking joint venture in Hong Kong, and is involved in two leasing companies, China Orient Leasing Company and the China Leasing Company, both incorporated in Hong Kong. In 1986 it took over the assets of the Ka Wah Bank in Hong Kong, and is a partner in the second cross-harbour tunnel project there. CITIC has offices in New York, Melbourne, Tokyo, Paris and Frankfurt.

Provincial/Municipal International Trust and Investment Corporations (*ITICs*)

There are many of these corporations, mostly licensed as financial institutions. In theory they can borrow from abroad and issue guarantees for foreign loans. They perform a limited range of functions, mainly attracting foreign investment and investing in projects. Not all have the initials "ITIC," for example Fujian Investment and Enterprise Company (FIEC).

The China Investment Bank (*CIB*)

Not to be confused in its investment functions with the CBOC, although the two work closely together, the CIB was established in 1981 as a channel for medium- and long-term loans to China from the World Bank and other multilateral organizations for small technical renovation projects as opposed to large aid-financed projects. It acts as on-lender in both renminbi and foreign exchange to developmental projects, and organizes syndicated loans and provides some capital participation in joint ventures. It also provides a consultancy service, and in 1985 formed a leasing company with Mitsui and Company, and the China National Technical Import Corporation.

State General Administration for Foreign Exchange Control (*SAFEX*)

This powerful organization draws up and implements foreign exchange regulations and approves guarantees given by Chinese organizations for foreign loans. Under the BOC until 1983, it now comes under the PBOC.

The People's Insurance Company of China (*PICC*)

Spun off from the People's Bank of China in 1984, the PICC has a monopoly on domestic and overseas insurance and reinsurance business. In recent years it has broadened its range of policies beyond the traditional marine cargo and hull and aviation insurance to include special policies for compensation trade, shipbuilding, contractor's all-risk and erection all-risk insurance. It also covers many major projects, and can provide most types of cover required, including third party liability and consequential loss insurance. It has two insurance affiliates overseas and has reinsurance relations with nearly 1,000 companies abroad.

The Bank of Communications (B.Comm) Active in Shanghai before the 1949 Revolution, the B.Comm has recently been revived there and has breached the state's monopoly on banking by building its capital base through share issues. A licensed financial institution, it can borrow from abroad and issue guarantees, and conducts all normal loan and deposit, settlement and remittance business in both renminbi and foreign exchange. It has participated in international lending syndicates and has invested abroad.

Shanghai Aijian Banking, Trust and Investment Company (Aijian) With activities similar to an ITIC, Aijian is non-governmental and was founded in 1986 by the largely overseas-Chinese-supported Shanghai Patriotic Construction Company.

Everbright Financial Corporation (EFC) A subsidiary of the Hong Kong-based Everbright Corporation, EFC was established in 1987 to handle a range of banking and financial activities, and may compete with organisations such as CITIC.

China Development and Investment Corporation (CDIC) Established in 1985 by the BOC Trust and Consultancy Company and the Ministry of Foreign Economic Relations and Trade's (MOFERT's) China National Export Commodity Base Construction Corporation, CDIC provides equity support for small and medium-sized export projects, including Sino-foreign joint ventures.

China Incomic Development Corporation Established in April 1985, Incomic provides consultancy, investment and foreign trade services.

It has authority to import equipment for ventures (including Sino-foreign joint ventures) in which it invests, and to act as agent for the venture's products.

China Venturetech Regarded as China's first real venture-capital organization, Venturetech is a joint venture between the State Science and Technology Commission, CITIC, three ministries (electronics industry, petroleum industry and coal), the Great Wall Industrial Corporation and the China National Petrochemical Corporation. Its brief is to work with and invest in small projects in the high-tech and materials-development areas, but it cannot engage in lending business.

BOC Trust and Consultancy Company This BOC subsidiary was founded in 1983 to act as a conduit for foreign investment and to invest in both domestic and Sino-foreign projects in China. It has stakes in two Sino-foreign leasing companies.

CCIC The Bank of China formed this licensed deposit-taking joint venture in Hong Kong with US and Japanese banks and China Resources (Holdings).

China International Finance Company (CIFC) This is a Hong Kong-based joint venture between the Bank of China's Shenzhen branch, the Bank of East Asia, Nomura Securities, Security Pacific Corporation and Sumitomo Bank.

Leasing companies China Orient Leasing, owned by CITIC, Japan Orient Leasing Company and one of the Beijing industrial bureaux, was the first Sino-foreign joint venture company of the kind to be established, in 1981. Since then the number of both domestic and joint venture organizations have grown, to about 50 by 1987. A prominent example is Trilease International, owned by BOC, Société Générale and Bank of East Asia. Attractive to Chinese importers of equipment as a way of circumventing credit restrictions, leasing business grew to an estimated $1bn-plus by 1985.

The markets

Markets of various types are appearing in the financial sector. Although still embryonic, they are already helping to solve some of the structural imbalances which hinder the development of financial resources.

The money markets

Interbank money markets have been created in Shenyang, Guangzhou, Changzhou, Chongqing, Wuhan, Shanghai, Beijing, Tianjin, Harbin and Xi'an. They enable banks to solve liquidity problems by borrowing surplus funds from other banks. Rates are fixed by the PBOC.

The domestic bond market has expanded rapidly as banks and enterprises have responded to credit restrictions by turning to the public for investment funds. Between 1981 and 1985 ¥23bn worth of bonds were issued to finance state deficits. Since 1985 banks have been allowed to discount treasury bonds, forming long-term secondary markets.

China's first bond market opened in Shenyang in August 1986, trading bonds issued by two local enterprises. Shanghai followed in September, then Beijing, Harbin and Tianjin in 1987.

Overseas bond issues were first made in 1982 (private placings in Tokyo). They have been used mainly to finance large infrastructural developments. Tokyo has been the main issuing centre, but both BOC and CITIC placed Deutschmark bonds in 1985 and both made Eurodollar issues in Japan. Hong Kong and Singapore have also been used. Following negotiations in New York over $30m of defaulted bonds, a syndicated $200m, loan was raised in the USA in 1987; previously all US bank loans were funded overseas. In the same year, following similar negotiations in Britain, the BOC made a $200m floating-rate note issue in London. Overseas capital markets borrowers include FIEC, SITCO and Guangdong and Tianjin ITICs.

The stock market

A stock market of sorts has emerged, although the "stock exchanges" in Beijing, Shanghai and Shenyang are mainly counters at banks where shares can be bought. There are no trading floors or specialized traders. Shanghai's exchange, which opened in September 1986, trades in the shares of two local companies. Beijing's exchange opened in January 1987.

Share issues curbed Although these "shares" are more like bonds, in that they yield a fixed interest rate plus a dividend when redeemed at maturity, the notion of stock ownership has not been easy to reconcile with the Chinese socialist system. Stock issues have also posed a threat to state attempts to control investment spending at the local level. Thus in April 1987 regulations were announced forbidding state enterprises from issuing stock to the public, restricting them to bond issues only, but under stricter conditions.

Foreign exchange trading

Foreign currency adjustment centres are another recent phenomenon – part of the Chinese government's efforts to assist enterprises by easing problems stemming from the inconvertibility of the renminbi. Centres were opened in Guangzhou and Beijing in mid-1986 for domestic enterprises, allowing them to trade surplus foreign exchange for renminbi at slightly higher than official rates. Centres for joint ventures followed in Guangzhou and Shanghai and then in the SEZs. Strict conditions were imposed on the uses to which purchased foreign exchange could be put, and the fixed rates of exchange in practice have failed to match the black market rate. Shenzhen, Zhuhai and Xiamen have since allowed rates to float.

Lawyers and accountants

Commercial law and accountancy were regarded with disdain from the 1950s until the 1980s. Now their importance is recognized as business with foreigners has become more complex.

Law

Foreign law firms are not permitted to represent clients directly in their dealings with Chinese organizations. However, major foreign law firms either maintain offices in China or have specialists in Chinese law on their staff. In practice Western companies turn to foreign law firms to represent their case in association with a Chinese firm. Foreign law firms have greater experience of commercial and international law than most Chinese firms.

Few local lawyers Chinese lawyers are few, and hardly any of them have experience in commercial and investment law. The leftist political campaigns in the 1960s and 1970s dramatically reduced the number of lawyers. Beijing had only 40 lawyers in 1979; there were still only 1,300 in 1987, serving a population of 8m. Chinese law firms thus tend to be comprehensive in their coverage.

Conciliation preferred Their experience in settling local domestic disputes predisposes many Chinese lawyers to aim for an acceptable compromise rather than pressing for full legal remedy. This conciliatory approach can at times work to the advantage of foreign companies, as can the Chinese lawyer's access to the unpublished guidelines which the bureaucracy have used, in the absence of formal laws, to control foreign companies in China.

Officially sponsored Since they are sponsored by ministries and quasi-government organizations, the independence of Chinese law firms cannot be guaranteed.

Western law firms

Baker and McKenzie, Suite 1803, CITIC Bldg, 19 Jianguomenwai Dajie, Beijing ☎ 5002255 ext. 1830 🄫 22907.

Coudert Brothers, 802 Noble Tower, 22 Jianguomenwai Dajie, Beijing ☎ 5123320 🄫 22291.
Paul, Weiss, Rifkind, Wharton and Garrison, 904 Noble Tower, 22 Jianguomenwai Dajie, Beijing ☎ 5123628 🄫 210169.

Chinese law firms

Beijing Foreign Economic and Trade Law Firm, Working People's Cultural Palace, Beijing ☎ 551343 🄫 22768.
China Global Law Office Room 1111 Noble Tower, 22 Jianguomenwai Dajie, Beijing ☎ 5128810 🄫 222222.
China Legal Affairs Centre, Sponsored by Ministry of Justice, 30 Dongjiaomin Xiang, Beijing ☎ 549527 🄫 22073.
C&C Law Office, Sponsored by China International Trust and Investment Corporation, 4th Fl, Temple of Heaven Hotel, 10 Tiyuguan Lu, Beijing ☎ 752831 ext. 352 🄫 20049.

Accountancy

Official audits for tax purposes can be undertaken only by Chinese accounting firms. However, foreign firms can provide advice on international tax planning (China has signed double-taxation agreements with most developed countries), on business registration and the preparation of tax returns. They can also provide management consultancy.

Foreign accountancy firms with offices in Beijing include seven of the Big Eight firms: Arthur Andersen and Company; Coopers & Lybrand; Deloitte, Haskins & Sells; Ernst & Whinney; Peat, Marwick, Mitchell and McClintock; Price Waterhouse; and Touche Ross and Company.

Trade promotion bodies

The numerous unknowns involved in all but the simplest transactions make it essential for the newcomer to business with China to seek advice. Fortunately, a wealth of advice and printed information is now available to offset the apparent inscrutability of China's trading and investment methods. However, for an accurate perspective of the market, it is worth consulting a wide range of sources.

The information sources

At the outset, contact should be made in the home country with the specialist trade promotion body, or the China section of the major trade promotion organization. They can usually advise on practical matters such as how to obtain a visa or find a translator, where to attend seminars and China briefings, and which government agencies in their country are involved in trade with China.

Lack of coordination Although Western governments lend considerable political and financial support to their companies' penetration of the relatively untapped China market, they rarely coordinate their efforts. Reports on China by the US Department of Commerce and the Central Intelligence Agency are prepared independently. There is a similar lack of coordination in business contacts between Chinese organizations and individual organizations at city or state level in the West.

Spreading the net Companies should find it worthwhile to make contact with the agencies for general information and studies in their field, including trade associations. Economic and market information is also available from embassies and consulates in China.

Research studies Academics in departments of Chinese and business studies in Western universities and institutes are now undertaking analytical work on the growing body of joint-venture case histories and other business concerns. Market research by consultancy firms exists for some sectors.

Exchanging experiences Experienced China business people in other companies (provided they are not competitors) are generally willing to share their experience and offer advice.

Trade promotion agencies

Belgium *Commission Economique Belgique-Chine*, Ave J B Van Gijsel 48, B-1810 Wemmel ☎ 479 99 94.

Europe *Directorate General for External Relations*, Commission of the European Community, 200 rue de la Loi, B1049 Brussels, Belgium ☎ 235 11 11.

France *Comité France-Chine*, 31 ave Pierre 1er de Serbie, 75784 Paris ☎ 47 23 61 61.

Italy *Camera di Commercio Italiana per la Cina*, Via Carducci 18, 20123 Milan ☎ 862765.

Netherlands *Nederland Centrum voor Handelsbevordering*, Bezuidenhoutseweg 181, PO Box 10, The Hague ☎ 478234.

Japan *Japan-China Association for Economy and Trade*, 1-2-3 Kitaraoyama, Minato-ku, Tokyo 107. *Japan External Trade Organization*, 2-2-5, Toranomon, Minato-ku, Tokyo 105 ☎ 582 3518.

Switzerland *Wirtschaftskammer Schweiz-China*, Löwenstrasse 119, CH-80901, Zürich.

UK *Sino-British Trade Council*, 5th Fl, Abford House, 15 Wilton Rd, London SW1V 1LT ☎ 828 5177.

USA *National Council for US-China Trade*, 1050, 17th St NW, Suite 350, Washington DC, 20036 ☎ 429-0340.

West Germany *Ost-Ausschuss der Deutschen Wirtschaft*, Arbeitskreis China, Gustav-Heinemann-Ufer 84–88, D-5000 Cologne 51. *Ostasiatischer Verein eV*, Neuer Jungfernstieg 21, D-2000 Hamburg 36 ☎ 3562557.

Business publications

Now that the major daily papers have active correspondents in China, many business people will probably need no more than one magazine subscription (such as *China Business Review*) and an investment guide or other handbook for background information. For those whose requirements are more extensive, there is a range of magazines and books, daily news reports from the New China (Xinhua) News Agency and on-line news services from Reuter's and other news agencies. Guides to trade and investment in China, as well as business newsletters, are distributed to clients (and potential clients) by the major legal and accountancy firms and by some banks. The Hongkong and Shanghai Banking Corporation produces reports on Beijing, Guangdong, Shanghai, Tianjin, Wuhan and Xiamen.

Business magazines

China-Britain Trade Review, published by the Sino-British Trade Council, London; 18pp, monthly. Sector and regional reports, contracts, exhibitions and other listings.

China Business Review, published by the National Council for US-China Trade, Washington DC; 62pp, every two months. Doyen of China business magazines. Comprehensive view on trading and investment, policies and methods, sectors and regions, statistics and analysis.

China Daily Semi-official newspaper published in Beijing, London and New York. Detailed and wide economic and business coverage from upbeat Chinese perspective.

China Database Economics and Foreign Trade, edited by the Economics Department, Sun Yat-sen University, Guangzhou, distributed by International Information Service Ltd, Hong Kong; 24pp, monthly. Wide range of material including new regulations, sector news and business opportunities based on raw material from Chinese agencies. No analysis or business perspective.

China Economic News, published by Economic and Information Consultancy Co, Hong Kong; 14pp, in English, weekly. Raw material drawn from semi-official Chinese-language *Economic Daily*; reliable and timely; new regulations, sector and provincial statistics, business opportunities.

China Economic Weekly, published by Anglo-Chinese Publications Ltd, UK; 24pp. Edited version of reports from *Economic Daily*, a semi-official Chinese-language publication.

China's Foreign Trade, published jointly by the China Council for the Promotion of International Trade and Longman, London; 48pp, monthly. Solid sector and regional reports, trade figures, business opportunities from Chinese perspective.

Chinese Newsletter, published by the Japan External Trade Organization, Tokyo; 24pp, every two months. Solid, analytical articles on aspects of economy and business methods.

China, North Korea Country Report, published by Economist Intelligence Unit, London; 40pp, quarterly. Comprehensive coverage and analysis of economic, trade and investment environment with selected sector developments; highlights economic trends.

China Trade Report, published by the South China Morning Post, Hong Kong; 16pp, monthly. Strong on sector and regional reports, trade and production statistics, business.

China Trader, published by Sino Communications Co, Hong Kong; 4pp, weekly. Selected news stories, sector and financial features.

Far Eastern Economic Review, Hong Kong; 116pp. Comprehensive weekly with punch of *Time* and economic clout of *The Economist*. Tailored for business reader.

Business Awareness

The vastness of the country and three thousand years of history combine to make China a self-contained world. Foreigners must accommodate Chinese national pride and use the language of "mutual benefit and equality" if they are to succeed in doing business in China. They must also adopt a long-term strategy and a patient attitude, and acknowledge the fact that the Chinese prefer to deal with people they know, by consistently fielding the same personnel.

The Chinese at work

Despite the opening-up to Western companies in the 1980s, few Chinese have more than a superficial grasp of what makes Western business tick.

Attitudes were already shaped by 2,000 years of bureaucratic life, and the Party's campaigns over the last 40 years to change the *zuofeng* (work style) have had little effect. The route to promotion depends on not making mistakes. Showing initiative may lead to trouble; no one is blamed for referring decisions upwards. After 30 years of a planned economy, the significance of efficiency and cost-effectiveness is not obvious to them. To operate successfully in China, the foreigner must bridge the perception gap.

Hours Government departments' official hours are 8–12 and 1–5, Monday to Saturday. Most offices follow this pattern. Chinese office workers take a relaxed attitude to time-keeping and, despite repeated exhortations to government employees to take only one hour off at midday, the break inevitably extends to two hours, to include a meal in the canteen and an after-lunch *xiuxi* (siesta). During the summer, office workers are often sent home early. Most offices are empty at 5.05pm. A cycle or bus ride to work of up to an hour is normal in the cities.

Communicating

Telephones Until recently there were no telephone directories in China. Establishing contact can still be difficult because the answerer, instead of naming the organization he or she represents, usually replies with a rather querulous "*Wei?*" (hello), a word which also punctuates most telephone conversations. Switchboard operators rarely speak any language other than Chinese.

Slow response Chinese organizations are notoriously slow at responding to telexes and letters. Frequently the delay is simply because the time is not ripe, the decision not yet made. In the meantime it may be a loss of "face" to admit to a delay. A notable exception is the China International Trust and Investment Corporation (CITIC), which has been successfully educating its staff in basic customer awareness with the slogan "Answer all letters, be willing to speak on the telephone, always be ready to see people." Authorization is necessary for junior staff to telex or write abroad.

Communication is poor between Chinese organizations. They are not encouraged to interact with each other, if they belong to different "systems" (which report to different ministries), without the highest approval.

Not in writing Most Chinese hold the information they require in their own notebooks and information is exchanged orally. Use of a Chinese typewriter is elaborate and time-consuming, paper may be in short supply, and photocopiers are few and liable to break down, so memos, meeting notes and the rest of the deluge of paper characteristic of Western offices are absent in China.

Hierarchies

Each Chinese factory and corporation is part of a hierarchy which is headed by a ministry or equivalent body. A handful of top people, centred on the Party's Politburo, take the key decisions. Major contracts are decided at ministerial level. Only those at the top of each organization are the "responsible comrades" (*fuze tongzhi*) who can make decisions.

The negotiators

Chinese team The Chinese team in a typical negotiation will include representatives from the plant, a foreign trade corporation and the plant's sponsoring bureau or ministry. The plant, which is often the originator of the discussions, may be represented by its manager and chief engineer. Since the plant probably has little experience in dealing with foreigners, the relevant trade corporation provides the expertise. The sponsoring department will have to give its permission for the deal, so it should, if possible, be represented in discussions. There may also be input from research institutes (especially for technology transfer) and, for investment discussions, a business matchmaker such as the China International Trust and Investment Corporation (CITIC).

Professional negotiators from the trading corporations will lead the discussion. Often there is no incentive for them to conclude a particular negotiation – it is usually the plant manager who wants an agreement quickly.

Decision-making

Decisions usually entail discussion among a number of people. Changes in the political line have in the past resulted in demotion for those who "stuck their head out." Junior officials are unwilling to act without prior permission: if the key decision-maker is away, the decision has to wait.

Slow talks Negotiations are often slow because the Chinese team does not have authority to take decisions. If the team does agree to a concession at the negotiating table, it may be denied the following day because higher authorities have taken a different view.

Rank

Rank is important. People are addressed according to their position, as "Chairman Wang" (*Wang zhuxi*) or "Party-secretary Bai" (*Bai shuji*), rather than as "Mr" (*Xiansheng*), which is reserved for foreigners. Titles take the same form, for men or women.

The main ranks are:

Zhuxi Chairman (of corporation)
Guwen Adviser (to any body)
Lishi Director (of corporation)
Jingli Manager (within corporation)
Changzhang Manager (of a plant)
Zonggongchengshi Chief engineer (of a plant)
Shuji Party secretary.

Seniority usually depends on age. The position of adviser has been popularized to encourage elderly figures to retire from active service.

Helicopters A few younger people, dubbed "helicopters" (*zhishengji*), do find fast promotion. There is general suspicion of them, not least because their rise may depend more on genealogy than on genius.

Visible status Rank is visibly expressed in clothes which have a finer cut or cloth than is generally available and in having sole use of a car and driver.

Cadres, not officials To dissociate itself from the elitism implied in the word "official," the Communist Party adopted the term cadre (*ganbu*) to describe specialists and administrators. Having a desk job nevertheless still gives immediate status in a country with 800m peasants.

Women in business

Industry and commerce in China are dominated by men, but there are enough women in responsible posts for a woman representing a foreign business not to be a novelty.

Chinese women

Confucian teaching, dominant for 2,000 years, has fostered the idea that "a woman does not talk about affairs outside the home" (in the words of the 5th-century BC *Book of Rites*). Moralists portrayed any woman who did become powerful as inevitably a source of national disaster. This theme was recently applied to Jiang Qing who, as wife of the ageing Mao Zedong, presided over the latter stages of the erratic and cruel regime of the Cultural Revolution.

Party policy has for half a century declared the equality of women, most famously in the slogan "Women hold up half of Heaven." The political and educational process has had a considerable effect on public attitudes. It is nowadays politically unacceptable, and therefore career-limiting, for men to belittle women in public.

Women in the work force

Training programmes in the 1950s and 1960s selected women to become engineers and join previously all-male professions, so that 27% of scientists and 24% of China's 20m officials are women. Women in top positions are few, however; one was Chen Muhua, formerly head of the Ministry of Foreign Economic Relations and Trade and later honorary president of the Bank of China.

Working mothers Few people remain unmarried after the age of 30. Most urban couples have only one child, and it is still largely the woman's responsibility to care for the child and look after the home. She also goes out to work, since few families are willing to forgo the wife's income. Large organizations have their own day nurseries and kindergartens. Alternatively the children may be looked after by grandparents or, with the increase of nuclear families, by nannies. There are more than 30,000 maids and nannies working in Beijing.

Dress By Western standards, Chinese women wear fairly conventional, albeit brightly coloured clothes. Although coloured blouses, skirts and scarves are common, it is rare for jewellery, perfume or make-up to be worn. For formal occasions many Chinese women wear Western suits, with either trousers or a skirt.

The foreign businesswoman

Chinese contacts are always wary of newcomers, male or female, unless their high status is immediately apparent by their holding a top position in business or government. Foreign middle management and technical people all have to work hard to establish the credibility of their organization, their position in it and their own level of expertise; gender makes little difference.

Drinking Negotiating sessions are interspersed with dinners, which may involve heavy drinking. Foreign women who join in the revelry and drink intensively – provided the hosts are equally inebriated – are considered strong characters. Chinese women often decline to drink alcohol – Westerners may follow suit but it is advisable to make preferences clear at the beginning of the meal.

Modesty best policy Western businesswomen should adapt to the Chinese style; short or tight skirts and low-cut or clinging dresses are best avoided. Trousers are, of course, acceptable.

Safety China is one of the safest places on earth. Even in large cities, or late at night, it is virtually unknown for a foreigner to be attacked, although young Chinese women are hesitant about going out alone at night in Shanghai.

Dress, manners and gifts

Chinese people are casual about dress; they know little of foreign fashion and are curious about Western clothes. Although the structure of meetings is formal, the atmosphere can be relaxed. Exchanging gifts is a mark of establishing a relationship.

Dressing for business

Chinese dress A Chinese government minister or corporation president may wear a suit and tie at a formal meeting, but the vast majority of Chinese people dress according to the weather. Thick sweaters may be worn under suit jackets in winter, jackets left at home in summer. The *zhongshan* or "Mao suit" is disappearing in favour of the Western suit for people in business.

Mix and match Foreign business travellers should match what their Chinese counterparts are wearing. At the first meeting, it is a good idea to dress formally, but men should remove jacket and tie if the Chinese have come without theirs. Chinese people show little self-consciousness about the needs of the body. If it is hot it is perfectly acceptable to roll up a trouser leg.

Gimmick To adopt outlandish hairstyle or clothes may distract the Chinese from the matters under negotiation. However, a personal foible, such as consistently wearing a bow tie, will make you (and thus your company) more memorable. It is worth remembering that the Chinese tend to think that Westerners all look alike.

Manners

Chinese people are invariably polite to foreigners, even when negotiations are at their hottest. Westerners should repay the compliment. Foreigners who lose their temper may also lose the possibility of gaining another entry visa.

Greetings and farewells are important to the Chinese. Business travellers usually go to China at the invitation of a host organization and until recently it was normal for the organization to send someone of appropriately senior rank to meet visitors at the airport and see them off at the end of their visit. As senior staff become more pressed for time, the custom is being abandoned, although a junior member of staff will be sent with a car to escort the visitors. Shaking hands is normal on meeting and departing.

Presents

Gifts are regularly given to foreign business contacts. They are usually traditional Chinese handicrafts and are presented at the end of the banquet hosted by the Chinese side. Although it is acceptable not to open the gift on the spot, unwrapping it for all to see and expressing appreciation is welcomed.

Presenting gifts Foreign visitors should give presents in return, either at the same occasion, or at the banquet they host. Gifts should be presented in a formal manner: they are a public token of friendship. They should be wrapped, preferably in red, the colour of happiness. Ideally there should be a gift for every member of the Chinese team, with a larger gift for the most senior member.

What to choose Care is needed in selecting gifts, since Chinese organizations may require all gifts received to be reported. Gifts may be presented "for the organization;" a VCR, for example, can be justified to prying eyes as necessary for educational purposes, even if it can also be used to entertain staff with foreign films. Otherwise, presents should be small enough to be kept by individuals. The best gifts are items which are inexpensive in the West but rare in China, such as silk ties, high-quality pens and scarves. A packet of foreign cigarettes is always appreciated by drivers.

Business meetings

The Chinese see business meetings as a method of eliciting information on foreign technology as much as a means of achieving a specific contract goal. The Chinese team rarely has full authority to negotiate; decisions involve many departments whose decision makers are not present. Negotiations can be infuriatingly slow.

Preparation

The Chinese will match whatever level of seniority is represented in the visiting team. Although it is important to attract senior Chinese to a discussion, the ground is best broken by middle managers and technical personnel. The company president can be held in reserve, ready to visit when pressure needs to be applied to speed up approvals at a higher level. The presence of senior management in initial discussions leaves the middle-level negotiating team with little authority.

Continuity is important once a team is chosen. Suspicious of foreign intentions, the Chinese prefer to deal with people they know. It is an advantage to be seen as a *lao pengyou* (old friend).

What's in a name? Having your name translated into a Chinese equivalent that is easy on the Chinese ear is essential. Chinese names usually have three syllables (each represented by a character). It is advisable for foreigners to keep theirs equally short and easy to remember: for example, Tomlinson could be shortened to Tang. Initials should be omitted. Long names transcribed mechanically into Chinese are difficult for Chinese people to remember as are Russian names for most Westerners.

Company names need to be translated with considerable care. Particular sounds in English may be transliterated into any one of a number of Chinese characters. Ideally the name should convey an idea of the company business and evoke the sound of the name in English. A certain soft drink has selected for its Chinese name characters which sound well in Chinese and mean "tasty and enjoyable" – *ke kou ke le*.

The meeting

Business meetings usually take place in a setting arranged by the Chinese counterpart, either in their offices or in a negotiation building. An endless supply of Chinese tea will be served to lubricate the proceedings.

Shaking hands On entering the negotiating room, it is customary for the whole foreign team to file round the room to shake hands with all the Chinese side. If there are large numbers of people, it is wise to leave the exchange of business cards until everyone is seated.

Introductions The senior Chinese may say a few words of welcome (*huanying*), after which it is firmly up to the foreign side to open the discussion. The foreign group leader introduces their team (giving ample time for each member to distribute cards) and invites the Chinese side to do the same. Since not all the Chinese team will have business cards, it is worthwhile passing round a piece of paper asking for each person's name, position and organization. It is necessary to repeat this process each time there is a change in the Chinese team. The foreign side then introduces the company and proposal.

Clear presentation The track record of a foreign company is an important factor in assessing its proposal, and should be presented in some detail. Some of the Chinese side may not know even the company name; few will be familiar with the overall company scope. Brand names famous all over the world may be unknown to the Chinese. The Chinese appreciate a step-by-step presentation, tracing a line from the corporation, to the specific company, to the specific product or service relevant to the negotiations. Wit is not expected, jokes best avoided.

A full explanation will be interpreted by the Chinese not as a reflection of their ignorance, but as a sign of frankness.

Explain as you go During the meetings, the foreign company is faced by a range of people on the other side of the table. These typically include trade officials with limited technical knowledge and technical personnel with no knowledge of foreign companies. Since the eventual decision relies on a consensus, it is essential that all the Chinese participants end up with a clear picture of what is on offer. For the benefit of the trade officials it may be important to explain in layman's terms why a product or technology is desirable; conversely, the technical personnel may stumble over management jargon unless the terms are explained. This is all the more necessary if the composition of the Chinese team changes from session to session.

Interest in technology Members of the Chinese team expect to use the negotiating session to extract the maximum information about both the company's technology and the latest developments in the technology worldwide. Restrictions on contact with the outside world in the 1960s and 1970s left Chinese specialists who have to assess foreign technology uncertain of the extent of their knowledge, despite a massive inflow of technical information into China in the 1980s. In certain fields, however, the Chinese already have considerable expertise, so there is always a risk of divulging key technology principles and methods only to find the Chinese going it alone.

Foreign initiative Although a business discussion may be starting as a result of an initial inquiry by the Chinese, the underlying expectation among the Chinese in many meetings is that the foreign side will be making proposals, the Chinese accepting or rejecting them, or proposing modifications.

Objectives undefined Priorities and plans are generally not agreed on the Chinese side before negotiations begin. Project definition takes place as the negotiations continue. In technology transfer discussions, only when the technology is explained can the Chinese side evaluate how it could be assimilated.

Formal proposals to higher bodies must include a description of the technology to be transferred and the terms offered by the foreign company: the higher body – often the relevant industry ministry or bureau – will want to shape the deal from its own perspective.

Chinese reluctance to reveal requirements to foreigners until as late as possible may be the classic negotiating ploy of the purchaser feigning indifference; it may also be that requirements are fluid, dependent on what the foreigner offers.

Attitude to foreigners China's introverted culture and 30 years of isolation from the West have left most Chinese people suspicious of foreigners, a feeling amplified by Party warnings not to become contaminated by too close a contact. Chinese counterparts are slow to divulge information: today's business information may be tomorrow's state secret.

Taking the foreigners for granted Little allowance is made for the fact that the presence of the foreign teams in China represents a considerable commitment by the foreign company of manpower and time. The Chinese assume that everyone is beating a path to their open door, an assumption justified by the rush of companies to China in the early 1980s. Foreign companies are treated as though they had limitless resources.

Communicating

Language is but one of the barriers to getting across the message. Pace and style also have to be adjusted in order to cross the cultural gap.

Chinese-language material introducing the company and specific product should be distributed to all of the Chinese team. It is treated as reference material and need not be expensively produced.

Diagrams are particularly useful in explaining the company hierarchy. They should be in English and Chinese, with a copy handed to each of the Chinese team.

Interpreters vary in their abilities, naturally. Because successful communication is so dependent on their efforts, it is worthwhile making their work as smooth as possible. Simple words and short sentences should be used. To avoid over-reliance on the interpreter's memory and to minimize the use of short-cut paraphrases, delivery should be in short paragraphs, with the interpreter translating paragraph by paragraph.

English is the major second language in China. A number of the Chinese team members may understand spoken English, although they may not make this obvious; they may also recognize the English – when they see it written – for obscure technical terms which may floor the interpreters.

Hospitality

The Chinese rarely entertain foreigners in their homes, which lack the facilities and space of residences in the West. Neither the theatre nor other entertainment is popular as a means of cementing business relations. The only exception is table tennis: anyone who can handle a ping-pong bat is on the inside track. The preferred method of getting to know foreign business partners is over the dinner table, in the private room of a restaurant or hotel. A dinner, or banquet, establishes the informal ties which facilitate business negotiations, at the same time giving the opportunity to probe positions and possibilities without any commitment: negotiations the following morning will ignore what has been said.

Banquets

Banquets are usually held in the early evening, at 6 or 6.30. This accords with Chinese custom and allows those on the Chinese side who do not have a company driver to return home by public transport (buses become infrequent after 9pm). The Chinese are hosts at the dinner which marks the visitors' arrival and the foreigners host the eve-of-departure dinner.

In most cases, older and more conservative Chinese prefer Chinese food, although they will be too polite to admit that they find Western food unpalatable. However, there is a new generation of Chinese who are as eager to learn about Western food and fashions as about Western technology; they would be delighted to be entertained in a European-style restaurant in an international hotel.

Advice In almost all cases, an interpreter will have been assigned to the foreign visitor or visitors by the host organization. It is often worthwhile to consult the interpreter, who may be able to advise on choice of restaurant for entertaining the Chinese team and on other matters of etiquette.

Invitations to formal banquets are usually arranged initially by telephone. Once it is established that someone is free to attend, a formal written invitation is sent.

Dining protocol No matter how informal a dinner may become, the host cannot forget his role. Even when seating arrangements appear casual, the Chinese host will ensure that his chief guest sits on his right, usually facing the door, the second guest on his left. The interpreter will then sit next to the chief guest. Considerable embarrassment, if not offence, may be caused if seating protocol is ignored.

Piling the plate The Chinese host will put food on his guests' plates. The host may select the largest piece of gelatinous sea-slug, or the eye muscle of a fish, to grace the plate of his chief guest. Although it is considered ungracious to refuse such morsels, it is acceptable to leave them on your plate. The faster you clear your plate, the more it will be replenished. It is wise to eat sparingly from the first courses, since there may be eight or nine to follow. Tradition dictates that there must be surplus food on the guest's plate and on serving dishes at the end of a meal. Rice is served only at the end of the meal. It is generally considered polite not to finish the rice; if you do, it indicates that you are still hungry.

Manners are primarily a matter of personal concern for others and have little to do with personal habits. It is important for a host to see that his guest is well looked after and that his plate is kept well stocked; it is not considered impolite to savour your soup noisily, or to spit out unchewed gristle on the tablecloth or floor.

Chopsticks An attempt should be made to use chopsticks (*kuaizi*) at least at the beginning of the meal, before recourse to knife and fork. Remarks on dexterity, or lack of it, should be taken in good part. The important thing is to join in the fun. Practice with chopsticks before visiting China is well rewarded, and anyway it is no disgrace to drop food on the pristine tablecloth.

Speeches set on record the framework within which negotiations are taking place. References to "mutual benefit" and "friendship between our two countries" are a necessary ritual for articulating a relationship which in the West would be left unstated.

Photos for the memory Taking photographs of the negotiating team together signals friendship and long-term commitment. A Polaroid picture which can be presented immediately is especially welcome. Every member of the Chinese team should receive a print. The foreigner may improve recollection of Chinese faces by asking each person to sign the photograph.

Drinking

A toast usually concludes any speech. The host may walk round the table to clink glasses before draining his with the word *ganbei* – literally "empty glass." Toasts are usually drunk in wine or spirits (including the high-octane *maotai*) and in fact this is the only occasion on which spirits are drunk. Beer (counted as a soft drink), lemonade and colas are always provided. Those who are prepared to join in and enjoy a drinking competition will be appreciated by more traditional Chinese. Those who prefer to drink more modestly should set the tone at the beginning of the meal. A non-drinker can always plead "doctor's orders," which will be most sympathetically accepted by the Chinese, who tend to be very concerned about their health.

Sightseeing

A pilgrimage to local scenic spots – in Beijing, the Forbidden City and the Great Wall – has been a standard requirement for foreign business travellers. In the past, refusal to participate was likely to be interpreted as an insult to China's cultural heritage. Since the mid-1980s, however, Chinese hosts have begun to show a more responsive attitude and to be very understanding if visitors say they have seen the Great Wall several times already; it is up to the foreigner if he or she prefers to spend a free afternoon roaming on a hired bicycle rather than being guided to tourist spots.

Cultural Awareness

A historical perspective

Since China was first unified in the 3rd century BC, central rule by the emperor (and subsequently, by the Communist Party) has been accepted as the norm, despite long periods in which the empire disintegrated, and despite Chinese people's deep-rooted loyalty to their home province. New dynasties were established by force, several by invaders such as the Mongols and Manchus. These were assimilated by the resilient Chinese culture, but the Europeans who arrived in the 19th century to trade and convert represented a force that could not be absorbed, and the Chinese were forced out of their centuries-long isolation.

Early history

The discovery of "Peking Man" and his fellows, whose fossilized bones have been found in caves at Zhoukoudian near Beijing, shows early human habitation in China 500,000 years ago.

The incised numbers and ideographs on pottery found at Yangshao, near Xian in the north, dating from around 4500BC, are probably the world's earliest examples of writing. Successive civilizations – the Xia, the Shang and the Zhou – flourished in the area under hereditary rulers, but by 700BC centralized control had given way to independent kingdoms. This diversity made possible the great age of Chinese philosophy, when "The Hundred Schools" flourished. Confucius (*Kongfuzi*) established the doctrine that officials needed to be scholars; the followers of the *Tao* (Way) explored the mysteries of man in the universe.

Early Emperors

The Qin The king of Qin united the kingdoms by force, to form the Qin empire (221–206BC). Existing fortifications were extended to form the Great Wall, which was frequently repaired and adjusted in later dynasties. The first Qin emperor was buried with a life-sized terracotta army, recently unearthed near present-day Xian.

The Han Dynasty, which survived from 206BC to AD220, established the pattern of the Chinese state and gave its name to the ethnic Chinese, the Han. A civil service was formed and trade with the West began – silk being the most important export.

The Tang Following the decline of the Han dynasty, the empire disintegrated and remained divided for nearly 400 years. Reunification by the Sui rulers laid the foundation for the Tang culture (AD618–907) and developed the Grand Canal. The Tang extended their rule to cover much of the territory which now comprises the People's Republic.

The Song presided over a rapid expansion of agriculture and manufacture, spurred by technical innovation. They made steel, used water-powered spinning machines, developed primitive cannons and grenades, and improved printing techniques.

Mongol hordes The expansion of the Central Asian empire had encompassed China by the time Kublai became Khan (ruler). In 1260 Kublai declared himself the founder of a new Chinese dynasty, the Yuan, and established his capital at Taidu (Beijing), in northern China.

Ming The early Ming presented their rule as a return to traditional Chinese forms, although they were no less autocratic than the Yuan. Confucian ideology was reaffirmed

and the civil service strengthened. In the early 1400s, Chinese expeditions ventured as far as East Africa.
The Qing The Manchu conquerors who came from the northeast (Manchuria), retained the Ming bureaucracy and founded the Qing (Ch'ing) dynasty (1644–1911). The Chinese had to wear their hair in a queue as a sign of subservience.

Confrontation with the West
Macao (Aomen), on the estuary leading to Canton (Guangzhou), flourished in the 16th century as the first European trade settlement in China. At times tolerated, at times harassed by the Chinese, it was never officially recognized by the introverted court which, like its predecessors, saw trade as a form of tribute from barbarians. In the 1700s and 1800s Dutch and English traders were restricted to Macao, and trade was allowed only in Guangzhou.
Opium wars Friction in Guangzhou over the British traders' practice of paying for tea and other commodities with opium instead of silver resulted in war with Britain (1840–42). Superior arms enabled Britain to force upon China a series of treaties allowing Western traders easier access to Chinese ports. One result of this first "Opium War" was that Hong Kong Island was ceded to Britain in 1842. Britain and France were involved in a second Opium War with China in 1857–60.
Punitive expeditions by Western navies in the mid-1800s anticipated the establishment later in the century of foreign "concession areas" in the major ports and the division of China into spheres of influence. The Russians and Japanese dominated in the northeast, the Germans in Shandong, the British along the Yangzi, the Japanese in Taiwan, the French in the southwest.
Rebellions against the Qing were directed against corruption at court and foreign encroachment. The Taiping Rebellion led to the formation of a breakaway kingdom

which lasted from 1850–64. A later popular uprising – that of the "Righteous and Harmonious Fists," called "The Boxers" by Europeans – foreshadowed the nationalist struggles which have shaped Chinese history in the 20th century. Missionaries, suspected of kidnapping Chinese children, and worse, were among their targets.

Nationalists vs Communists
Efforts by intellectuals to modernize China and make it more powerful and to reform imperial rule proved ineffective against the conservative empress dowager, Zi Xi (1860–1908). A republic was declared in Nanjing in 1912 but a first attempt by Sun Yat-sen, leader of the emerging nationalist movement, at forming a democratic state was thwarted by the provisional president, Yuan Shikai, who planned to restore imperial government, with himself as emperor.
May Fourth movement Student demonstrations broke out in Beijing on May 4 1919, when it was learned that under the Treaty of Versailles, German territories in Shandong would not be returned to China but given to Japan. A nationalist movement quickly developed.
The Nationalist Party (Guomindang or Kuomintang), with the support of the new Soviet Union, built up a training base in Guangzhou. Sun Yat-sen died before the Nationalist forces achieved any significant success but he came to be revered as the founder of the Chinese republic.
The Chinese Communist Party, founded in Shanghai in 1921, pursued the strategy of joining the Nationalist Party to overthrow the warlords (the military barons who effectively controlled large areas of China) to unite the country and to expel foreigners.
Shanghai slaughter Communists and union organizers had already taken over the centre of Shanghai by the time the Nationalist forces

arrived in 1927. The Nationalists carried out a sudden purge of left-wing members, killing or imprisoning the revolutionairies. The Nationalist government established in Nanjing under Chiang Kai-shek was supported by warlords, industrialists and foreigners fearful of a Marxist revolution.

Jiangxi Soviet The Communist Party, illegal from 1927, founded small soviets in remote areas across the country. The political commissar of the largest of them in Jiangxi was Mao Zedong, who had led an abortive peasant uprising in Changsha.

The Long March Campaigns by the Nationalists continued, and the Communist bases had to be abandoned. To escape the Nationalists, in 1935, Communists started to trek towards the remote west, ending up a year later in the mountains of Shaanxi. During the trek, which came to be called the Long March, Mao Zedong emerged as paramount leader of the Communist forces. Of the 100,000 who started out on the 9,000km/5,600-mile march, only 10,000 survived. They formed an inner brotherhood within the Party leadership which still existed in the 1970s.

Japanese invasion Chiang Kai-shek's main concern was the extermination of the Communist "bandits". When the Japanese bombed Shanghai in 1932, Chiang signed a peace agreement with them. He offered no resistance to the Japanese annexation of northeast China, and his failure to respond to widespread anti-Japanese feeling lost him considerable public support.

A united front of Nationalists and Communists followed the full-scale Japanese invasion in 1937. The Japanese held central China and key routes south. The Nationalist government retreated to Chongqing (Chungking), where it was supplied and supported by the Allies. The Communists conducted guerilla warfare against the Japanese from the bases in the northwest.

Civil war The defeat of Japan in 1945 was followed by a scramble for territory, the Communists moving from Yan'an to take north China, the Nationalists from Chongqing into central China and the south. Despite attempts by US envoys to arrange a compromise, civil war followed, and the Nationalists were forced to flee to Formosa (Taiwan).

The People's Republic

The peace and stability which followed the establishment of the People's Republic, proclaimed on October 1 1949, earned the new government widespread support. The foreigners living in China on privileged terms were expelled.

Fanshen The process of "turning over the body" *(fanshen)* – that is, of distributing land among the peasants – had begun in the Communist-led areas in 1946, and continued elsewhere until 1951. Village meetings often ended with landlords being beaten up or killed.

Nationalization of private industry was completed by 1956. Heavy "fines" and "taxes" were levied on foreign and large companies in the early 1950s, but many former owners received compensation.

Soviet assistance The USSR helped China with 150 key projects which formed the basis of many industries, and gave China moral support in international affairs. Collision with UN forces in the Korean War left China isolated from the USA and the West in general.

The "hundred flowers" failure Mao Zedong's call in 1956 to let "a hundred flowers blossom, a hundred schools of thought contend" aimed to revive the diversity and liveliness of ancient Chinese thought. Intellectuals used the occasion to attack not just isolated examples of the Party's pettiness but the very principle of the Party's monopoly of power. But then a campaign of meetings and press articles in 1957 smothered the growth of free expression and led to many arrests.

Great Leap Impatience with the slow pace of social change led Mao to unleash what he considered an untapped force capable of overcoming physical restraints – the human will. The Great Leap Forward of 1958–59 aimed to build socialism through the rapid development of communes and rural industry. The ensuing disruption and chaos were exacerbated by two years of natural disasters and failed harvests. Mao temporarily retired.

Soviet split Disagreements over the USSR's interference in Chinese politics and its refusal to pass on nuclear technology made Mao impatient. China's patriotic pride and desire for "self-reliance" finally resulted in the withdrawal of Soviet assistance in 1960.

The Cultural Revolution When the minister of defence Peng Dehuai expressed the view in 1959 that the Great Leap had been a gigantic mistake, Mao had him sacked. The traditional method of circumventing censorship under imperial rule, through historical plays and allegories, was revived. The idea that Mao was another autocratic despot was implied in the play *Hai Rui Dismissed from Office*, performed in 1966.

Mao and his supporters organized a campaign of criticism against the play which developed into an overall attack on "revisionism." Officials and intellectuals were reviled in the press and paraded at mass rallies, while zealous "Red Guards" responded to Mao's call to "Carry on the Revolution to the End." Physical abuse was commonplace; many people were killed. Loyalty to "Mao Zedong Thought," embodied in the "Little Red Book" of Mao's quotations, became the chief criterion for survival in power for anyone in authority. Foreign films and books, as well as traditional Chinese operas and novels, were generally banned.

By 1969 the People's Liberation Army had been called in to end the chaos. Revolutionary Committees, which included the military, replaced the anarchic rule of rival Red Guard factions, many of whose members were dispersed to the countryside. However, nearly a decade passed before the Great Proletarian Cultural Revolution was officially declared a disaster. Chinese people now frequently refer to the Cultural Revolution as "the lost decade" or the "ten bad years."

The death of Mao Zedong in 1976 marked the end of the excesses. The trial of Mao's wife Jiang Qing and of a few others exorcised to a degree the disgrace and denigration experienced by intellectuals and officials. For the many young people involved, the abrupt policy reversals brought disillusionment with the Party, but the retention of Mao as a figurehead of the revolution indicated unity as a central political aim.

Democracy Wall became a symbol of free expression in 1978 when liberals used wall posters pasted up at a central bus station in Beijing to debate the nation's political predicament. These spontaneous expressions were curtailed by the authorities.

World welcome for China The instatement of the People's Republic in China's seat at the UN and the visit to China of President Nixon in the early 1970s marked the re-entry of China into the mainstream of world affairs.

The reformist line The post-Mao leadership, centred round Deng Xiaoping, won the firm loyalty of the educational and administrative establishment by a return to orderly government. A bold programme of political and economic reforms was introduced in the mid-1980s: the people's communes were abolished, a limited degree of private enterprise was allowed, travel abroad became easier, consumer goods were more readily available and socially acceptable and, as part of the new "open door" policy, China began to encourage foreign investment.

Key dates in Chinese History

500,000BC Prehistoric "Peking Man".
551–479BC Life of Confucius (Kongfuzi).
475–221BC The age of philosophers.
221–206BC Qin dynasty. First Great Wall.
206BC–AD**220** Han dynasty.
581–618 Sui dynasty.
618–907 Tang dynasty.
970–1127 Song dynasty.
1280–92 Marco Polo in China.
1260–1368 Yuan (Mongol) dynasty.
1368–1644 Ming dynasty.
1644–1912 Qing (Manchu) dynasty.
1840–42 First Opium War with Britain.
1842 Hong Kong Island ceded to Britain.
1850–64 Taiping Rebellion.
1898 New Territories leased to Britain for 100 years.
1899–1901 "Boxer" Rebellion.
1912 Declaration of Republic by Sun Yat-sen.
1919 May Fourth Movement.
1921 Chinese Communist Party founded.
1923–27 Nationalist-Communist collaboration.
1927 Nationalist "White Terror" against the Communists.
1928 Soviet established in Jiangxi. Nationalist government in Nanjing.
1930–34 Nationalist "Bandit Suppression" campaign against Communists.
1934–35 The Long March.
1937 United Front formed against Japan.
1938 Nationalist capital moved to Chongqing.
1945 Nationalist-Communist Civil War begins.
1949 Foundation of People's Republic of China (PRC).
1950 Friendship Pact with Soviet Union. Chinese enter Korean War.
1956 Hundred Flowers period of limited free expression.
1957 Anti-revisionist campaign ends Hundred Flowers.
1958–59 Great Leap Forward. Formation of communes.
1960 Split with Soviet Union begins.
1964 China explodes nuclear device.
1966–76 Great Proletarian Cultural Revolution.
1971 Rapprochement with USA; PRC takes China seat at UN.
1976 Death of Mao Zedong.
1978 Democracy Wall. Beginning of economic reform.
1982 Communes abolished.
1984 14 coastal cities look for foreign investment. Sino-British agreement on the return of Hong Kong to Chinese sovereignty.
1987 13th Party Congress reaffirms reformist line.
1989 June 4 suppression of pro-democracy students.

Beliefs, attitudes and lifestyles

The Chinese way of life is shaped by certain ideals which are centuries old and unchanging, despite political changes. Respect for age and rank, and a strong need to belong – to the family, the organization, the Party – are deep-rooted in Chinese society. Belonging to a group implies readiness to conform, which in turn makes for very correct and formal behaviour in official and business dealings. However, the formality is dropped for private occasions, when the Chinese show the relaxed and fun-loving side of their nature.

Politics and society

Politics hold no particular interest for most Chinese, who have painful memories of the campaigns which for a generation have periodically disrupted their work and leisure. Cynicism towards Marxism has grown since official pronouncements and daily reality parted company during the Great Leap Forward in the 1950s. Anyone with ambition must join the Communist Party, however.

Unobtrusively present Party policies are disseminated through a hierarchy of Party branches in every institution, from investment corporation to kindergarten. When crucial decisions are made, what counts is seniority in the Party rather than public rank: a plant director might defer to the branch secretary or Party committee.

Neighbourhood committees see and hear everything that happens in their locality. If an unemployed youth suddenly arrives home with a new TV set, the committee will ask his parents for an explanation. Rising living standards and political apathy have made the committees less prominent, but they remain an effective brake on crime and social disorder. The committees are backed up by the Public Security Bureau, always ready to clamp down on anti-social behaviour.

Collective responsibility makes the group answerable for the individual's behaviour. This concept can extend to foreigners: if a visitor abuses his credit card facility in a Chinese hotel, the hotel may suddenly decide to refuse all credit cards.

Regional allegiances

Most Chinese, when asked – abroad – where they are from, give the name of a province or city rather than "China." Loyalty is to your home town (*laoxiang*). Speaking the same dialect, not to mention sharing culinary tastes, encourages people from the same province to band together.

North/south Southerners regard northerners as dour and unimaginative, while southerners in turn are seen as garish and exuberant.

Religion and beliefs

Religious belief was discouraged after 1949 and suppressed during the Cultural Revolution (1966–76). In the late 1980s, the government has become tolerant of religious organizations, provided they accept the regulation of the Religious Affairs Bureau under the State Council.

Confucianism The dominance of Confucianism as the establishment philosophy under successive dynasties has framed attitudes and thinking. The essence of Confucian conformity lay in obedience to authority and respect for superiors. While everyone carried out their duties according to their social position, the world and heaven would remain in harmony. Confucian rites included respect for, even worship of, ancestors and a veneration of the elderly which survives even today.

Taoism complemented Confucian regulation of public and family life with reflections on the place of the self in the cosmos. Contemplation of the Tao (Dao), or "Way," brought inner peace and attunement with all being. Harmony was achieved through a balance of the Yin and the Yang, representing male and female, among a range of dualities. Taoism looked also for practical means to the achievement of immortality through gymnastics and herbal medicines. It also developed as a religion, with a number of deities who could be propitiated by the correct offerings.

Buddhism, introduced to China in the first century AD, was at first regarded as alien and unwelcome but in time was adapted and assimilated. The Amitabha sect minimized the role of contemplation and unworldliness: meritorious deeds and devotion alone guaranteed entry to paradise. Although Buddhist sculptures and architecture are common, practising monks and nuns are few.

Non-exclusive The beliefs of Confucianism, Buddhism and Taoism, all of which are permeated by a certain acceptance of fate, tended to become intermingled.

Islam became established in China in the 7th century. China has more than 20m Muslims, most of them the "minority nationalities" (Hui, Uygurs, Kazaks, Uzbeks) of the northwest. Muslims are exempted from the most rigorous strictures of birth control policy.

Christianity made a limited impact during the Tang (through Nestorians) and the Ming (through Jesuits). The Opium Wars of the 19th century opened China to a widespread influx of Protestant and Roman Catholic missionaries. By 1949 there were about 3m Catholics and 500,000 Protestants in China. Association of missionary activity with foreign dominance of China has left a suspicion of Christianity among many Chinese.

After 1949 the Protestants grouped themselves into the Confederation of Protestant Churches, acceptable to the Chinese authorities because it is independent of any foreign organization. However, a gulf still divides the officially sanctioned Roman Catholic body, the Patriotic Christian Association, and the Vatican, which insists that Chinese bishops be appointed from Rome.

Although overt proselytizing is still difficult, sacred texts are no longer banned and congregations, though small, now meet for collective worship and they include some young people.

Marxism appealed to Chinese reformers in the early 20th century as a modern panacea, a strong medicine to cure an ailing China. In China it has a distinctly Chinese flavour. Official ideology is termed "Marxism-Leninism-Mao Zedong Thought."

Attitude to foreigners

Chinese people are invariably friendly and polite to *waibin* (foreign guests), although small children may point them out as *changbizi* (long noses) or *yangguizi* (foreign devils). A foreigner surrounded by Chinese people in a small town is in a sea of curiosity, not hostility.

Nevertheless, at official level, even under the new "open door" policy, foreigners (*waiguoren*) are still regarded as intruders. Mixing with foreigners outside official business is discouraged. The Party aims to combat the encroaching corruption of Chinese culture by Western influences and prevent the leakage of official secrets. Any contacts with Western journalists can generate suspicion, and hotel staff may monitor Chinese visitors.

Marriage between Chinese and foreigners is permitted but frowned upon. Discovery of a sexual relationship with a foreigner may result merely in expulsion for the foreigner, but for the Chinese person it may mean reform-through-labour and the end of any career prospects.

Foreign food Chinese are extremely wary about the rest of the world's cuisines, which are often lumped together as *xican* (Western food). Knives and forks are considered clumsy, rare beef steak as barbarian. **Overseas Chinese**, or *huaqiao*, are honoured as "compatriots." No matter for how many generations they have lived abroad, they remain Chinese. Entry formalities into China are easier for them than for other foreigners, accommodation and food bills lower. To the government, they are a source of foreign exchange through their remittances to families, who cherish them as providers of all manner of foreign consumer goods.

The family

The family remains the focus of life for most Chinese people. Very few people remain unmarried and most rely on their children for support in old age. In the countryside, following the decollectivization of the late 1970s, livelihood depends on the abilities of the family. Following the political upheavals of the 1960s and 1970s, when youngsters were encouraged to denounce their parents, there has been a resurgence in family loyalty.

Marriages are still frequently arranged through the traditional matchmaker, who liaises between the two families. Most marriages are made within the village or place of work. Despite official disapproval, the groom's family usually seals the engagement with a payment of furniture, food or money to the bride's parents. In urban areas, the bride will normally move in with her parents-in-law, although modern nuclear families are becoming more common.

Romantic love as a basis for marriage is a rarity. The family requires a union based on economic good sense. However, political constraints (romance was seen as bourgeois in the Cultural Revolution) and parental authority are both declining as a younger generation asserts its independence.

Weddings are an occasion for lavish expenditure. At urban weddings, the bride may wear a Western-style white wedding dress instead of the more traditional red gown. A tiered wedding cake reinforces the modern image.

Children Late marriage is officially encouraged, with a legal minimum age of 22 for men and 20 for women. The "one-child" policy in the 1980s offers cash incentives to parents who agree to have only one child, while birth of a second child not authorized by the local family planning officer may mean, in urban areas, a fine of 15% of a couple's income. Peasant couples in particular hope for a son, who will be able to care for them in old age.

Generation gap Blue jeans, sunglasses, colas, even owning a motorbike, represent the image which now attracts many urban youths, to the consternation of their parents.

Leisure

Leisure time is limited. There is a six-day working week for most people, and few households have washing machines or other labour-saving devices. What free time there is, is usually spent with the family, at home or in a stroll in the park. Until recently, few Chinese took vacations, the only major break being a few days' holiday at Chinese New Year (Spring Festival), often involving a visit to parents. However, an increasing number of families are spending vacations away from home so that, in summer, trains are even more crowded than usual.

Television has become accessible to an estimated 300m of the population. Programmes range from practical tips on crochet to extensive coverage of life and politics abroad, interspersed with foreign films.

Hobbies and pets, considered a bourgeois indulgence during the Cultural Revolution, are popular. Goldfish, songbirds and crickets are kept as pets, and there are clubs devoted to kite-flying, stamp-collecting and other enthusiasms.

Education

Young Chinese are preoccupied with their career prospects. White-collar jobs, which have status and financial attractions, depend on achieving the right education. The current system favours the children of officials and intellectuals. In the countryside, children leave school early to join in farm work and increase family income.

The Cultural Revolution

Education was severely disrupted by the Cultural Revolution (1966–76). Many people now studying are those who missed their chance during the "lost ten years." At the height of anarchic activity (1966–69), teachers were reviled and physically abused. They did not regain their respected status until the 1980s.

Red and expert During the Cultural Revolution, entry to university depended on social background, political activism and recommendation by the place of work. It was compulsory to spend two or three years on productive labour before any tertiary education. The aim was to redress the elitism of a system which was seen to discriminate against the children of "workers, peasants and soldiers" and to produce more egalitarian intellectuals who were both "Red and expert."

The education system

Streaming, or tracking, of students by ability was re-instituted in 1977 in the revived "key" schools (*zhongdian*). There are key schools at primary, secondary and tertiary levels, and they receive extra funding and employ the best teachers. In theory they cream off the most gifted children. In practice, however, it is the children of the establishment who attend the key schools – most of which are in urban areas – while the children of peasants go to locally run schools (*minban*), and those of urban workers attend technical schools.

Primary schooling reaches an estimated 93% of children in the relevant age group (usually 7–11 years).

Secondary education is divided into junior secondary (12–14 years) and senior secondary (15–17 years). In rural areas many children do not attend secondary school.

Tertiary education In 1977 academic criteria were reinstated for entrance to universities. Competition for university places is intense: there are places in tertiary education for only 4% of secondary-school leavers. The number of places is being increased through expansion of evening colleges and correspondence courses, and in particular through a national TV university and numerous provincial TV universities.

Postgraduate research, suspended during the Cultural Revolution, has returned in the 1980s. The emphasis remains on the sciences, but it is also permissible to study politically controversial areas, even in the social sciences. Free access to libraries and to foreign publications and international exchanges of academics, have helped Chinese academics to "liberate their thinking."

Study abroad Several thousand Chinese study abroad, financed by the government, their family or a foreign institution. Senior officials ensure that their own offspring benefit from this open door. Today's returned students are tomorrow's high flyers.

Youth unemployment has been a problem since enrolment in secondary schools expanded rapidly in the 1960s and 1970s. One solution was to send "educated youth" to work in the countryside. However, many of those sent have since drifted back to the cities. In the 1980s, expansion of light and service industries has increased job opportunities.

Language

Most foreign visitors to China are escorted by a bilingual guide. They also benefit from the current fashion for learning English. There is little need to learn Chinese, but an ability to greet and thank in the language is always appreciated.

The spoken language

Chinese is based on only 400 monosyllables, each syllable represented by a different character depending on its meaning. In other languages a variety of meanings for one word can be implied by varying the intonation – for example, in English, with "Hello?". In Chinese, totally different words are produced, according to which of four different tones is used. Each character (word or part of a word) has a specific tone: *Mā* pronounced with a level tone means "mother," *Má* with a slightly rising inflection means "hemp" *Mǎ* with a full "down and up" intonation means "horse," *Mà* with an abrupt downward tone means "curse."

In modern Chinese many words have more than one syllable, so that the chances of causing confusion – or offence – are diminished.

The written language

Chinese characters were originally pictograms and ideograms, and the pictures and ideas represented are still discernible in some characters. A knowledge of 4,000 characters is necessary to read the *People's Daily*. Happily, Chinese characters conform to patterns: for example, most words associated with water have on their left-hand side the "three drops of water," three vertically arranged dots.

A major simplification of characters took place in China in the 1950s, but the Chinese people in Taiwan, Hong Kong and elsewhere abroad retain the "complex forms."

On the mainland, Chinese texts now read horizontally, from left to right instead of vertically, starting on the right hand of the page, as in the classical system.

Numbers Arabic numerals are commonly used, but translation of figures is often confused because the Chinese count by the ten thousand (*wan*), not thousand. It is wise to ask for all large numbers to be written down.

Dialects

Although written Chinese is the same throughout China, dialects differ sufficiently to make Cantonese incomprehensible to Mandarin speakers. Mandarin (*guanhua*), as the name suggests, was the language of officialdom, based on the most widespread dialect of the north. Its spread is officially encouraged, under the more democratic name of "common speech" (*putonghua*), although most Chinese resort to their dialect with family and friends. The majority of Chinese people who emigrated to the West came from the southern provinces and speak the dialects of Guangdong and Fujian.

Romanization

For transliteration of Mandarin Chinese into the Western alphabet, the "Pinyin" system has now gained wide acceptance, replacing the various systems used in different countries, such as the Wade-Giles and Yale systems. Hence Peking has become Beijing, Canton City is Guangzhou. Pinyin, which means "spelling by sound", was developed by the Chinese and officially adopted in 1958, but had its precursors in systems which started to be used in the 1930s. It is now learned at school by all Chinese children, but many of the older generation are not familiar with it. Computers use English input but there are a number of Chinese systems, some based on Pinyin and some on Chinese characters.

Key phrases

	Pinyin	Phonetic
Welcome	Huānyíng	(Huan-yeeng)
Hello	Nǐ hǎo	(Nee-how)
Hello (on telephone)	Wei	(Way)
Is there anyone who	Yǒu meí yǒu rén	(Yoe may yoe ren)
speaks (English)?	shuō (Yīngwén)	(shwaw) (Yeeng-wun)
German	Déguóyǔ	(Dur-gwaw-yew)
French	Fǎguóyú	(Far-gwaw-yew)
Italian	Ìdàliyǔ	(Ee-dah-lee-yew)
Japanese	Riyǔ	(Rur-yew)
Please give me	Qǐng geí wǒ	(Ching gay wo: "o" as in hot)
Please	Qǐng	(Ching)
Thank you	Xièxie	(sye-sye)
Sorry!	Duibuqǐ	(Dway-boo-chee)
Goodbye	Zaijiàn	(Zye-ji-en)
Good	Hǎo	(How)
Cooperation	Hézuò	(Her-dzwo)
I don't understand	Wǒ bùdǒng	(Wo boo-dung; "o" as in hot)
I'm unwell	Wǒ bingle	(Wo bing-la)
Ladies	Nǔ cèsuǒ	(New tse soo-or)
Gentlemen	Nán cèsuǒ	(Naan tse soo-or)
Western food	Xīcān	(See-tsan)
Chinese food	Zhōngcān	(Joong-tsan)
Beer	Píjiǔ	(Pee-joe)
Knife	Dāo	(Dow)
Fork	Chā	(Chah)
Tea	Chá	(Chah)
Siesta	Xiūxi	(See-oh-see)
Taxi	Chūzū qìchē	(Choo-zoo-chee-chur)
(Peking) Hotel	(Běijīng) Fàndiàn	(Bay-jing fan-dyen)
Embassy	Dàshiguǎn	(Dah-shh-gwan)
Luggage	Xíngli	(Sing-lee)
Key	Yàoshi	(Yow-shh)
Telephone	Diànhuà	(Dyen-hwa)
Telex	Diànchuán	(Dyen-chwan)
(It's) broken, out of order	Huàile	(Hwai-luh)
Sold out	Méiyou	(May-yoe)
I am...	Wǒ shì...	(Wo shh...; "o" as in hot)
Englishman/woman	Yīngguórén	(Yeeng-gwaw-ren)
American	Měigguórén	(May-gwaw-ren)
German	Déguórén	(Dur-gwaw-ren)
Frenchman/woman	Fǎguórén	(Far-gwaw-ren)
Italian	Yidàlìrén	(Ee-dah-lee-ren)
Canadian	Jiānádàrén	(Jya-nah-dah-ren)
Japanese	Riběnrén	(Rur-bun-ren)

City by City

China is the third largest country in the world. It is more than 5,500km/3,400 miles from the Nansha Islands of the south to the Heilong river in the north and it is some 5,000km/3,100 miles from the eastern seaboard to the Pamir mountains in the west. It encompasses the extremes of climate, vegetation, population and topography, from the sub-zero winters of Harbin to the tropical humidity of Guangzhou, from the typhoons of the southeast coast to the sandstorms of the Gobi desert, from the heavily populated cities of the eastern plains to the sparsely populated mountains of Tibet.

For administrative purposes China is divided into 22 provinces (including Taiwan). In terms of land mass and size of population they are often equivalent to a European country. Provincial identity is very strong and during periods of unstable government many provinces have effectively been independent states (see *The structure of government*).

Travelling between the cities of the east China plain, where every inch of land seems to be cultivated, one does not realize that less than one-third of China's total land mass is suitable for agriculture. Sixty per cent of China's terrain is mountainous or hilly. The highest mountains are in the west, where the Himalayas, rising to 8,000 metres/26,200ft, form the borders of Tibet; then come the Pamirs, the Karakoram mountains and the Tianshan (the Heavenly mountains), bordering on the Soviet Union. Gradually descending eastwards the extensive plateau of Qinghai and Tibet averages 4,000 metres/13,200ft in height. East of Lanzhou in the north and Kunming in the south, the terrain is altogether gentler: the highest mountains are between 1,000 and 2,000 metres/3,000 and 6,500ft. These are the Great Xingan range or the Changbai mountains of the northeast, the Wushan mountains of central China which isolate fertile Sichuan, and in the south the Wuyi mountains of Fujian and the gentle Yun-gui plateau of southwest China.

The rivers and waterways of China evoke powerful images. The Yellow river, which has its source in the Qinghai plateau, winds through the northern provinces of Gansu, Ningxia, Nei Menggu, Shaanxi, Shanxi and Henan, before emerging through Shandong province in the Bohai Gulf. The river is yellow because of its silt. In the past it has often flooded with disastrous consequences. Chinese culture began on the banks of the Yellow river: it is China's Nile. The Changjiang or Yangzi river rises in the Tangla mountains of Qinghai, passes through Yunnan and Sichuan before cleaving its way through the Wushan mountains to emerge in the provinces of central China, where it widens and the flow becomes slower, till it ends its journey in the Yellow Sea just north of Shanghai. The Yangzi provides the main means of transport between Sichuan and eastern China. Major rivers of the south are the Pearl and the Huai.

USSR

HEILONGJIANG

● Harbin

JILIN

● Changchun

Shenyang ●

LIAONING

NORTH KOREA

Sea of Japan

Hohhot ●

ENGGU
NGOLIA)

✈ BEIJING
Tianjin ●

Dalian ●

● Seoul

SOUTH
KOREA

JAPAN

Taiyuan ●

Shijiazhuang ●

HEBEI

SHANXI

● Jinan

SHANDONG

Qingdao ●

Yellow Sea

Kian ●
AANXI

Zhengzhou ●

HENAN

JIANGSU

ANHUI

Nanjing ●
Hefei ●

✈ SHANGHAI

HUBEI

● Wuhan

✈ Hangzhou

ZHEJIANG

East China Sea

HOU

Changsha ●

HUNAN

Nanchang ●

JIANGXI

Fuzhou ● ✈
FUJIAN

Taipei ●

Guilin ●

✈

Xiamen ●

TAIWAN

ANGXI

GUANGDONG

✈ GUANGZHOU

● Nanning

Zhuhai ●
Macau ●

Shenzhen
● Hong Kong
✈

Shantou ●

South China Sea

The Grand Canal, extending from Beijing to Hangzhou, was dug mainly during the sixth century and remained in constant use until the mid 19th century. Parts of it have been repaired, and it is intended to re-open the canal over its whole length; certainly on the stretch south of the Yangzi it has remained the principal means of local transport. In northwest China, a system of "interior drainage" feeds the depressions of the Taklamakam desert. Qinghai lake (Kokonor lake) is the largest saltwater lake in China, while the biggest freshwater lakes are Taihu lake in Jiangsu, Dongting lake in Hunan and the Poyang in Jiangxi.

The cities featured in this section are in the front line of China's programme of modernization. They are principally on the "East China Plain," already have a fairly strong if outdated industrial base, and possess a large workforce and relatively developed communications. However, what there is available to the business traveller varies considerably.

The north and northeast

The north, encompassing the provinces of Shandong, Hebei, Shanxi and Nei Menggu, and the northeast with those of Liaoning, Jilin and Heilongjiang (which were formerly known as Manchuria) and the municipalities of Beijing and Tianjin, tend to be cold, bleak and arid in the winter. The summers are warm, with a short wet season. In recent times Manchuria was dominated by the Japanese and the Russians, who left behind a network of railways and a foundation of heavy industry. In the far north the border with the Soviet Union is marked by the Heilongjiang or Ussuri river; to the southeast it touches North Korea. The eastern seaboard, giving on to the Bohai Gulf, possesses some of China's major ports, Tianjin, Dalian, Qingdao and Yantai. Inland, the area is principally wheat growing, with some other grains – maize, sorghum, millet – some cotton and some market gardening in the vicinity of the cities. Nei Menggu is principally given over to cattle-rearing: the people are still nomadic. The north and northeast have rich mineral resources, particularly coal in Shanxi and oil in Heilongjiang at Daqing and at Shengli in Shandong, but both industry and transport are outdated.

The northwest

China's northwest is bleak and remote, yet often fascinating. Xian, today as in the past, is a gateway to the area: it was from this ancient capital (then called Chang'an) that merchants and travellers set out along the "Silk Road" through the northwest to India and the Middle East. From the fertile loess plateaux of Shaanxi and parts of Ningxia and Gansu, one enters the Gobi desert's inhospitable terrain of grey gravel-like sand, in which the oases are fed by underground channels from the melting snows of the nearest mountain ranges. The border is with Outer Mongolia and the Soviet Union. In the far west of Xinjiang Uygur are the Taklamakam desert, the depressions of Turfan and the Tarim basin, the dramatic Tian mountains and the Pamirs. Summers are hot and dry, winters cold and dry, with sand storms in the spring. Many people here are Muslims, speaking their own Turkic language. Their features are Caucasian rather than Chinese and the architecture, cuisine and culture all have a flavour of the Middle East. The oases are a source of fine fruit (such as melons, grapes, apricots) and of cotton. There is little industry (only at Xian and Lanzhou), and the mineral resources including important oil fields (already in production at Karamayi) are relatively unexploited.

The centre
Central China comprises Jiangsu, Zhejiang, Anhui and Hubei. Though Jiangsu and Anhui are relatively poor and undeveloped, the remaining provinces are fertile and intensely cultivated, producing three crops a year, principally rice, cotton and silk. These are areas of dense population, with industry concentrated around the major cities of Shanghai, Nanjing, Hangzhou, Wuhan and Hefei, and major iron and steel works at Baoshan near Shanghai and Maanshan in southern Anhui.

The west
Western China includes the densely populated province of Sichuan, reaching up to mountainous Tibet and the Qinghai plateau. Sichuan is situated in a fertile basin, surrounded by mountains; its main contact with the rest of China has traditionally been the Yangzi river. Due to the associations that leading government figures had with the province, Sichuan was a front runner in political and economic reforms and experiments with the "responsibility system" in the countryside. Chengdu used to be the only gateway to Tibet, but this is changing. Sichuan also backs on to Qinghai – remote, sparsely populated, largely Muslim.

The south
The provinces of Fujian, Jiangxi, Guangxi, Guizhou, Guangdong and Yunnan comprise the southern region, bordering the South China seas, with the Wuyi mountains of Fujian and the Yun-gui plateau of Guizhou and Yunnan. The climate is subtropical to tropical on the southern borders with Vietnam, Burma and Kampuchea. While there are pockets of wealth along the coastal areas, and certain cities benefit from their proximity to Hong Kong, the interior has long been neglected. Communications are poor, and there is little industry. The most typical products are in light industry and crafts. The terrain is difficult to farm; principal crops are rice, tea, tobacco, ramie, tropical fruits and sugarcane. An important source of income in Yunnan and Guangxi, with their exotic scenery, is tourism. Hainan Island, which produces rubber and coffee, is being promoted as a resort, and has recently been given provincial status.

BEIJING
Area code ☏ 01

Taken as a whole, the city of Beijing (Peking) is not beautiful, for its outstanding monuments – the Imperial Palaces of the Forbidden City and the Temple of Heaven – are isolated in their glory, surrounded by dreary apartment blocks and grimy industrial complexes, none of which exhibits a distinctly Chinese character. The city would be oppressive but for the tree-lined boulevards which divide it into a network of rectangular blocks and attract the eye upwards and outwards to the encircling hills (when they are visible through the dust).

Though it is an ancient city, Beijing became the capital of China only in comparatively recent times. It was rebuilt on its present site in the 13th century by Kublai Khan, under whom it became the capital, and this was the flourishing city that Marco Polo visited and admired for its sophistication and culture. Other Westerners followed and, from 1860, exploited the weakness of the later Qing emperors. The last Qing emperor was forced to abdicate in 1911, and throughout the first half of the 20th century Beijing was a hotbed of revolutionary ideas, strikes and civil disturbances. In 1928, the ruling Guomindong (Nationalist) Party, under Chiang Kai-shek, moved the capital of China to Nanjing. Later, Beijing came under increasing Japanese domination. It was occupied by the Japanese at the outbreak of the Sino-Japanese War, in 1937, and remained so until 1945.

After the civil war that followed World War II, on October 1 1949, Mao Zedong declared the founding of the People's Republic of China from Beijing. The city began to develop its austere character during the next ten years, when large areas of Beijing were cleared of congested slums and replaced by public buildings and industrial zones using Soviet aid and technology. During the Cultural Revolution, Beijing became divided against itself. Particularly here, the professional and intellectual classes were sought out, beaten and humiliated.

Industrially, Beijing is a centre for communications equipment, electronics, military supplies, textiles and man-made fibres, and other light and heavy industry. It also has a substantial suburban population who farm the surrounding 100km/50 miles and early in the morning fill the roads into the city with their laden trucks, bicycles and horse-drawn vehicles carrying produce to the open markets and street stalls. But Beijing is pre-eminent as a diplomatic and administrative capital and it now houses well over 100 embassies, a large community of press, TV and radio journalists, and more than 2,000 foreign companies. Although foreign business people can now conduct and conclude negotiations in many other cities without reference to Beijing, they still find it worthwhile to cultivate contacts in the capital, since the ministries here are the ultimate arbiters in the making of major or sensitive business decisions.

Arriving

Foreign visitors to Beijing usually arrive by air. CAAC flies between Beijing and all the main cities of China. On international routes CAAC shares the timetable, generally on alternate days of the week, with other major airlines, most of which have better check-in and inflight arrangements than CAAC.

Shoudu (Capital) airport

Passengers arrive at one of two circular halls connected to the main terminal building by automatic walkways; when these break down, as they regularly do, passengers are faced with a 200-metre walk. Quarantine and immigration checks are speedily done; baggage arrives by automated carousel after a 20min wait. It may take a further 15min to clear customs, making an average of 45min from touchdown to airport lobby. This has an information desk and bank and is usually crowded with people meeting flights.

Arrangements for departing passengers are better than at most Chinese airports, but be prepared for much jostling. Check-in procedures take an hour at least. Airport tax of ¥15 on departing international flights has to be paid at a separate desk before proceeding to immigration. Beyond that is a hall with a Bank of China desk for converting FEC back to foreign currency (but opening hours are erratic), a post office, an international telephone office, and a souvenir and duty-free shop. Passengers then line up for the final security check and proceed to the departure lounges, where there is a small coffee shop. The first-class passenger lounge differs only in having more comfortable seating. The airport is well signposted with indicator boards. Airport inquiries ☎ 552515, 557396, 555402; foreign airlines 522931.

City link The airport is 32km/20 miles east of the city centre. Hotels will meet guests from the airport by prior arrangement, but most visitors take a taxi from the rank situated to the far left of the airport exit doors. Before reaching the ranks, you will be approached by touts offering a fare comparable to the metered rate but they will then attempt to talk you into black market currency transactions throughout the long journey into town. It is best to ignore them. The journey normally takes 40min, but allow 60min in rush hours (8–9 and 4.30–6). There is an airport bus costing ¥2.5, but it deposits passengers at the CAAC building, which is a mile northeast of the city centre, and has an erratic taxi service.

Railway station

The busy, crowded Beijing terminus is within a mile of the city centre. All passengers leave by the same exit, usually in a rush to be one of the first in line for onward transport. Always anticipate having to wait longer for a taxi than you spend in it. The central hotels are a short ride away (15min maximum), but too far to walk with baggage.

Travelling out by rail, you are best advised to obtain tickets through hotel travel desks or CITS although, if necessary, you can buy them at the 24hr reservations office in the station which has a foreigners' section.

Getting around

Few people who do not speak Chinese are prepared to brave the city's subway system or buses, so visitors usually rely on taxis. Bicycling, however, is another option.

Taxis The number of taxis has steadily increased in Beijing to the point where visitors need no longer freeze on a hotel doorstep during winter while waiting 20min or more. It has also become much easier to hail one in the street. There are ranks only at hotels (where dispatchers will help with directions), at the CITIC Building, the Friendship Store and the International Club. The *Shoudu (Capital) Taxi Company* ☎ 557461 has English-speaking dispatchers but cannot be relied upon to have a taxi when you need one, especially at night. Other radio cab companies are *Beijing Auto Service* ☎ 594290, *Beijing Taxi Company* ☎ 781184 and *Beijing Travel Service* ☎ 755246.

Cabs are mostly kept clean and in good repair and are often new Japanese imports. All have meters and indicate whether they are free by means of a red circular flag on the passenger side of the windscreen or a roof light. In Beijing taxi-driving is a popular form of entrepreneurship and carries its own status symbol, the in-car stereo playing imported tapes. If you are lucky enough to find an English-speaking driver he will tell you frankly much about daily life and work in the capital. Fares, depending on the model, start at ¥2.80 and go up by ¥0.8 per kilometre. Always carry small change; taxi-drivers never seem to have enough, though they will get change from other drivers, given no alternative.

Hotel transport Top hotels, such as the Great Wall Sheraton, have fleets of limousines and taxis which can be used by non-residents. Hotels out of town, such as the Lido (Holiday Inn), run a morning and evening shuttle service and make their buses available for excursions.

Limousines and minibuses
Vehicles with drivers can be obtained at inexpensive rates from the *Shoudu Taxi Company* ☎ 557461 or the *China International Travel Service* (*CITS*)☎ 554192 ext. 2339, open 7.30am–8.30pm. *Union Car Rental* at the Great Wall Sheraton ☎ 5005566 has luxury limousines. A chauffered Mercedes costs ¥180 a day and a Cadillac ¥360.

Walking Maps of Beijing deceptively make the city look compact. In fact, even though they are on adjacent blocks, it is a good 10min walk to Tian'anmen Square from the Beijing Hotel, and from the Jianguo a very brisk 45min.

Bicycling Many visitors use a bicycle for the occasional day off as a means of exploring the city centre; younger expatriates often buy one and use it as their chief means of transport. Bicycles can be rented for ¥5 an hour or ¥25 a day from the *Sports Centre* at the Great Wall Sheraton ☎ 5005566, open 8–8. The rate is high, but the bicycles are modern and well maintained. It is cheaper to rent from the *Jianguomenwai Bicycle Repair Shop* ☎ 592391, which has one outlet opposite the Friendship Store and another at 94 Dongchongmenwen Dajie, near the railway station; both open 7–7. Charges are ¥10 per day plus a small, refundable deposit.

Bicycles must be parked in designated areas – unmistakable because of the ranks of other bikes. Usually these areas are attended by elderly women with red armbands who provide a numbered ticket and charge ¥.05 when the bike is collected.

Subway The subway is fast and clean, though not much used by visitors because its station entrances are difficult to find and because it is unpleasantly busy in the 7–9 and 4.30–6 rush. The circular route follows the ring road around the city, linking Tian'anmen Square, the railway station, the Workers' Stadium and Beijing Zoo. There are maps in every subway carriage. The flat fare is ¥0.10; tickets are purchased at kiosks in the station entrance and given up at the end of the journey.

Buses and trolley buses Such is the confusion of routes, signs and fares, and the general overcrowding, that these are best avoided.

Area by area
Beijing is as varied as it is big, and visitors' experience of it will be coloured by the atmosphere of the area in which they stay, from the quiet, leafy avenues of the consular district around the Great Wall Sheraton at one extreme to the busy, historic heart of the city around the Beijing hotel at the other. The city is

laid out in a series of concentric squares.

Central Beijing

At the heart of the capital is the Forbidden City (now the Palace Museum), considered by the emperors who conceived it to be the centre of the world. Tian'anmen Square, to the south, immediately outside the Forbidden City, is a huge ceremonial parade ground of 40.5ha/100 acres, thronged during the day with Chinese and foreign sightseers.

To the west of the square is the Great Hall of the People. China's parliament, the National Peoples' Congress, meets here, and the largest assembly room can accommodate up to 10,000. The Hall contains numerous conference rooms which are used for receiving and entertaining foreign guests and delegations. To the east of the square are museums of the Chinese Revolution and of Chinese history. These contain few artifacts but many vast tableaux interpreting human evolution in terms of the primitive, slave, feudal, capitalist and, finally, socialist eras.

To the south of Tian'anmen Square is the Monument to the People's Heroes, an obelisk carved with scenes representing the major events of the Revolution. Behind that is the Mao Zedong Memorial Hall which contains a huge white marble statue of the late chairman and a crystal coffin preserving his body. At the southern extremity is the Qianmen Gate and pavilions, part of the Ming dynasty city wall and originally reserved for the emperor's exclusive use when, on rare excursions from the Imperial Palace, he would pass through to commune with the gods in the Temple of Heaven.

One block west of the Forbidden City is the high-walled compound called Zhongnanhai after the two lakes contained within. This is the political heart of China, and the headquarters of the Central Committee of the Chinese Communist Party and the homes of government leaders are located here.

The eastern district

The next concentric square is formed by the first, or inner, ring road built on the line of the former outer city wall. Most of the interest for business visitors lies in its southeast quarter. The busy three-mile-long boulevard which starts as Chang'an Avenue (Dongchang'an Dajie), then becomes Jianguomennei Dajie and finally Jianguomenwai Dajie, has a number of international hotels and offices along its northern side and in the streets running north from Dongchang'an Dajie.

Some way east, in Jianguomenwai Dajie, are the headquarters of the China International Trust and Investment Corporation, which channels foreign investments (much of it from overseas Chinese) into various projects and raises venture capital through bond issues on the international markets. It also houses a large number of foreign companies.

Directly north of Jianguomenwai Avenue and stretching for several miles, is the Sanlitun district, which contains more than 100 embassies, agencies of the United Nations and offices of the correspondents of the world's media. Here, also, foreigners are privileged to live in low-rise mansions and compounds, surrounded by well-maintained gardens and guarded by the People's Armed Police.

The nearest Beijing equivalent of a central shopping district is Wangfujing Dajie, running north from Dongchang'an Dajie. Street traders have begun to colonize the surrounding streets, setting up temporary stalls or simply displaying their wares on the ground, but the local Chinese buy most of their daily needs from the flourishing free markets located around bus termini and housing estates in the suburbs.

To Summer Palace
and Beida University

N

INNER RING ROAD

12   17   2

XIZHIMENWAI   DAJIE

13

NANDAJIE

FUCHENGMEN

XIDAN BEIDAJIE

FUXINGMEN
BEIDAJIE

FUXINGMENWAI DAJIE   FUXINGMENNEI DAJIE   XICHANG

12 5

FUXINGMEN
NANDAJIE

XUANWUMENWAI DAJIE

0   1 mile
0   1 km

HOTELS

1   Beijing
2   Great Wall Sheraton
3   Jianguo
4   Jinglun (Beijing-Toronto)
5   Majestic
6   Lido (Holiday Inn)
7   Shangri-La
8   Zhaolong
9   Guoji (International)
10   Heping (Peace)
11   Shoudo (Capital) Guesthouse
12   Minzu (Nationalities)
13   Xiyuan

RESTAURANTS

1   Donglaishun
2   Fangshan
3   Fengzeyuan
     International Club (Building 8)
4   Maxim's de Paris
5   New Beijing Duck
6   Qianmen Roast Duck
7   Ren Ren
8   Sichuan
9   Window of the World (Building 4)

BUILDINGS AND SIGHTS

1   Beijing Arts and Crafts Store
2   Beijing Exhibition Hall
3   Beijing Gymnasium
4   CITIC Building
5   Cultural Palace of the Nationalities
6   Friendship Store
7   Great Hall of the People
8   International Club
9   International Post Office
10   Mao Zedong Memorial Hall
11   Qianmen Gate
12   Shoudu Gymnasium
13   Shoudu Theatre
14   Temple of Heaven
15   Union Medical College Hospital
16   Workers' Gymnasium
17   Zoo

24 km/
15 miles

8 km/
5 miles

OUTER RING ROAD

INNER RING ROAD

5

2

8

INNER RING ROAD

16

OUTER RING ROAD

Beihai
Park

2

Jingshan
(Coal Hill)
Park

1

Zhongnanhai

PALACE
MUSEUM
(Forbidden
City)

13

WANFUJING DAJIE

Sanlitun

10

1

4 15

1

9

DONGCHANG'AN DAJIE

9

JIANGUOMENNEI DAJIE

8 4 6

3 4

JIANGUOMENWA I DAJIE

DAJIE

11

7

TIAN' ANMEN
SQUARE

Main railway
station

10

NMEN XIDAJIE

6

11

QIANMEN DONGDAJIE

8

5

LIULICHANG LU

7

QIANMEN DAJIE

3

Tiantan Park

14

3

105

The southern district

Areas of low-density housing are becoming an increasing rarity in Beijing: large plots between the inner and the second, or outer, ring road are under development for local housing, factories, schools and government buildings. But old Beijing can still be seen in the narrow streets east and south of Tian'anmen Square. Cars cannot pass here, and it is much quieter. Some of the grey brick and pantiled houses, built round courtyards, have finely carved marble door jambs and lintels. Broken querns are used for paving, and proud householders cultivate tiny gardens along the street.

The northwestern district

Beijing has a large population of students and academics in more than 200 universities, colleges and research institutes. These are all in the northwestern outer suburbs of the city. The most prestigious of all is Beijing (Beida) University, with its spacious campus sited between the Zoo and the Summer Palace. Some 100,000 students compete for 10,000 places in annual nationwide entrance examinations, much as under the former feudal system the brightest scholars competed for places in the imperial civil service. The university also has a large number of expatriate Westerners teaching and studying on the campus.

Hotels

The hotels recommended here dominated the market in the late 1980s. It is hard to find fault with either the Shangri-La or the Great Wall Sheraton, and all of the others have their strong points. However, although the municipal government imposed a moratorium on new building in the city centre, which halted the growth of new hotels for some time, the demand for beds has so increased that large areas of low-rise housing have been cleared and new sites released. Thus, the hotel scene will have changed completely by the early 1990s. Twenty new hotels were under construction within a radius of a mile from the Beijing Hotel, and many of the existing hotels in the northwest of the city, which were badly dilapidated, are being improved in line with the new developments.

Beijing ¥¥¥
33 Dongchang'an Dajie ☎ *5007766*
🆃🆇 *22426 • 910 rooms and suites,*
5 restaurants, 2 bars-cum-coffee lounges
People with an affection for the past will choose the grandeur of the Beijing in preference to any of the city's modern hotels. But the hotel will only accept guests who have been introduced by a Chinese host organization or by one of the long-established foreign banks and trading companies which have their offices in the hotel. It is in a good position, just two blocks from Tian'anmen Square, has fine views (from the rooms at the rear in the west end) over the golden rooftops of the Forbidden City, and its impressive dining halls (see

Restaurants) serve first-rate Chinese food. The hotel is made up of four wings. One of these, the "Distinguished Guests Building", was opened in 1987 while the others were all refurbished during the 1980's. All of the rooms have colour TV and refrigerators, but no minibars. In characteristic Chinese style, the main restaurants all close by 9pm, but by popular demand a 24hr restaurant with a limited menu has been opened in the middle wing. The bars remain lively well into the night. Extensive shopping arcade, travel service • fax, cable, secretarial services, typing, photocopying, courier services, 20 meeting rooms, ballroom.

Great Wall Sheraton ~~¥¥¥¥¥~~
Donghuan Beilu ☎ *5005566* ㊟ *20045*
• *AE DC MC V* • *1,004 rooms and suites,*
4 restaurants, 2 bars, 2 coffee shops
The Great Wall was far and away
Beijing's top hotel until the Shangri-
La opened, and even now it scores
higher for its location. It is a world
unto itself, where guests are
pampered and the real China is kept
well at bay. Colour TVs show in-house
movies, the minibars are well stocked
and, unusually for Beijing, guests
enjoy 24hr room service. The
excellent restaurants (see
Restaurants) have a reputation for
being expensive, but several now
offer fixed-price lunches. Shopping
arcade, travel centre and airline
counters, limousine hire, beauty
salon, barber shop, disco, 24hr
medical services • pool, tennis
courts, gymnasium, whirlpool and
sauna • business centre providing
secretarial services, translation,
copying, fax and international
telecommunication services,
6 meeting rooms, all with audiovisual
equipment, 230-seat theatre,
ballroom accommodating up to 1,600.

Guoji (International) ~~¥¥¥¥~~
9 Jianguomennei Dajie ☎ *5122324*
㊟ *22350* • *AE DC MC V* • *1,047 rooms*
and suites, 11 restaurants, bars, cafes
This 29-storey luxury hotel is
situated a few blocks away from
Tian'anmen Square opposite
Beijing's main railway station. All
rooms have refrigerators and there is
24 hour room service. A superb view
of the city can be enjoyed from the
revolving roof-top restaurant.
Shopping arcade, hairdressing salon,
beauty parlour, massage centre, post
office, bank, travel service • tennis
courts, bowling centre, billiards
room, health club with pool and

For general information about
hotels and an explanation of the
price symbols, see *Planning and
Reference.*

sauna • business services, ballroom
(capacity 1,000), 20 banquet and
meeting rooms.

Jianguo ~~¥¥¥¥¥~~
Jianguomenwai Dajie ☎ *5002233*
㊟ *22439* • *Peninsula Group* • *AE DC*
MC V • *445 rooms and suites,*
4 restaurants, 1 bar, 1 coffee shop
Many have commented that this
American-designed hotel resembles a
West Coast roadside motel. When it
opened in 1982, the Jianguo
immediately became the hotel to
which foreign residents flocked for
home comforts, from dry cleaning
services to freshly brewed coffee. It
has remained a favourite with them
even though other hotels now offer
comparable facilities, because it is
only a short walk from the diplomatic
district. The atmosphere is always
lively and informal as old China
hands and newly arrived visitors meet
and exchange news. All the rooms
have wall-to-wall carpeting, well-
stocked minibars, and verandahs.
Waves of visitors arrive at lunch time
for the buffet spread in Charlie's Bar,
and again in the evening for after-
hours socializing. The bakery-cum-
delicatessen sells fresh bread,
sandwiches, fancy cakes and a good
range of imported cheeses and cooked
meats. The ballroom is frequently
used for shows by visiting musicians
and dancing troupes. Travel desk,
medical clinic, beautician and barber
shop • pool, fitness centre •
photocopying, fax, telex, 3 meeting
rooms and ballroom.

Jinglun (Beijing-
Toronto) ~~¥¥¥¥¥~~
Jianguomenwai Dajie ☎ *5002266*
㊟ *210011* • *AE DC MC V* • *Nikko*
Hotels International • *659 rooms and*
suites, 3 restaurants, 1 bar, 1 coffee shop
The Jinglun, also known as the
Beijing-Toronto, is on the eastern
limit of Beijing's business axis,
immediately south of the Sanlitun
consular district and next door to the
Jianguo. But although it shares with
its next-door neighbour all the

advantages of its position, it hasn't become such a social centre for expatriates as the Jianguo. Perhaps this is because the staff, though polished and efficient, maintain a polite aloofness. The delicatessen shop at the back of the lobby is a favourite with Americans craving cheesecake and also sells freshly baked bread. The Tao Li restaurant (see *Restaurants*) is the best in Beijing for fresh fish, cooked Cantonese-style. A Swiss chef presides over the Dynasty Continental restaurant. Post office, extensive shopping arcade
• indoor pool, sauna and massage
• business centre offering typing and photocopying; 3 meeting rooms and a banqueting hall for up to 400 people.

Majestic ¥¥¥¥¥
21 Liang Ma Qiao, Chaoyang district
☎ *5003388* ☎ *210327* • *AE MC V*
• *853 rooms and suites, 7 restaurants, 2 bars, 1 coffee shop*
First-time visitors to Beijing nearly always experience a moment of disbelief when they see two virtually identical hotels, on opposite sides of Donghuan Beilu. The Majestic (formerly the Kunlun) is built to the same design as the Great Wall Sheraton opposite, although it is clad in alternate bands of marble and glass rather than burnished aluminium. The managers of the Majestic, the China International Travel Service, see the hotel as every bit as good as its neighbour but the truth is that, despite willing staff, the hotel lacks the Sheraton's luxury and sophistication. However, it has all the facilities necessary to attract business travellers, with 74 rooms designated as executive suites. The tower at the top of the 30-floor structure contains a revolving restaurant, furnished with Louis XIV-style furniture and serving Continental cuisine. Above it is a helipad from which trips can be taken to the Great Wall. The hotel's other dining rooms provide ample choice, including Japanese, Muslim, Cantonese and seafood restaurants,

and Western fast food is served in the coffee shop. A Hong Kong firm runs the Glass House Disco. Large shopping arcade, medical clinic, beauty salon and barber, post office
• tennis courts, health club, pool and gym • business centre offering fax, typing and photocopying; ballroom and several meeting rooms with audiovisual and simultaneous translation facilities.

Lido (Holiday Inn) ¥¥¥¥
Jichang Lu, off Jing Tai Lu
☎ *5006688* ☎ *22618* • *AE DC MC V*
• *1,029 rooms and suites, 3 restaurants, 1 bar, 1 coffee shop*
The Lido is situated midway between the airport and the commercial district, a 30min trip by taxi or hotel shuttle bus. Although this is a deterrent for the long-term resident, it makes little difference to those staying less than a week. The advantage the Lido has over other hotels is space, and it has used this to create a miniature village, including the best-stocked supermarket, delicatessen and pharmacy in China, run by the Hong Kong-based Wellcome chain. Apart from its Chinese and European restaurants, the Lido runs many special promotions, usually based on one of Asia's ethnic cuisines, in an effort to attract expatriates to the hotel. Post office, hairdressing salon, shopping arcade, disco, medical clinic •
bowling centre, health club and sauna • 24-hour fax, and typewriter rental; secretarial support can be arranged.

Shangri-La ¥¥¥¥¥
29 Zizhuyuan Lu ☎ *8312211*
☎ *222322* • *Shangri-La International*
• *AE DC MC V* • *786 rooms and suites, 2 restaurants, 2 bars, 1 coffee shop*
The recently opened Shangri-La is 30min–1hr from central Beijing, depending on traffic density and the driver's knowledge of back roads. This is the only drawback to a hotel which in all other respects is stylish, welcoming and efficient. The interior

design reveals an unusually well balanced combination of Chinese decoration and Western feeling for light and space. Minibars are well stocked, and there are in-house movies and 24hr room service. The hotel has two excellent restaurants (see *Restaurants*) and a delicatessen which sells bread, chocolates, cakes and imported cooked meats and cheeses. Shopping arcade, hairdressing salon, shuttle bus to central Beijing, medical clinic • health club with pool, gymnasium, sauna, solarium and steam bath • business centre providing secretarial assistance, translation, interpreting, copying and binding, courier service, fax; 13 meeting rooms and a grand ballroom, all equipped for simultaneous translation and audiovisual presentations.

Zhaolong ¥¥
2 Gongren Tiyuguan Beilu, Chaoyang district ☎ *5002299* ⊺ˣ *210079* • *AE DC MC V* • *270 rooms and suites, 6 restaurants, 1 bar, 1 coffee shop*
There is nothing outstanding about the Zhaolong but it is surprisingly good for a relatively low-cost hotel. Others in this price category are neither so central (15min by taxi to Tian'anmen Square) nor so well equipped and efficient. The Zhaolong was one of the first hotels in China to be built with overseas funding. Perhaps for this reason, and as a showpiece for the open-door policy, it was equipped to a high standard, with Western furniture and marble bathrooms with Japanese

fittings. Other hotels have since overtaken it in grandeur, and tourists now form the major clientele, but it is a very adequate base for those visiting Beijing on business. Travel desk, post office, hairdressing salon • pool, sauna • typing and fax.

OTHER HOTELS
Heping (Peace) (¥) *4 Jinyu Hutong* ☎ *558841*. Reasonably priced, this hotel is centrally situated near the main shopping area. It also has business services.
Minzu (Nationalities) (¥¥) *Fuxingmennei Dajie* ☎ *658541* ⊺ˣ *22991*. Two miles west of Tian'anmen Square, in a dead part of town, but inexpensive and with good restaurants which stay open late.
Palace (¥¥¥¥¥) *Wangfujing* ☎ *5005202* ⊺ˣ *210370*. A central location and full business facilities make this new hotel an attractive choice. There is also the option of exclusive business services in the "Palace Club" on the 12th and 13th floors. Good transport services.
Shoudu (Capital) Guesthouse (¥¥¥) *9 Qianmen Donglu*. Newly opened in the heart of the city (opposite the Beijing) this hotel has 120 offices and 320 rooms along with good business and sports facilities.
Xiyuan (¥¥¥) *Erligou, Xijiao district* ☎ *8313388* ⊺ˣ *22831*. A vast hotel located 13km/8 miles northwest of Tian'anmen Square but convenient for those with business at the nearby Erligou Trade Negotiation Centre or Beijing Industrial Exhibition Hall. Equipped with a pool, gym and sauna.

Restaurants
Business entertaining in Beijing, as throughout China, centres on the major hotels, simply because of the prestige attached to them. They excel in making the arrangements for a set piece banquet, and will give guidance in protocol. It is usual to rent private function rooms both for pre-dinner drinks, which are an important part of the ritual, and for the banquet itself.

The Beijing business community does a great deal of dining out, partly to share news and information, partly to break the tedium of a relatively slow pace of business life and also to increase the number of dishes that can be sampled. Breakfast-time meetings are common, and all the hotels provide fixed-price breakfast buffets on a lavish scale. Lunch is also taken in hotels because this is usually more convenient. Several specialist restaurants listed here are suitable for entertaining, though they also attract large parties of tourists and might be considered too informal for some occasions.

Reserving a table soon in the day is essential for all restaurants and dining early is the rule in Beijing even more than in other Chinese cities. Hotel restaurants close at 9 and local ones at 7.30. Unless otherwise stated, hotel restaurants will accept major credit cards and local restaurants will not.

HOTEL RESTAURANTS
Western food *The Brasserie* (¥¥¥¥) at the Shangri-La is currently regarded as the best restaurant in Beijing, though this reflects the natural prejudice of visitors for Western food rather than Chinese. Although the style is Parisian, with waiters in long aprons, the food is rather more English: venison, rib of beef and delicately roasted lamb. *Le France* (¥¥¥¥) at the Great Wall Sheraton is directly comparable. Purists may scoff at the bad French of the menu (even the definite article in the restaurant's name is the wrong gender), but there is nothing to denigrate about the food or service. *Justine's* (¥¥¥¥) at the Jianguo, which is always busy, suffers from slow service.

Chinese food For entertaining Chinese guests there is a wide choice of restaurants serving distinguished food in smart surroundings. Once more, the Shangri-La heads the list because the service at the *Shang Palace* (¥¥¥) is so good, and the restaurant takes the trouble to find genuine Cantonese vegetables and seafood rather than using local substitutes. The *Fan* (¥¥¥), at the Great Wall Sheraton, is decorated with sandalwood and silk fans of every size. Even some of the delicious barbecued meats, *al dente* vegetable and seafood dishes are presented in

fan-shaped arrangements. The *Tao Li* (¥¥¥) at the Jinglun invites guests to select their own fish live from tanks as proof of their freshness and specializes in steamed fish with ginger and spring onions. The Great Wall Sheraton's roof-top restaurant, the *Yuen Tai* (¥¥¥), provides Sichuan food: instead of rice, guests are served rich, yeasty, steamed white bread, the proper accompaniment to this food. The *Four Seasons* (¥¥¥) at the Jianguo has an eclectic menu, ranging from jellyfish and scallops to Beijing duck.

Eating at the Beijing Hotel (no credit cards) is a different experience. The hotel has not adopted the Western restaurant model of small rooms and widely spaced tables; its vast main dining rooms can each seat well over 1,000, and at lunch time are always full. The *main dining room* (¥¥) in the east wing has a long menu. Highlights are the cassia flower duck, chicken in oyster sauce and duck web with mustard for *hors d'oeuvre* and shark's fin with chicken shreds, lamb shashliks and steamed fresh fish for the *entrée*. The *middle dining room* (¥¥) is Sichuan, with no allowances for Westerners. The third of the Beijing's restaurants, called the *Chinese Restaurant for Gourmet Specialities* (¥¥), is quieter and known only by word of mouth or discovered by accident, since it is hidden away on the top floor of the west wing. Its best dish is Mongolian hotpot, described on the menu as "mutton in chafing dish."

Japanese food Beijing now has two fine Japanese restaurants, reflecting the number of Japanese businesses based in the city. The *Nakabachi* at the Jianguo (¥¥¥) is superior and more expensive. The restaurant at the Beijing (¥¥) is geared to executives working in the hotel and serves good value, fixed-price set lunches.

Late night and snacks The *Greenery* at the Jianguo (¥¥), the *Orient Express* at the Great Wall Sheraton (¥¥) and the *Coffee Garden* at the Shangri-La (¥¥) all open until 11. The Greenery has the best pizzas and cheeseburgers in Beijing. The Sheraton *Coffee Lounge* is so good that it is used for business entertaining. It serves Chinese dishes as well as salads, smoked and grilled fish, a choice of pasta dishes, beefburgers, kebabs and even American ice-cream cakes of indulgent richness.

Reservations Beijing ☎ 5007766, Great Wall Sheraton ☎ 5005566, Jianguo ☎ 5002233, Jinlun ☎ 5002266, Shangri-La ☎ 8021471.

LOCAL RESTAURANTS

Donglaishun ¥¥
16 Jinyu Hutong ☎ 550069
Two can eat quietly here without being overwhelmed by the number and size of dishes. It is a Muslim restaurant, specializing in lamb hotpot. Diners cook their own lamb slices in seasoned broth over a charcoal-fired table stove. Gourmets attribute the flavour and tenderness of the meat to the breed of sheep used: the Donglaishun raises its own lambs on the Inner Mongolian grasslands. The restaurant will also serve a quarter or half Beijing roast duck, which is suitable for smaller parties.

Fangshan ¥¥
Yilan Hall, Beihei Park ☎ 443481 • AE
In order to dine here, you must make a reservation a week in advance, since it is much in demand for banquets and high-level entertaining, and you need to set out earlier than usual. To reach the restaurant, enter Beihai Park by the main entrance, then cross the Yong'an (Eternal Peace) Bridge to Qiong Island and follow the right-hand path to the covered way which leads to the restaurant on the northern shore in Yilan (Flashing Ripple) Hall. Your journey will be rewarded by the most tranquil surroundings and food in the style of the Qing imperial kitchen. The restaurant was established in 1925 by former cooks of the Empress Dowager Ci Xi, who have handed down their skills to the present generation.

Fengzeyuan ¥¥
38 Zhushikou Xidajie ☎ 332828 • AE
A very simple, unadorned restaurant in a forbidding concrete building, the Fengzeyuan is nevertheless regarded as one of Beijing's best for unusual delicacies: for instance, asparagus, steamed prawns, soup flavoured with octopus roe or braised bear's paw.

International Club ¥
Ritan Lu ☎ 522188
Next door to the CITIC Building, this is a Sino-Japanese venture, run by Japanese. There are three restaurants serving Cantonese, Western and Japanese food.

Maxim's de Paris ¥¥¥¥
2 Qianmen Dongdajie ☎ 5121992 • AE DC MC V
Maxim's is heavily patronized by foreigners because it is such an unlikely restaurant to find in China. It is a joint venture with Pierre Cardin and an exact replica of Maxim's in Paris. Everything is elaborate Art Nouveau, from the staircase to the table lamps and the lush vines of the stained-glass windows. The food and the wine list are French, naturally, and both can be superb, although it is not unknown for tough meat and soggy vegetables to be served.

New Beijing Duck ¥¥
Xinhua Lu ☎ *334422* • *AE DC MC V*
Because it can seat 2,500 people and
processes Beijing ducks with
assembly line precision, this
establishment is also known as the
"McDonald Duck." The restaurant
is supplied by farms in the Beijing
suburbs where ducks are force-fed
until they reach the required degree
of plumpness. Besides the traditional
dish of duck skin wrapped in
pancakes with plum sauce, the
restaurant serves complete duck
menus which might include duck
bone soup, deep-fried duck liver,
duck heart with sautéed vegetables,
or duck served in a variety of
combinations with nuts, vegetables or
mushrooms.

Qianmen Roast Duck ¥¥
32 Qianmen Dajie ☎ *5112418*
• *AE DC MC V*
Beijing duck is just as good in other
parts of China, but many visitors
expect it to be more authentic here.
Hence the many duck restaurants
that are thriving. The Qianmen at
this address is one of two that can be
recommended for their general
cleanliness and good service. It is
quieter and more intimate than the
other, the nearby New Beijing Duck.
It is also the first Beijing duck
restaurant (opened in 1966) and
the original of what is now a
government-run chain of a dozen, all
of which bear the same name.

Ren Ren ¥¥
18 Qianmen Dongdajie ☎ *5112314*
• *AE DC MC V*
The Ren Ren is a good alternative to
the Sichuan (see below) for business
entertaining. It is smart, clean and
nearly always full of overseas
Chinese, the managers of Hong Kong
trading companies for the most part.
The restaurant stays open late by
Chinese standards (11.30) and
specializes in *dim sum* and such
delicacies as barbecued pigeon,
scallops and steamed mandarin
fish.

Sichuan ¥¥
51 Rangxian Hutong ☎ *656348*
• *AE DC MC V*
This is one of two restaurants (the
other is the Ren Ren) much used for
entertaining senior Chinese officials.
In fact, Deng Xiaoping and other
Communist Party leaders sometimes
personally entertain guests here. The
restaurant is housed in the former
mansion of Prince Chen Ke, 24th son
of the Qing Emperor Kang Xi (1662–
1723). The service is slow but few
complain, preferring to relax, fanned
by breezes that blow in through the
open windows of the pavilions with
their red pillars and painted roof
beams. The dishes are more
descriptive of their appearance than
their content: "panda playing with
bamboo," "magpie in a plum tree"
and "goldfish in lotus pond" are all
works of culinary art, though
ingredients such as preserved egg are
not palatable to all Westerners. Not
so the stuffed cabbage, braised duck
breast, tea roast duck and stewed
carp. The kitchens are personally
supervised by Chen Song Ru, whose
cookbooks have made him famous
throughout China.

Window of the World ¥¥
*CITIC Building, 19 Jianguomenwai
Dajie* ☎ *5003335* • *AE DC MC V*
There are two restaurants on the top
two floors of the China International
Trust and Investment Corporation
(CITIC) building; one is Western and
the other Chinese. Both are heavily
patronized by the business
community housed in the offices
below. The Western restaurant serves
a lunch-time buffet and, in the
evening, rack of lamb, beef
Wellington, crêpes Suzettes and
chocolate soufflé. The larger Chinese
restaurant serves Cantonese food, and
is particularly known for its
"beggar's chicken," so called because
it used to be baked in mud over an
open fire. Nowadays, this popular
dish is baked in a clay pot and it must
be ordered at least six hours in
advance.

Bars

Some of the embassies have bars for staff and accompanied guests, with imported drinks sold at cost (the best are at the British, Irish and Australian embassies), and you may be able to barter news from home in return for an invitation. Otherwise, it is a choice among the hotel bars. *Charlie's*, at the Jianguo, became the best-patronized bar in town when it opened in the early 1980s because it was the first bar in Beijing serving cocktails and imported beer. Visitors can no longer be sure of meeting the Beijing correspondents of the world's media here, but it remains popular. The Great Wall Sheraton has Beijing's most elegant cocktail lounge, the *Orchid Pavilion Court*, underneath a glass-roofed, seven-floor, tree-lined atrium, and featuring a pianist of concert-hall standard. The same hotel's *Summit Lounge*, 21-floors high above Beijing in the octagon, is quiet and remote from all that is mundane about the city.

Travellers on their own seeking company should visit the coffee bar to the left of the lobby of the *Beijing*, a meeting place for travellers of every nationality and level of affluence. Strangers readily strike up conversations.

The Beijing also has a bar which ought to be better known than it is. Called the *Long Corridor Club*, and situated in the west wing, with a roofed-in veranda, a good view and old-fashioned furniture, it is always quiet and suitable for private conversations.

Entertainment

In Beijing there is tourist entertainment, hotel entertainment, and, best of all, the parties put on by the local expatriate community. If visitors can get invited to these they will come away with the impression that Beijing is the liveliest city in China. Highlight of the week is the Friday night party, put on by the embassies in rotation. Drinks, a buffet supper or barbecue, swimming in fine weather and a disco later in the evening are the usual ingredients, plus the latest news from home and local business intelligence. Once every three weeks or so, *Maxim's de Paris* restaurant holds open house for foreign residents. The star of the evening is a Chinese musician called Cui Jian, who was dismissed from the Beijing Philharmonic for his progressive experimentations in music.

Nightclubs All the main hotels have discos. *Juliana's* at the Lido (Holiday Inn) is the most popular with young visitors at the weekend, despite the distance from central Beijing. The *Cosmos Night Club* at the Great Wall Sheraton suits all tastes, providing a Filipino band which alternates between middle-of-the-road favourites and the latest chart hits in Hong Kong and the West. Smart dress essential.

Acrobatic displays Chinese acrobatics, popular in China for some 2,000 years, combine something of the Western circus – juggling acts and animal routines – with mime and gymnastics. The chief venues are *Beijing Gymnasium*, Longtan Lu ☎ 757231, the *Shoudu Gymnasium*, Baishiqiao Lu ☎ 890281, and the *Workers' Gymnasium*, Chaoyangmenwai Dajie ☎ 592961. Performances are nightly.

Music, drama and dance The *Beijing Philharmonic Orchestra* has a varied repertoire, from popular Western classics to traditional Chinese folk dance, but no permanent concert hall. It is also frequently away from Beijing on tour. The Central Opera and Ballet Company and the China Opera and Ballet Company perform Western opera and ballet at the *Beijing Exhibition Hall Theatre* ☎ 890661. Visitors also go to performances of Chinese opera by any of the four opera companies in Beijing, but most find the piercing singing hard to enjoy, even when interspersed with lively acrobatic and comic routines.

Westerners are usually taken to the *Shoudu (Capital) Theatre* ☎ 550978.

Regional Chinese music and dance is performed by visiting troupes from all over China at the *Cultural Palace of the Nationalities*, Fuxingmen Dajie ☎ 668761.

Hotels also often put on entertainments, typically featuring dancers and musicians from a neighbouring Asian state.

Information and reservations
The *China Daily* carries details of what's on, and hotel travel desks will arrange tickets and transport (and even dinner-inclusive packages) for anything from acrobatic displays to the opera.

Shopping

Liulichang Road Visitors with limited time should head for the Liulichang Road, which was restored and opened in 1980 as a pedestrian mall lined with 18thC antique and crafts shops. It is mostly state-run, but a handful of the shops are private enterprises, one of which boasts "Fassination for tourists and the only smiling faces in Beijing." All shops take the major credit cards and are open daily 8.30–6.30. All have in abundance jade, pearls, jewellery, cloisonné, porcelain, seals, ink stones and calligraphy brushes, reproductions of famous scrolls and bronzes, embroidery and fans. Among the best shops are no. 80, which has the finest Qing dynasty porcelain, with prices starting at ¥80,000; no. 96, which has a large stock of good, contemporary watercolours; and no. 108, which stocks giant fans for use as wall decorations. Other shops specialize in paintings and stock everything from hand-painted greeting cards and woodblock-printed stationery to fine watercolour reproductions of famous paintings from China's museums.

Wangfujing Dajie is the main shopping street in Beijing and has the Beijing *Arts and Crafts Store*, China's biggest. This doesn't mean that it is

the best, however. It simply has more varieties of the standard Chinese artifacts, with showcase after showcase of carved jade, inlaid lacquerware, cloisonné, pottery, embroidery and bamboo sculpture. It also has a counter for credit card sales and shipping (open 8–8). Other stores of note in the street are no. 235, the *Foreign Languages Bookstore*, which has a large collection of fine art books with superb pictures of China's main historical monuments; no. 265, the *Beijing Paintings Shop*, which sells reproductions of famous Chinese paintings and exhibits work by modern artists; and no. 293, the *Huaxia Arts and Crafts* shop, which has smaller antiques such as lacquer jewellery cases and silver pipes.

The Friendship Store The store, in Jianguomenwai Dajie, is massive. Its stock is much like that of the Beijing Arts and Crafts Store. Exotica include Chinese typewriters, musical instruments, and innumerable varieties of chopstick. There is also a florist, a carpet shop, a refreshment hall, a currency exchange and credit card sales desk and a supermarket which sells excellent Chinese yogurt and cheeses.

Qianmen Dajie Immediately south of the Qianmen Gate is another district of stores, mainly of curiosity appeal, although bargain-priced furs can be bought at the *Beijing Silk Shop*, 5 Qianmen Dajie ☎ 331859 open 8.30–8. This is the finest building, architecturally, in a muddle of narrow, crowded lanes. It has a splendid green and gold cast-iron balustrade and pillared doorway. The furs are upstairs, and a coat can be made to any design from as little as ¥300. Farther down, by the Qianmen Stationery Store, turn right into a small lane called Dazhalen. Here, many of the shops have elaborate façades of carved wood, rubbed brick and ironwork. Every available surface is decorated. One to try is no. 33, the *Jui Fu Hsiang Hsi Hung Chi Store*, which proclaims "superior stuffs, moderate prices, nice selection."

Sightseeing

Beijing's major tourist sights cannot be seen in a spare hour or two. Half a day is the minimum you need to invest in a visit to the Forbidden City or the Temple of Heaven. Both the Great Wall and the Ming Tombs are 2hrs away by taxi, and the excursion normally takes a whole day, although there is a half-day helicopter excursion covering both sights which departs 9am daily from the Lido and returns at 2pm. Contact the CTS Helicopter Desk ☎ 506688 ext. 3388. Hotel travel desks sell tickets for group tours, and will organize taxis and guides for one to four persons. Group tours tend to be rushed and regimented, so the latter option, though more expensive, is preferable. Typical costs for a day trip to the Great Wall and Ming Tombs are ¥300 for one person, ¥170 per person for two or three, and ¥130 for four to nine. Leading tour operators with multilingual guides are *Hua Yuan Travel Service*, Great Wall Sheraton ☎ 5005566 ext. 2336 and CITS *Tours*, main office, Room 2041 Jinglun ☎ 5002266 ext. 2041.

Palace Museum (Forbidden City) The imperial palace is a grand scale architectural masterpiece, and it demands considerable stamina. Although the distance from north to south is only 960 metres/1050 yards, sideways excursions into some of the hundreds of smaller court rooms and gardens can easily turn the visit into a hot, but satisfying, trek of several hours. The site of the palace was first laid out during the Yuan dynasty (1279–1368). All of the present buildings, however, were erected by the third Ming dynasty emperor, Yong Le (1403–24) and the Qing dynasty Dowager Empress Ci Xi (1835–1908).

The imperial palace was conceived as the main seat of government and the setting for coronations and important state ceremonies. It housed the emperor, his family, ministers, court officials, servants and craftsmen. It was only during the 18th century that the palace began to take on the aspect of a Forbidden City from which the emperor rarely emerged. The palace was looted during the Japanese occupation, and by the defeated Nationalists before 1949. Many of the greatest treasures are now in Taiwan.

Visitors enter first through the Gate of Heavenly Peace, which forms the northern boundary of Tian'anmen Square. However, the entrance proper is through the Wumen (Meridian) Gate beyond, from which the emperor reviewed his armies and prisoners of war and the imperial astronomers announced the dates of the calender for the coming year, based on the moon's cycles. Through its arches lies the most delightful of all the palace's ceremonial courtyards, bisected by the winding Golden Water Stream, which is crossed by five marble bridges. Through the arch to the east of the courtyard is a series of cool, quiet gardens shaded by cypresses.

The Gate of Supreme Harmony leads to the largest of the palace's courtyards, dominated at its northern end by the Hall of Supreme Harmony, which houses the emperor's throne.

In the next building, the Hall of Harmony, the emperor used to greet distinguished foreigners, address his household and inspect seed-grain before planting. The Hall of Preserving Harmony, beyond, was used for examining candidates who wished to enter the highest levels of the administration. The world-famous Flying Horse of Gansu is displayed here, along with ancient embroidery. The next building, the Palace of Heavenly Purity, was the setting for the last imperial ceremony, the marriage in 1922 of Pu Yi, puppet emperor of Japanese-occupied northern China.

The main path then divides into numerous branches, taking visitors through scores of smaller halls, palaces and gardens which formed the living quarters of the Ming and

Qing rulers and which are now museums. The best lie to the east, and visitors with limited time should seek out the Hall of Paintings as a priority. *Open 8.30–4.30.*

Jingshan Wansui (Coal) Hill
Directly opposite the northern exit to the imperial palace, in Jingshan Park, is an artificial hill constructed from the earth dug from the moat surrounding the palace. Visitors with the energy to climb to its summit are rewarded with outstanding views of the Forbidden City.

Temple of Heaven The Temple of Heaven is the collective name given to three ceremonial structures set in Tiantan Park, in the southeastern corner of the city. These beautiful buildings are not only a remarkable feat of 15thC architecture; they once played a crucial ceremonial role in the Chinese calendar. Two of the buildings are circular, remarkable both for their acoustic properties and for their nail-less carpentry.

Beihai Lake and Park The lake was excavated in the 12th century, and the Mongol emperor Kublai Kahn established his palace at the southern end of the park in 1260. The most prominent building is the white-domed Dagoba, built in Tibetan style in 1651. During the week the park is a beautiful spot to walk in, but crowded at weekends.

Beijing Zoo In the 19th century, an imperial park in the northwestern corner of the city was given over as a menagerie and originally called "the Garden of 10,000 animals." In fact, a rather sorry and primitive affair by modern standards, Beijing Zoo stocks about 500 species including, of course, the pandas.

The Summer Palace The palace where the imperial court stayed during the summer months to escape the heat of Beijing is no more than a 45min drive from most of the city's hotels. Its best-known attraction is the marble pleasure boat at the western end of the lake, which was completed for the Dowager Empress Ci Xi in 1888.

Out of town

The Great Wall This is said to be the only man-made structure visible to the naked eye from the moon. Sections were begun as early as the 4th and 3rd centuries BC. To link the piecemeal sections into one continuous rampart, Qin Shi Huangdi (221–206BC) used a conscript army of 300,000, many of whom are buried in the rammed earth and sand-core. Although the Wall was said to be impregnable, it was frequently breached by northern invaders by the simple expedient of bribing the sentries. The Wall took on its present form in the Ming dynasty (1368–1644), when the earth ramparts were reinforced with stone, and beacon towers were built at regular intervals. From its eastern starting point at the Shanhaiguan Pass in Hebei province to its western end at the Jiayuguan Pass in the Gobi Desert, it can be traced for 6,000km/3,750 miles, though much of its masonry has been stolen or has suffered natural erosion. The Badaling stretch of the Great Wall attracts 1.3m tourists a year, and at peak times over the summer weekends there are so many sightseers it is difficult to move. For this reason, visitors should go to the newly opened 1.7km/1-mile stretch of the Wall at Mutianyu. Apart from being less crowded and having a modern restaurant and shopping complex, it has a cable car to the highest point of the Wall. The views are just as good as those from the Badaling section, which are familiar the world over from tourist guides and posters.

The Ming Tombs A visit to the Ming Tombs, 50km/30 miles north of Beijing, is usually combined with an excursion to the Badaling stretch of the Great Wall. Only two of the 13 tombs have been fully excavated. The rest are spread out over a considerable area and are in a sad state of disrepair, with collapsed, monumental masonry left to become overgrown. Beijing residents frequently picnic among the ruins.

The mausoleum that tourists usually visit is that of Emperor Wanli (1573–1620). It is approached down the mile-long Avenue of Animals, lined with huge statues of lions, elephants, horses, camels, mythical beasts and soldiers, administrators and servants from the household of the deceased emperor. The tomb was defended against robbery and has revealed finds of great splendour, including well-preserved clothing, wood and leather. These rich treasures are now displayed in exhibition halls.

Spectator sports
The *Shoudu (Capital) Gymnasium*, Xizhimenwai Dajie ☎ 890281, is Beijing's main venue for local and international sporting events, although the *Workers' Gymnasium and Stadium*, Gongren Tiyuchang Lu, also hosts events. The popular local sports here are soccer, volleyball, basketball, table tennis and gymnastics – also ice-hockey and figure skating at the Shoudu Gymnasium. Forthcoming events are announced in the "What's On" section of the *China Daily*, and a certain number of tickets reserved for foreigners can be obtained through CITS ☎ 5122211 or hotel travel desks.

Keeping fit
Fitness facilities in Beijing are sparse, though most hotels have swimming pools and saunas. Guests at the Great Wall Sheraton are best served, with a resident trainer to supervise use of the gymnasium, tennis courts, large swimming pool and sauna. Nonresidents are charged admission to the swimming pool and the gym and can use the tennis courts on payment of a membership fee (¥220 a month). The Lido also has tennis courts but these are reserved for guests only.

The *International Club*, entrance on Ritan Lu ☎ 522188, has an Olympic-size swimming pool but to use it you must first go to the Shoudu Hospital for a medical check and obtain a licence from the pool attendant. Only long-term visitors will consider the effort worthwhile. There is no such ceremony for the use of the Club's indoor and outdoor tennis and badminton courts, but they are popular and have to be reserved several days in advance. The Club does not lease equipment.

Joggers are thwarted by the fact that the central parks are not open before 8.30 and usually close by 5. Thus the relatively traffic-free, shady streets of the Sanlitun consular district offer the best running.

Local resources
Business services
The best of a limited choice is the Business Centre at the Great Wall Sheraton ☎ 5005566. It offers secretarial and translation services, photocopying, telex and fax.

Communications
International couriers DHL *Sinotrans* is at the Beijing, Room 1149 ☎ 486004, 485681. *OCS* and *TNT Skypak* are both at the Beijing Air Cargo Centre, in the lobby of the Beijing ☎ 5007766 ext. 727.
Post office Hotel post offices handle most transactions but sometimes refuse to accept international parcels. The main post office handling parcels is at 23 Dongdan Beidajie ☎ 555265; the same building houses a section for express mail ☎ 336621.
Telephone International collect calls can be made from any telephone by calling the International Telephone Service ☎ 115. Otherwise, telephone calls can be arranged through the hotel switchboard. At the present time IDD is available in a few hotels but may extend only to Japan and Hong Kong.
Telex and fax Nearly all hotels now provide this service; if it is not available, use the Great Wall Sheraton Business Centre ☎ 5005566 during normal office hours, and the Lido ☎ 5006688 for 24hr telex service.

Conference/exhibition centres

Beijing Exhibition Hall, Xizhimenwai Dajie, northwest suburbs ☎ 890661, is the main showcase for Chinese manufactured goods. It has a huge central hall, two smaller ones in each of the wings, a theatre, cinema and restaurant. The *Great Wall Sheraton* ☎ 5005566 has the best hotel conference facilities.

Emergencies

Bureaux de change The exchange desk at the *Friendship Store* ☎ 593531 is open daily 9–7; the Great Wall Sheraton, Jianguo, Jinglun, Lido and Shangri-La desks are open 8–9, depending on demand.

Hospitals The *Beijing Union Medical College Hospital*, Dongdan Beidajie ☎ 553731, was funded by the Rockefeller Foundation until 1949 and continues a tradition of Western medical practice. Dial ext. 217 for emergencies, 24hrs; otherwise ext. 274 or 251 for foreigners' section. The *Beijing Friendship Hospital* ☎ 331631 has a dental clinic for foreigners, but you are advised to use it only in cases of extremity.

Pharmacies *Watson's Pharmacy*, Lido Hotel ☎ 5006688, has a comprehensive stock of imported drugs. Open 8.30–9.

Police Emergencies ☎ 110. Otherwise ☎ 552729 for foreigners' section.

Government offices

The list of ministries and state trading corporations with offices in Beijing is extensive. The most reliable, locally available published source of information is the annual *China Phone Book and Address Directory*, available by post from the Hong Kong publisher, The China Phone Book Company Ltd, GPO Box 11581, Hong Kong ☎ 5-264073 ⊠ 84958. Useful organizations include the *Beijing Customs Office* ☎ 595568, the *Foreign Trade Bureau* ☎ 554808, the *Public Security Bureau* ☎ 553102 and the *State Statistical Bureau*, Information Centre ☎ 863547.

Information sources

Business information It will save time and frustration if visitors begin their search for information with the commercial section of their own embassy (see *Embassies* in *Planning and Reference*). Otherwise, the three main Chinese organizations which handle general inquiries are the *Bank of China, Trust and Consultancy Company* ☎ 656550; the *China Council for the Promotion of International Trade* (CCPIT), Liaison Department ☎ 867504; and the *China International Trust and Investment Corporation* (CITIC) ☎ 5002255.

Local media The *China Daily*, also available in English, is published in Beijing and distributed to hotels, with a Business Supplement every Sunday. It is an official national newspaper, and the types of story it covers are a good indication of the projects and attitudes of which the government approves.

Tourist information Hotel travel desks are the best starting point; otherwise contact the CITS ☎ 5122211. CAAC has an inquiry desk ☎ 558861 ext. 2525; an office for domestic flight reservations and confirmations ☎ 553245; and another office for international flight confirmations ☎ 557319. For rail inquiries ☎ 5581032.

Thank-yous

The florist at the *Friendship Store* ☎ 593531 has a good selection of flowers and will make up bouquets but does not deliver. The *Delicatessen* at the Lido (Holiday Inn) ☎ 5006688 has the best range of luxury chocolates. All hotels stock imported wines and spirits, but the choice of quality wines is best at the Lido Delicatessen.

CHENGDU

Area code ☎ 028

Chengdu, the capital of Sichuan province, was at the centre of Deng Xiaoping's initial experiments with economic reforms in the late 1970s. Deng himself is a native of the province and at the time Zhao Ziyang was governor here. Chengdu has a total population of 8m and Sichuan is China's most populous province with 109m. The city is situated in the heart of Sichuan's fertile basin, where grain, tea and silk production flourish, and animal husbandry is important. While the city maintains a broad-based light and heavy industry, including textiles and garments, the province is rich in minerals and chemicals. Chengdu is also a principal point of access to Xizang (Tibet), although this may begin to change as Lhasa is linked by air to other parts of China.

The city is hot and humid in the summer; the winters are fairly mild. In the Qing dynasty Chengdu was famous as a beautiful city but, unfortunately, has largely given way to the drabness which typifies China's cities today. But local identity is strong and people still gather in tea houses to gossip and listen to storytellers. The markets are strung with bundles of chilies and the exotic herbs and spices of pungent Sichuanese cuisine.

Arriving

Chengdu is well served for flights to Beijing (2hr 15min), Guangzhou (2hr), Shanghai (2hr 30min), Lhasa (2hr), Kunming (2hr) and Chongqing (1hr). You can fly on from Hong Kong on the same day via Guangzhou. The airport is 22km/14 miles from the city centre.

Chengdu is connected by rail to Shaanxi, Yunnan and Guizhou provinces, and to Chongqing (7hr).

Hotels

While the accommodation in Chengdu is comfortable, standards fall short of international.

Chengdu (¥) Dongfeng 3-Lu ☎ 44112 or 43312 ⊠ 60164. Built in 1984 and renovated in 1987 in a joint venture with a Hong Kong company, the hotel is not very conveniently situated, but neither is it expensive. It has a small gym. Telex and photocopying.

Jinjiang (¥¥) 36 Renmin Nanlu, Erduan ☎ 24481 ⊠ 60109. This 500-room hotel in the city centre, built in 1961 and refurbished in 1984, is found adequate by most business travellers. Some suites are available.

There is also a tennis court. The World Trade Centre Club in the lobby (open 9–9) provides photocopying, secretarial services, interpreting and consultancy.

Minshan (¥¥) 17 Renmin 2-Nanlu ☎ 52611 ⊠ 60247 • AE DC MC V. Completed at the end of 1987, facing the Jinjiang, the Minshan is Chengdu's newest hotel. The rooms are comfortable and well appointed. IDD, telex and photocopying; good conference and meeting rooms.

Restaurants

In Chengdu it will not be hard to develop a liking for Sichuan cuisine. For entertaining and informal dining try the *Garden* in the Jinjiang, a joint venture restaurant, and one of the few to offer Western as well as excellent Cantonese cooking. Also worth trying is *Wenjun Fandian* (¥) 1 Qintai Lu ☎ 24397. Attractively located in a traditional setting, it offers over 300 kinds of *dim sum*.

For informal dining and lots of local atmosphere there is *Yaohua Fandian* (¥) Chunxi Lu, Xiduan, one of Chengdu's oldest restaurants, in the heart of the shopping area.

119

CITY BY CITY

Relaxation

Shopping There is a strong local crafts tradition specializing in silver filigree, lacquerware and anything made from bamboo, including bamboo weaving. Silk, brocade and embroidery are also excellent. The main shopping and commercial area is around *Renmin Lu* and *Dongfeng Lu*; specialist craft shops are on Chunxi Lu, and the *Sichuan Antique Store* is on Shangyechang Jie. There is a calligraphy and painting street market near the Jinjiang.

Sightseeing Chengdu has many scenic spots and historic monuments to absorb any free time you may have. Sights within the city itself include *Du Fu Cao Tang* (Du Fu's Thatched Cottage), an attractive little park of bamboo groves, galleries, a house and a small museum which commemorate the life of the famous Tang dynasty poet Du Fu, who retired here to write. You may also visit the *Temple of Wu Hou Ci* (the Marquis of Wu) and the *River View Pavilion Park*.

Mt Emei, approximately 150km/93 miles south of Chengdu, is one of the sacred mountains of Buddhism, rising over 3,000 metres/9,800ft. As well as having various temples, it abounds in monkeys and some interesting plant life. There is a panda reserve at *Wolong* to the northwest, beyond the Qingcheng mountains. *Leshan*, 167km/105 miles from Chengdu, is famous for its 70-metre/230ft tall statue of the Buddha, carved into a cliff face and overlooking the confluence of the Qingyi, Min and Dadu rivers. There is good, though simple, accommodation available at both Mt Emei and Leshan.

Local resources

For all business support services use the *World Trade Centre Club* in the lobby of the Jinjiang ☎ (028) 24481 ext 681 or 682 ℡ 60216, 60217 fax (028) 24481 ext 683. The Jinjiang also has comprehensive mailing services. The *Provincial Foreign Economic Relations and Trade Bureau*, Chenghua Jie ☎ 32372 or 32587 ℡ 60131 has an information centre ☎ 32105. The main *Import and Export Corporations* are located at 16 Renmin Bei-3 Lu. The *Sichuan Corporation of Industrial and Commercial Development*, 211 Xinhua Donglu, Erduan, and *Sichuan Changjiang Business Enterprise Corporation*, 34 Fuqing Lu ☎ 33396 may provide useful information.

For travel arrangements and interpreters, contact *CITS* ☎ 28225 or 28731 ℡ 60154; its office is in the Jinjiang. *CAAC*, 31 Beixin Jie ☎ 23990; airport inquiries ☎ 22304. *Bureau of Public Security*, 438 Xinhua Donglu ☎ 22951.

CHONGQING
Area code ☎ 0811

Chongqing is Sichuan's second city. During the war with the Japanese in the 1930s, the capital was relocated here. Its importance derives from its position at the confluence of the Yangzi and Jialing rivers, for until recent years the only way to reach Sichuan was along the Yangzi river and through the Three Gorges. Unusually for a Chinese city it is built on hills. It was first opened to foreign trade in the late 19th century. Chongqing's major industries include iron and steel, machine tools, electrical engineering, electronics and textiles, and in 1986 the city made news when the former millionaire owner of the well-known Minsheng Shipping Company was allowed to recommence trading. The total population is currently 13m. Chongqing tends to get foggy particularly in the winter, hence the local saying "dogs bark when the sun comes out." The summers are very hot and humid, the winters fairly mild.

120

Arriving

There are regular flights to Beijing (2hr 10min), Chengdu (1hr), Guangzhou (1hr 45min) and Xian (1hr 45min) and also less frequent flights to other cities. Chongqing airport is 27km/17 miles from the city; you should arrange to be met.

Chongqing is connected by rail with Chengdu and Guiyang.

Hotels

Accommodation in Chongqing for business visitors has at last begun to improve. There are now four comfortable hotels.

Chongqing Guesthouse (¥¥) Xiaoshizi ☎ 49301 or 42332 ℡ 62193 • AE DC MC V. A modern comfortable hotel, which enjoys a good central location.

Renmin (People's) (¥¥) 175 Renmin Lu ☎ 551555 or 55156 ℡ 62126 • AE DC MC V. This central hotel set in attractive gardens was first built in 1955, with a large conference hall in the style of Beijing's Temple of Heaven. The hotel underwent extensive renovation in 1987: the generously sized rooms are now well-appointed and the service has improved. Travel desk.

Yangtze Holiday Inn (¥¥) Dian Zi Ping and Nan Ping Xiang ☎ 483380 ℡ 62220 • *AE DC MC V* • Recently opened in the Nan An district this is a comfortable and well-equipped hotel.

Yuzhou (¥) Yuanjiagang ☎ 811829 ℡ 62201. A medium-range hotel with generously sized rooms set in beautiful grounds in the suburbs.

Restaurants

Highly recommended for entertaining is the *Wei Yuan* (¥) 37 Zhouyuan Lu ☎ 43592. The main restaurant of the *Chongqing Guesthouse* is suitable for both entertaining and informal dining. The *Xiao Dong Tian* (¥) Jiao Chang Kou ☎ 43910, popular with the locals, is for informal dining.

Relaxation

Shopping Popular local products include bamboo scrolls and utensils, household ceramics, silk and traditional medicinal herbs. The commercial area is around *Jiefang Bei* (Liberation Monument).

Entertainment Chongqing has its own acrobatics troupe and a local, very boisterous, opera.

Sightseeing The city's two principal parks are *E Ling* (Goose Neck) *Park* and *Pipa Shan Gongyuan* (Loquat Hill Park), the city's highest point.

The best sights are outside Chongqing, where the journey is as fascinating as the destination; the vegetation is lush and rural life seems timeless. There are two hot spring spas in the area, *Southern Hot Springs*, 30km/20 miles from Chongqing on the Yangzi river, and *Northern Hot Springs*, 50km/30 miles upstream from Chongqing, close to the Jialing river. The latter offers not only pools and bathhouses but also ornate temple buildings dating from the Tang dynasty, and caves with stalagmite formations. Nearby is a favoured summer resort known as *Jinyun Mountain*, covered in dense forest and rare and varied flora. However, most interesting of all are the *Dazu Buddhist Grottoes*, some 160km/100 miles northwest of Chongqing. Created between the 9th and 13th centuries, the grottoes contain numerous sculptures.

Local resources

There are limited business support services in Chongqing, although the main hotels do have telex. Initial contacts can be made through the *Bureau of Foreign and Economic Trade*, 35 Linjiang Lu ☎ 42766 ℡ 60174. *China Council for the Promotion of International Trade* is also in this building ☎ 42847.

For travel arrangements, contact the *Chongqing Tourism Company*, Renmin Hotel ☎ 53421 ℡ 62126, or *Yangzi River Travel Service*, 4 Shaanxi Lu ☎ 45942 ℡ 62170.

Bureau of Public Security, Linjiang Lu ☎ 44400.

DALIAN
Area code ☎ 0411

Since 1984 the port of Dalian has experienced a change in fortune. It has begun to encourage foreign investment and to resume its role as an entrepôt for the hinterland of the northeast provinces of Liaoning, Jilin, Heilongjiang and Nei Menggu.

In 1898, Dalian was leased by the Russians, who took advantage of its natural ice-free harbour where ships of up to 10,000 tonnes/11,025 US tons may dock. The Russians named it "Dalny," whence Dalian; it is now also known as Lüda. They redesigned the city, creating the wide, tree-lined avenues which still characterize it. In 1905, the city was ceded to the Japanese, whence another name by which the city is known, Dairen. Today the total population has grown to 4.8m. Principal industries include shipbuilding, oil refining (oil is sent by pipeline from the oilfields of Daqing), machine tools, petrochemicals and electrical goods. The Liaodong Peninsula is fertile, and important for the production and processing of soy beans and providing a large proportion of the country's apples. There is also good fishing. The climate is warm and pleasant in the summer, and the winters, while cold, are by no means as gruelling as in the northeastern hinterland.

As part of the drive to promote Dalian and the northeast, since 1984 the city's harbour, airport and communications have been expanded. In 1987, approval was given for the expansion of the port at Dayaowan to the northeast, in order to create extra container and multipurpose berths able to handle 26m tonnes/28.6m US tons of cargo by 1991. A new international exhibition centre has been built. The municipality may independently handle and approve projects which require investment of up to $10m, and it has trade links with 140 foreign countries. Representatives of enterprises from the provinces of the northeast have set up offices here as well as several – mostly Japanese – foreign firms and banks. Dalian also hosts the National Centre for Management Development, which is jointly sponsored by the State Economic Commission and the US Department of Commerce.

Arriving
Daily flights from Beijing take 1hr and from Guangzhou (daily except Thursday) 3hr 30min. There are also flights from the major cities of the northeast, and four flights a week from Tokyo. The airport is 18km/11 miles from the commercial centre (taxis available).

Dalian is well connected by rail; it is 5hr from Shenyang, 18hr from Beijing.

Hotels
Bangchui Island (¥) 1 Bangchui Island ☎ 25131 ⊠ 86236. This is a resort hotel, on the seafront 11km/7 miles from the city centre, but it offers amenities such as several meeting rooms and conference halls.
Dalian Guesthouse (¥)
4 Zhongshan Guangchang ☎ 23111. On the central square of Dalian, the hotel dates from 1905. It has long enjoyed a reputation for its seafood.
Friendship (¥) 137 Stalin Lu ☎ 24121 ext 250. Built in 1961 close to the harbour and the offices of the foreign trade corporations. Only 39 rooms.
Holiday Inn (¥¥) 18 Sheng Li Sq, Zongshan District ☎ 808888

86383. Dalian's newest quality hotel offers a convenient location, health facilities and a business centre. **International** (¥¥) 9 Stalin Lu 238238 86363. This new joint-venture hotel was completed in late 1987. It offers a business centre and all other normal international-class amenities, and is highly recommended.

Nanshan (¥) 56 Fenglin Jie, Zhongshan District 28517. The hotel opened in 1980, with a further wing added in 1985. It is in the north of the city and has a swimming pool.

Restaurants
Every visitor to Dalian must try the seafood. Recommended restaurants are *Dalian Seafood Restaurant* (¥) 85 Zhongshan Lu 270767 and *Huibin Canting* (¥) 3 Jinbujie 35362. For entertaining, the *International* hotel offers the best facilities.

Relaxation
Shopping Local crafts include shell carving and glassware. The principal commercial area is around *Tianjin Jie*, with the main department store at 199 Tianjin Jie and the *Dalian Antique Store* at 229 Tianjin Jie. *The Friendship Store* is at 137 Stalin Lu.

Sightseeing For the summer visitor, there are many pleasant beaches. *Tiger Beach Park*, to the southeast of the centre, also has pleasure steamers to Ginseng Island. *Xinghai Park*, 5km/3 miles to the southwest of the centre, has several amenities; the attractive beach is reached through a cave. In the city itself the only other main park is *Qingniwa Park*, also known as Labour Park, which is famous for its cherry blossoms in May and houses a sports ground and theatre. There are no monuments of note in the city. There is a *Natural History Museum* at 3 Yantai Jie and a *Zoo* which has tigers from the northeast.

Local resources
For business support, Dalian has been relatively undeveloped. However, the *International* hotel now offers a range of business services; as does the *Holiday Inn*. The offices of the *Foreign Trade Bureau of Liaoning* are in Zhongshan Square 25679 86151. *The Bank of China* 23625 86163 and the main post office are also in Zhongshan Square. *CITS*, 3 Changtong Jie, Xigang 331080 86485. *CAAC*, 12 Dagong Jie 35884.

FUZHOU
Area code 0591

While Fuzhou, the provincial capital of Fujian, has a long-standing tradition as a busy sea port with international contacts, the hinterland is mountainous, inaccessible, difficult to farm and poor. These hardships led to mass emigration in the 19th century.

In 1979, the province was among the first to be given special overseas trading rights. At the suggestion of the Japanese Nomura Bank, Fujian has raised loans worth ¥5bn and ¥10bn through the issue of bonds. The revenue has been used to extend and improve the airport of Fuzhou. The port of Fuzhou, at Mawei 48km/30 miles downstream, has also been extended and with a loan from a US bank the province has financed its own fleet, which is already producing a healthy revenue. A well-publicized – if controversial – joint venture with Hitachi has begun to produce colour TVs. Other plans include a major hydroelectric project financed by a loan from Kuwait and the construction of steel plants and an oil refinery. The city has a population of 1m.

Arriving

There are daily flights to Beijing (2hr 20min) and regular flights to Guangzhou, Shanghai, Nanjing and Hangzhou. There are also charter flights to and from Hong Kong. The airport is 14km/9 miles from the city centre and the main hotels (taxi available).

By rail from Xiamen takes 15hr, from Guangzhou or Shanghai, 36hr.

Hotels

In its new capacity as a Special Economic Development Zone, Fujian has invested heavily in hotels, many of which are joint ventures of a high standard. The new hotels have IDD telephones.

Donghu (East Lake) (¥) 44 Dong Dalu ☎ 57755 ✆ 92171. The centrally located hotel has both an old and a new wing. Not expensive; fax and photocopying services.

Foreign Trade Centre (FTC) (¥¥) Wusi Zhong Lu ☎ 550154 ✆ 92158 fax 550358 • AE DC MC V. This is a well-appointed hotel in a central location, with a business centre. The Foreign Trade Exhibition Centre is also here.

Haishan Guesthouse (¥) Wusi Lu, Drum Tower ☎ 56444 ✆ 92136. Centrally located resort hotel. Each room has a balcony.

Minjiang (¥¥) Wusi Lu, Gulou (Drum Tower) District ☎ 57895 ✆ 92146. Centrally located resort hotel which was completed in 1984. It has a hot spring-fed swimming pool and a tennis court.

Wenquan Dasha (Hot Spring) (¥¥) Wusi Zhong Lu ☎ 551818 ✆ 92180 fax 535150 • AE DC MC V. This new central hotel is part of the Pearl International Group. It has water from local hot springs and all amenities, including a tennis court and a business centre.

Restaurants

For entertaining guests, you cannot do better than the new hotels, particularly the Western-style *Tropicana* (¥¥) and the local-cuisine

Ming Palace (¥¥), both at the Wenquan Dasha ☎ 51818. For informal dining, try the *Jiu Yuan Chun* (¥) 817 Beilu ☎ 553038.

Relaxation

Fujian is famous for its banyan trees and its hot springs, the waters of which are considered beneficial. The hotels offer a good range of sporting activities.

Shopping One of the major products of the region is lacquerware, often fashioned into attractive household goods and furniture. Visits can be arranged to the ateliers, where you can also buy. Local stone and cork carvings are also worth looking out for. The *Arts and Crafts Store* is on Wuyi Lu, and the *Tourism Products Service Co* is on Wusi Lu.

Sightseeing *Gushan* (Drum Mountain) has noteworthy art and architecture, including the Yongquan Temple, the early Song-dynasty porcelain *Thousand Buddha Pagoda*, a jade Buddha and numerous manuscripts. In West Lake Park, in the northwestern suburbs of the city, is a small *Cultural Museum*.

Outside Fuzhou, in the northern part of the province, are the *Wuyi* mountains, an attractive area of waterfalls and gorges and twisting waterways which has been designated a nature reserve. The area is also famous for its Oolong tea.

Local resources

For business support services including general advice, you should contact the *Foreign Trade Centre* or the *Wenquan Dasha* hotel. Prominent in Fuzhou's present development are *The Provincial Foreign Economic and Trade Commission*, Dongda Lu ☎ 554981; *Fujian Foreign Trade Corporation*, Wusi Lu ☎ 551340; *Fujian Import Export Corporations* branch office, Wusi Lu ☎ 550154 (next to the Foreign Trade Centre). *Exhibition Centre* ☎ 556107.

CITS, 44 Dongda Lu ☎ 556293 or 551950 ✆ 92201.

GUANGZHOU
Area code ☎ 020

Hong Kong people say that Guangzhou (Canton) is not really part of China. Of course, politically it is, but because of its proximity to Hong Kong, just over 80km/50 miles away, it has always been more cosmopolitan, and its 6m citizens more affluent, than anywhere else in China. Many residents of Guangzhou have relatives in Hong Kong who give them televisions, cameras, washing machines and refrigerators. The young are quick to emulate Hong Kong fashions; and petty crime, black market dealing and organized begging are among the less beneficial influences that have crossed the border. On the other hand, the people of Guangzhou, like those of Hong Kong, are often hardworking and ambitious. Many have learned English and are used to doing business with foreigners. The city is one of 14 "open cities" granted a high degree of economic autonomy in China, and within the province of Guangdong, of which Guangzhou is the capital, are three of China's four Special Economic Zones (Shenzhen, Zhuhai and Shantou).

Guangzhou is surrounded by rich tracts of fertile river delta, densely cultivated to supply the supermarkets and restaurants of Hong Kong. The local farmers are among the chief beneficiaries of the responsibility system, which allows them to sell surplus produce on the open market once they have reached the targets set by the government. Factories in the region are busy handling unskilled sub-assembly work for Hong Kong firms, and since the cost of labour compares favourably with Hong Kong, the trend is likely to spread into increasingly sophisticated types of production. Oil companies prospecting in the South China Sea and tourists have also brought employment to the city and surrounding province (see Shenzhen). Guangzhou has a growing population of overseas management and technical personnel, and prior to the events of June 1989 foreign investment generally was increasing at a healthy 15% a year.

Hong Kong commentators often point to the growing integration between the Territory and Guangzhou as an example of the way things will be after 1997 when Hong Kong reverts to Chinese sovereignty. Hong Kong will have a greater influence on China than *vice versa*, so the argument runs, infecting the mainland with its energy and pragmatism in a reverse takeover on a grand scale.

Guangzhou has often played a leading role in China's history. The Portuguese arrived here as early as the 16th century, and in the 19th century it was the first city in China to be opened to foreign trade, when the British were permitted to settle at Whampoa, 24km/15 miles south of the city. At first they traded Indian silver for Chinese silk and tea; then later, colluding with local merchants, they found it more profitable to pay for Chinese commodities with opium. Attempts by the Chinese authorities to crush this illicit trade led to the two Opium Wars. The second war ended in 1861 after the British occupied Shamian Island, to the south of the city, and with it gained control of the river routes to the city. In the 20th century Guangzhou has played an important role in national politics. A native of Guangzhou, Dr Sun Yat-sen, led the Chinese Nationalist Party (Kuomintang) to overthrow the Qing dynasty in 1911. The city's outward-looking attitude is evident in the fact that even during the 1950s and 1960s, when the rest of China was closed to foreigners, Guangzhou managed to hold its twice-yearly Trade Fair.

Guangzhou today is a city of memorials to great leaders and past conflicts, a mélange of traditional Chinese and run-down European-style buildings. It may not be typical of China, but it is one of the easiest cities in which to do business and different enough to provide visitors with a novel experience.

Arriving

Guangzhou is easy to get to. There are direct daily flights from Manila, Bangkok and Beijing, and several a day from Hong Kong. Visitors from Hong Kong can also travel by train or hovercraft. The Hong Kong and Yaumati Ferry Company operates a hovercraft service from Kowloon to Guangzhou three times a day (journey takes just over 3hr). The Kowloon–Canton railway operates four through trains in each direction daily, also with a total journey time of just over 3hr. Although it is not possible to do the return trip in a day and have time for business in Guangzhou, rail and hovercraft offer a comfortable and scenic alternative to air travel for anyone making more than a brief visit. Tickets for both services can be reserved through CITS or purchased in Hong Kong at Ticketmate booths in all MTR (Mass Transit Railway) stations.

Guangzhou (Baiyun) airport

Guangzhou airport is strictly no frills. Arriving passengers walk to the arrivals hall, where the health declaration desk, passport control and baggage reclaim are all within a compact area. Formalities are quickly completed, but baggage takes 20min to unload. It is deposited on the arrivals hall floor, and there may be a mêlée as passengers search for their bags. There are few trolleys, but the distance to customs is no more than

30 metres. Passengers with no goods to declare are quickly processed. At the exit from customs the Bank of China currency exchange desk and CITS inquiry desk are both to the left; the meeting area is to the right. For cabs, turn left out of the exit past a row of food stalls and left again to the taxi rank, a walk of 100 metres. Total time from arrival to exit rarely exceeds 30min.

The airport has only basic facilities for departing passengers: small shops selling a limited range of Chinese crafts and duty-free cigarettes and liquor, and a post and telecommunications desk. On the first floor is a café selling tea, coffee, beer, soft drinks and snacks. CAAC inquiries ☎ 661843; flight confirmations ☎ 662969.

City link The airport is about 8km/5 miles north of the city. Travellers who have arranged hotel transport in advance will be met in the meeting area and helped with their bags. Those going by taxi will have to carry their own and are usually approached by touts offering transport at many times the correct rate. The journey into town takes less than 30min and should cost around ¥8.

Railway station

Guangzhou Station presents no particular challenges. The arrivals hall is well signposted and has a special channel for foreigners where formalities are quickly completed. The distance to walk is short. If you have requested hotel transport you will be met at the exit. The White Swan has a reception desk and operates a free minibus service to the hotel. There are always plenty of taxis on the ramp in front of the station. The Dong Fang and China hotels are only a 2min walk away; others no more than 15min. Inquiries ☎ 661789.

Hovercraft terminal
Zhoutouzui Pier is 2km/1.5 miles from Guangzhou's business centre. Allow up to 45min to clear entry

formalities. It is best to arrange hotel transport in advance, since the number of passengers sometimes exceeds the number of taxis. The journey into town should take no more than 15min. Inquiries ☎ 447560.

Getting around
Most visitors rely on taxis to get around Guangzhou, but in the area around the Trade Fair Exhibition Hall and the China and Dong Fang hotels it is pleasant enough to walk. Farther south, walking is more difficult because paving is erratic, and construction work often creates

	HOTELS		RESTAURANTS		BUILDINGS AND SIGHTS
1	China	1	Banxi	1	Friendship Store, Baiyun hotel
2	Dong Fang	2	Beiyuan	2	Friendship Store, China Hotel
3	Garden	3	Caigenxiang	3	Guangzhou Antique Store
4	White Swan	4	Datong	4	Guangzhou First People's Hospital
		5	Guangzhou	5	Guangdong Gymnasium
		6	She Can	6	Guangdong Provincial Museum
		7	Yeweixiang	7	Guangzhou Museum
				8	Peasant Movement Institute
				9	Sun Yat-Sen Memorial Hall
				10	Trade Fair Complex

large puddles and other obstacles.
Taxis are cheap and plentiful,
outnumbering any other kind of
vehicle on the road. They come in
every colour imaginable, and some
are old and dilapidated but newer
red Toyotas, which formerly plied
the streets of Hong Kong, are kept
in better repair and are
air conditioned. Taxis can be hailed
in any of the main avenues and
tourist haunts – a circular red flag on
the passenger side and, at night, an
illuminated roof sign indicate the
taxi is free; but when it is raining
the best bet is a hotel taxi rank. Few
drivers speak English, but some
carry a card with the major hotels
and tourist sites written in both
Chinese and English, to which you
can point.

Limousines The China, Garden
and White Swan hotels all have fleets
of chauffeur-driven Mercedes for the
use of guests (the Swan also has
three Rolls-Royces). The average
cost is ¥35 per hour, which includes
the first 15km. Thereafter it is ¥1.70
per km. Hotels will also negotiate
half- or whole-day rates for guests
and will try to find an English-
speaking driver.

Area by area

Guangzhou is neither big nor
complex. The two main highways
which divide the city into quarters
are the east/west Zhongshan Road
and the north/south Jiefang Road.
The city has no recognizable heart
but does have a business district in
the north around the Trade Fair
Exhibition Hall and a shopping area
to the south by the river.

Northern Guangzhou The low
glass-and-steel buildings which
house the twice-yearly Chinese
Export Commodities Fair, better
known as the Canton Trade Fair,
also house the offices of most of the
foreign trade corporations. Naturally
enough, the surrounding area has
gradually developed into the business
centre of Guangzhou, and its status
was confirmed with the opening here

of the luxurious China Hotel in
1984, followed shortly afterwards by
the hotel's 15-floor office annex,
which now houses all the trading
companies and banks that were
formerly in the Dong Fang. Business
visitors are likely to spend most of
their working day in this area.

The district bustles during the two
months of the Trade Fair: Apr 15–
May 15 and Oct 15–Nov 15. From
its foundation in 1957 the Fair has
been the major showcase for Chinese
products and was once virtually the
only opportunity for the Chinese to
trade with foreigners. It has
diminished in importance as a result
of the greater commercial freedom
which has been created by the new
open-door policy but still attracts
more than 25,000 foreign visitors a
year and accounts for 10% of China's
foreign trade.

Surrounding the business district
are three attractive parks for early
morning and evening walks: the
Liuhua Park and its many lakes; the
delightfully secluded Orchid Garden,
with its teahouse and gazebo; and
the Yuexiu Park, which has fine
views of the city from the Zhenhai
Lou watchtower, built in the late
14th century.

Downtown Most of the local
Chinese shops and restaurants are in
the stretch of Renmin Road closest
to the river (Renmin Nanlu), 20min
from the China Hotel by taxi. Here
are rows of characteristic Chinese
shop-houses with covered walkways.
Some date from the 1920s, when
large sections of the city were
pulled down and rebuilt as part
of a slum-clearance programme,
and have a solid classical
appearance. Immediately to the west
of this area is Shamian Island. It
occupies a commanding position at
the junction of two branches of the
Pearl River and was held by the
British until World War II. Today
it is a traffic-free haven of peace
and a popular place for a stroll
among relics of Guangzhou's
colonial past.

Hotels

Of the five hotels listed three are among the best in China and generally attract superlatives: the China for its all-round service, the Garden for its comprehensive facilities and the White Swan for its setting.

The city no longer suffers a shortage of rooms except during the Trade Fair when all hotels are heavily booked. However China trading firms usually reserve large numbers of rooms in advance in anticipation of the needs of the companies they represent. Guangzhou was the first city in China to have been linked, via Hong Kong, into the international telephone network, and all rooms in the hotels below have IDD telephones.

China ~~¥¥¥¥~~
Liuhua Lu ☎ 666888 ⊠ 44888 Fax 677014 • New World Hotels International • AE DC MC V • 944 rooms, 60 suites, 6 restaurants, 2 bars
The China aims to attract well-heeled Western business travellers, or the "merchant princes of today" as its slogan goes. The China's central position (opposite the Trade Fair complex and on the airport road), its well-trained staff and its luxurious appointments are indeed inducements. Though the red-marble lobby is poorly illuminated, the rooms are light and spacious, and many have views of the surrounding parks and city. There are several floors of residential apartments with kitchens for families and long-stay guests. The China is well provided with places to eat (see *Restaurants*), besides its large Veranda coffee shop. 24hr room service, medical clinic, florist, beauty salon, disco • tennis, gym and health club, outdoor pool, 9-lane bowling alley • photocopying, printing and binding, word-processing and secretarial services, interpreters and translation, telex and fax, auditorium (capacity up to 1,200) with simultaneous translation.

Dong Fang ~~¥¥~~
Liuhua Lu ☎ 669900 ⊠ 44439 Fax 662775 • AE DC MC V • 1,200 rooms and suites, 13 restaurants, 1 bar
The Dong Fang is next to the China, which has creamed off most of its custom at the top end of the market.

Having once been the foremost hotel in Guangzhou, it is very busy now only during the Trade Fairs and is regarded by some as old-fashioned. Nevertheless, it provides a fair degree of comfort and friendly service, is good value, and could not be more central for business. The hotel is built around a courtyard containing a typical Chinese garden. The restaurants serve a wide range of Chinese regional cuisines – Mongolian hotpot in the Nationality Court, Sichuan in the Garden Restaurant and Cantonese in the Jade Palace – as well as European dishes, in the Orchard. For privacy and for formal entertaining it is best to use one of the hotel's 50 private dining rooms. Disco, medical centre • gym, tennis, badminton, billiards, bowling alley, pool • small business centre providing word processing and translation; separate offices in the ground-floor arcade handling photocopying, fax, telex and mail.

Garden ~~¥¥¥¥~~
368 Huanshi Donglu ☎ 773388 ⊠ 44788 Fax 338989 • AE DC MC V • Peninsula Group • 1,100 rooms, 53 suites, 7 restaurants, 1 bar
The Garden has the most congenial atmosphere of the leading Guangzhou hotels. It has a substantial number of long-stay residents, including families, and is an easy place to meet people and find out what is going on. The staff are friendly, speak good English and provide swift, attentive service. It is

5 min by taxi from the Trade Fair complex. The building itself successfully balances the grand and the intimate. Leading off the enormous lobby are a number of excellent restaurants (see *Restaurants*) and a large peaceful garden. Sports facilities are extensive and serve as the focus for much of the social life of the hotel. The business services are the best in town; they are run by the Hong Kong-based Sullivan Business Centres, which employ many expatriate wives. 24hr room service, extensive shopping arcade, delicatessen, travel desk, disco, in-house nurse, limousine service
• large pool, gym, sauna, jacuzzis, plunge pools, squash, tennis
• photocopying and binding, word-processing and secretarial services, translation, interpreters, meeting rooms (capacity up to 60), auditorium (1,800 seats) with simultaneous translation and audiovisual facilities.

Holiday Inn City Centre ¥¥¥¥
Huanshi Donglu ☎ *753141* ⊤ˣ *441045 Fax 753126* • *AE DC MC V* • *431 rooms and suites, 3 restaurants, 1 bar, 1 coffee shop*
This 24 storey hotel opened in 1989. It adjoins a large exhibition centre and offers business and convention facilities. Visitors can choose between a grill room and two restaurants offering different types of local fare. Fast food is also available. Shopping arcade, cinema, disco • health club, pool • business centre, convention facilities, meeting rooms (capacity up to 500).

White Swan ¥¥¥
1 Shamian Nanjie, Shamian Island ☎ *886968* ⊤ˣ *44688 Fax 861188*
• *AE DC MC V* • *Leading Hotels of the World* • *822 rooms, 62 suites, 6 restaurants, 2 bars*
The White Swan is for travellers who consider setting and environment to be paramount and who do not mind being half an hour by taxi from the business district, or living in what is essentially a tourist hotel. The location could hardly be better, on the southern point of Shamian Island, amid the shady streets and elegant mansions of the former British and French colonial settlements, and beside the Pearl River. When the White Swan opened in 1983 it was China's first international-class hotel, an ambitious joint venture between the Guangdong Tourism Bureau and Goodyear Investments of Hong Kong, and they spared no expense. The atrium features a large waterfall, surrounded by lush greenery and crowned with a mountain-top pavilion. Little is done to deter the large numbers of local people who come to stare. The rooms come with a choice of river or island view, and all have balconies. The restaurants provide ample choice (see *Restaurants*), and they are popular: Guangzhou business people like to be entertained in the White Swan. 24hr room service, Elizabeth Arden hair and beauty salon, bakery, limousine service, disco • golf driving range on the roof, pool, sauna, massage, gym, squash, tennis • secretarial services, translation, telex, fax, auditorium (600 seats) with simultaneous translation.

Restaurants
For business entertaining a hotel restaurant is the usual choice. Besides being reliable and convenient, these restaurants can suit any mood, from casual to formal, and a variety of tastes, providing Western-style food and the best of Cantonese and other Chinese regional cuisines. Dining in Guangzhou's local restaurants, however, is altogether better than elsewhere in China. Decor is often magnificent compared to the austere

character of restaurants in Beijing. The food is fresher, subtler and more varied, to the point that the menus can be intimidating unless a choice is made of one of the set banquets; the local tourist guidebook claims that Guangzhou's restaurants combined serve 5,400 regional dishes. Parties of Hong Kong Chinese come to Guangzhou for its unusual fare: dog (eaten in winter) and game such as pangolin (spiny anteater), monkey and civet, which are protected species in Hong Kong. These exotic foods need seeking out, however. Most of the restaurants listed here present menus more acceptable to Western palates. Reservations are advised in all cases; the information desk at most hotels will do this for you and will order special dishes in advance. Most restaurants expect guests to arrive by 7.30pm and will close not long after 9pm. None of the independent restaurants listed accepts major credit cards. The hotel restaurants do, but may prefer non-residents to pay cash. Inquire when you make the reservation.

HOTEL RESTAURANTS
Western food Two restaurants stand apart from the rest for formal dining and Continental cuisine. The *Connoisseur* (¥¥¥¥¥) at the Garden is for the serious gourmet and is in a dignified white-pillared room overlooking the front garden of the hotel. It has an extensive but pricey wine list, with ordinary Burgundies starting at ¥160. The *Roof* (¥¥¥¥¥) at the China is busiest at lunch time, when the fine views of the surrounding parks can best be appreciated.
Chinese food in all its regional varieties is available in abundance in Guangzhou and presented with a flair uncommon in the rest of China. The *Four Seasons* (¥¥¥) at the China is widely regarded as the best, with high marks going to its fresh local steamed fish, although the chefs have a tendency to overburden the *hors d'oeuvre* with piped mayonnaise in their attempts to present a pretty dish. The *Peach Blossom* (¥¥¥) at the Garden has a peaceful atmosphere with seven private dining rooms and a further five tucked away in a pleasant garden setting. Both of these are the flagship Cantonese restaurants of their respective hotels and expect relatively formal dress.

Regional-style restaurants are generally more relaxed. The *Ming*

Yuen (¥¥) at the Garden specializes in Beijing duck. The *Garden* (¥¥) at the Dong Fang serves rich, spicy Sichuan cuisine. The *Taste of China* (¥¥) at the White Swan covers the spectrum. The *Chao Zhou* (¥¥¥) at the China serves fine seafood. The *Nationality Court* (¥¥) at the Dong Fang is the only one to serve Mongolian hotpot.
Other cuisines Restaurants that provide a complete change from Chinese fare include the Japanese *Hirata* restaurant (¥¥¥) at the White Swan, and the *Songbird* (¥¥¥) at the same hotel, which serves Mexican food.
Informal dining Popular places for lunch are the *Village* (¥) at the China, which serves *dim sum*, and at the Garden the cheerful *Pizzeria* (¥) and the *Carousel* (¥), which has the best-value buffet with hot and cold Western and Oriental food plus a 360-degree view.
Reservations China ☎ 666888, Dong Fang ☎ 669900, Garden ☎ 338989, White Swan ☎ 886968.

LOCAL RESTAURANTS
Banxi ¥¥
Longjin Xilu ☎ 889318
This restaurant is within the grounds of Liwanhu Park, to the southeast of the city, and overlooks the Liwan Lake. To build up an appetite it is

pleasant to stroll around the paths and admire the traditional architecture of what is, in fact, not one restaurant but a series of linked teahouses artfully designed to appear haphazard and present changing vistas. Visitors are generally led to the air conditioned and newer foreigners' section, but can ask to dine in one of the many older pavilions. Despite the restaurant's capacity of 1,000 people the style is sedate. It is well-known for its *dim sum*, which can be ordered as part of a larger meal. The *hors d'oeuvre* are shaped to picture a bird. The winter-melon soup (in season) is an example of Cantonese delicacy and inventiveness: broth enriched with chicken, ham, mushrooms and lotus seeds is cooked inside a whole melon and served at the table with a ceremonious cutting open of the carved melon lid.

Beiyuan (North Garden) ¥¥
Xiao Beilu ☎ *332466*
A short taxi ride from the China, Garden and Dong Fang hotels, the Beiyuan is located at a busy intersection but the traffic noise disappears once you are inside the small rooms surrounding the inner courtyard. The rooms resemble an old-fashioned luxury railway carriage (though larger), with screens of inlaid wood, stained glass and heavy dark wood furnishings. Dishes include shark's fin soup with chicken, deep fried crab balls arranged around the pink claw, chicken cooked in red Shao Xing wine, fish with pine kernels, and rich sweet-and-sour goose.

Caigenxiang (Vegetarian) ¥¥
167 Zhongshan 6-Lu ☎ *886835*
This restaurant will suit both the vegetarian and the meat eater, since its famous Six Treasures dish succeeds in re-creating the flavour and appearance of everyday Cantonese chicken, pork and duck entirely out of rice, bean curd and vegetables. The vegetable balls are also excellent, and servings generally

feature a wide selection of mushrooms.

Datong ¥¥
63 Yanjiang Xilu ☎ *885933*
The top floors of this restaurant, overlooking the Pearl River, are reserved for foreigners. Cool breezes blow in through the terrace in the evening. The best dishes include roast suckling pig, peacock-shaped chicken with ham and vegetables, fish with pine kernels, and the seasonal straw mushrooms on shredded crab.

Guangzhou ¥¥
Wenchong Nanlu ☎ *884339*
This is a noisy, good-natured restaurant in the heart of the city with rooms on several floors. Foreigners eat on the top floor, above the hubbub. The food is highly regarded; dishes include boiled shrimps (in season) eaten with various sauces, braised chicken with frogs' legs, and roast goose.

Nanyuan ¥¥
120 Qianjin Lu ☎ *449781*
On the south bank of the Pearl River, 30min from the main hotels but well known by taxi drivers, the Nanyuan is entirely surrounded by a white wall which conceals a charming water garden and several small pavilions. It is known for its "goose stewed after frying," a rich dish for the climax of a meal which might also include elaborate *hors d'oeuvre* and steamed fish to make a variety of tastes and textures.

She Can ¥¥
41 Jianglan Lu ☎ *882517*
This is a restaurant for the adventurous. "She" means snake, and snake is served in an unbelievable number of forms, including snake bile in Maotai liquor (for virility!), soup with three kinds of snake, snake meat balls and a casserole of snake and civet cat called "dragon and tiger" stew. The flavour of snake is surprisingly delicate – though you

may lose your appetite after seeing them skinned alive before your eyes as proof of their freshness.

Yeweixiang (Game) ¥¥
249 Beijing Lu ☎ 330997
The Yeweixiang is noisy but will appeal to those who like novelty. Dog meat, wild duck, quail and lark are all on the menu.

Bars
The two most popular rendezvous points in Guangzhou hotels are the *Tavern* at the Garden and the China's *Corner Bar*. The Tavern looks like a smart London pub, with etched smoked glass and velvet-upholstered seats. It serves draught Carlsberg and delicious canapés while the Corner Bar serves good cocktails.

Entertainment
Western-style nightlife consists of a choice of four nightclubs and discos located in the main hotels. At the White Swan, the *River Room* has a resident three-piece Filipino band singing middle-of-the-road pop and cabaret classics. The same hotel's *White Swan Disco* attracts mainly European and American tourists. The *Checkmate* disco at the China has two female disc jockeys and is the most sophisticated. *Parrot's* at the Garden is popular with the smart young Hong Kong Chinese business set and plays the latest chart hits.

Shopping
Guangzhou has little to tempt anyone except the most compulsive shopper. Visitors passing through Hong Kong will find the same stock on sale there in far greater variety and at similar prices.
Hotel shops The *Garden* has the best shopping arcade, with shops stocking top-of-the-market clothing, jewellery, rugs, porcelain and antiques.
Friendship Stores Opposite the Garden at the foot of the Baiyun Hotel, is one of Guangzhou's two *Friendship Stores*. It takes AE and DC

cards and also has a shipping service. Here you can purchase a wide range of items. Good buys include sequined silk ladies' evening wear and, for inexpensive gifts, sandalwood fans and wickerwork ducks and swans. The other Friendship Store, behind the China hotel, stocks imported foods, toiletries, cosmetics and clothing, as well as the usual local arts and crafts.
Other shops The *Guangzhou Antique Store*, 146 Wende Lu, houses a number of shops selling largely 19th and early 20thC porcelain, seals, jade and scrolls and both Qing and modern reproductions of Ming pottery and bronzes. The crowded streets around Zhongshan 5-Lu and Beijing Lu are best for small shops and street stalls. There are also some shops near the Trade Fair Centre.

Sightseeing
Guangdong Provincial Museum Housed in the Old Guangzhou University building on Wenming Lu, this collection of archeological finds in the province includes Ming celadon porcelain, clothing and some fine clay tomb figurines depicting everyday activities. *Open 9–12, 2–8.*
Guangzhou Museum Exhibits include maps and models of the city's development and rooms devoted to the Opium Wars with amusing contemporary paintings, depicting the British as seen through Chinese eyes. The museum is in Yuexiu Park in the oldest building in Guangzhou, the five-floor Zhenhai Tower, originally built in 1380 as a lookout post. *Open 8–12, 2–8; closed Mon.*
Guangzhou Zoo Popular primarily because of its pandas, the zoo also has a representative collection of other Chinese wildlife, including the rare clouded leopard, elephants, yaks, hippopotami, monkeys, reptiles and birds. *Open 8–5.30.*
Peasant Movement Institute Among Guangzhou's several memorials to past leaders and revolutionaries, the Peasant Movement Institute is the most

rewarding. Mao Zedong was the director in 1926–27, working alongside Zhou Enlai to train members to spread Communist ideology throughout China. Shortly afterwards the Institute was closed when the Kuomintang, under Chiang Kai-shek, sought to root out Communism from the party. In the brutal suppression that followed more than 5,700 citizens were murdered. Visitors can see the schoolrooms and a reconstruction of Mao Zedong's office. *42 Zongshan 4-Lu. Open 8–12, 2–8.*

Shamian Island Until it was occupied by the British during the Second Opium War in 1861, Shamian Island was an uninhabited sandbank. Subsequently it became a foreigners' enclave, a miniature Europe. The noble villas and gardens built by the residents still stand, and some are now being redecorated, though none is yet open to the public. The wide, traffic-free, tree-lined boulevards of Shamian Island are perfect for strolling.

South China Botanical Gardens Among the attractions at these extensive gardens are some 2,000 varieties of tropical and subtropical plants, the most comprehensive collection in China. *Northeast of the city in Longyandong. Open 8–6.*

Out of town

If you are staying in Guangzhou for more than two weekends you will soon exhaust the local sights. The travel desk at the China hotel ☎ 773388 has two-day tours to the first two of the following destinations at around ¥120 per person for groups and ¥240 for individuals and couples.

Conghua Hot Springs About 80km/50 miles northeast of Guangzhou are a group of mineral springs yielding colourless, tasteless water with a surface temperature of 60°C/140°F which is said to be a cure for diverse ills from hypertension to rheumatism. The local hotel has bathrooms supplied with spring water, and there are several public

indoor and outdoor baths. Conghua is very crowded at weekends.

Seven Star Crags This dramatic grouping of karst towers, 100km/60 miles southwest of Guangzhou, has weathered into the precipitous crags familiar from traditional Chinese paintings and unique to southern China. Visitors stroll along pathways and arched bridges connecting the crags or row in the small lakes and the many large caves beneath. Very busy at weekends.

Guilin Inquire at your hotel for tours to the district of Guilin, where the most abundant and beautiful karst crags are to be found. Or take the 45min CAAC flight and stay at the lakeside Holiday Inn ☎ 3950 ⊤ₓ 48456, 20min from the airport. From the hotel you can take the day ferry trip up the Li River to Yangshuo and admire the enchanting hills which have inspired many generations of Chinese landscape painters and poets. Guilin has now become one of the popular scenic spots in China.

Keeping fit

Jogging Chinese and foreigners alike jog in any of Guangzhou's parks, but especially around the lakes of Liuhua Park, conveniently close to the China and Dong Fang. Foreigners need ¥0.20 for admission. *Open 8–8.*

Golf An 18-hole, 6,000-metre/6,500-yard, par 72 golf course designed by Arnold Palmer was opened in 1985 at the *Chung Shan Hot Spring Golf Club*, Zhongshan ☎ (07654) 24019. It is 3hr from Guangzhou by taxi, and visitors can stay at the Hot Spring Resort Hotel.

Local resources
Business services

If your hotel cannot supply the services required, try *Sullivan Business Centres* at the Garden ☎ 338989 ext. 3194. It is expatriate-run and open virtually around the clock during the Trade Fair, otherwise 8.30–6.30, Mon–Fri; 9–5, Sat.

Communications

Intelpost ☎ 677870 provides courier services, but most expatriates use the informal network of friends and colleagues travelling between Guangzhou and Hong Kong, where the courier services are faster and cheaper. The city's four main hotels have telex, fax, IDD and full mailing facilities, so there is no need to resort to the public post and telecommunications.

Conference/exhibition centres

The *Canton Trade Fair* complex is immediately south of the railway station and north of the Dong Fang and China hotels. The *Garden* ☎ 338989 has the best convention facilities, with a column-free floor area of 1,580 sq metres/1,900 sq yards, seating for up to 1,800, simultaneous translation equipment and full audiovisual facilities.

Emergencies

Bureaux de change The White Swan ☎ 886968 has a 24hr currency exchange service.

Hospitals All hotels listed here have a resident nurse and a clinic for minor ailments and casualty cases, and will refer more serious cases to the most appropriate hospital or dental clinic. However, visitors with dental problems are best advised to wait and seek treatment in Hong Kong. The *Guangzhou First People's Hospital*, Renmin Beilu ☎ 333090, and the *First Hospital*, attached to the *Zhongshan Medical College*, Zhongshan Dong-2 Lu ☎ 778223, both have 24hr emergency clinics for foreigners.

Pharmacies Hotel shops stock basic pharmaceuticals.

Police Normally, you should report any incident immediately to the hotel, which will pass the matter to the police. US citizens can call the Garden ☎ 338989 and ask for the consulate duty officer. Others can call the Public Security Bureau, Foreign Affairs Section ☎ 331060.

Government offices

All the official bodies that assist with foreign trade affairs are located in the corridor off the lobby of the old (east) wing of the Dong Fang Hotel ☎ 669900. They include the *Guangzhou Foreign Trade Development Corporation*, the *Labour Services Corporation* (which deals with the hiring of local staff), the *Guangdong International Trust and Investment Corporation*, the *Foreign Economic Law Office* and the *Municipal Tax Bureau* (both of which will advise on the current legal and tax situation on foreign trade), and the *Bank of China*, which introduces potential partners and acts as foreign trade consultant and as guarantor to the Chinese partner in joint ventures.

Information sources

Business information The *Guangzhou Foreign and Economic Affairs Centre*, at the Dong Fang, Room 2110 ☎ 669900 ext. 2110, functions like a Chamber of Commerce, and its members include local representatives of the major state corporations.

Tourist information CITS main office, 179 Huanshi Lu ☎ 661369; branch office at the Dong Fang, Room 2366 ☎ 669900 ext. 2366.

Thank-yous

Imported whisky and brandy, particularly Hennessy XO, are the gifts most appreciated by senior Chinese business representatives and officials. They can be bought at the *Friendship Store*, Jiefang Beilu, behind the China, or at the *Delicatessen Corner* at the Garden ☎ 338989. This also has the best range of luxury cakes and chocolates, which can be wrapped in attractive presentation boxes. The *Flower Shop* at the China ☎ 666888 will deliver locally.

HANGZHOU

Area code ☎ 0571

Hangzhou, renowned as a scenic resort, is a delightful place in which to conduct business. Sited on the shores of Xi Hu (West Lake), the city is celebrated in the saying "Above is Heaven, below are Suzhou and Hangzhou." Tourism (indigenous and from overseas) as well as silk and tea, reputed to be the finest in China, are the major contributors to the city coffers; fruit, rice and fish are also important.

The last ten years have seen the introduction of the manufacture of a wide range of modern consumer goods. Because it is the capital of the province, the important local industries have offices here. Zhejiang University specializes in engineering and the sciences and has many overseas contacts.

Arriving

Hangzhou may be reached by air from the principal cities in China, and direct from Hong Kong four times a week. The airport is 14km/9 miles from the city centre.

The city is on the main Shanghai–Guangzhou railway and the journey from Shanghai takes a little over 4hr; from Guangzhou 30hr. The railway station is in the eastern suburbs of the city; taxis are usually available if you take the "soft class" exit, where there is a CITS desk.

Getting around Taxis can be arranged through hotel reception desks. For relaxation and exercise, Hangzhou is an ideal place to rent a bicycle; contact the hotel reception desk or CITS.

Hotels

Most of the city's hotels are scattered around West Lake, while the commercial and residential quarters spread out east of it, and heavy industry is located as far from the lakeside as possible. Hangzhou has a good stock of hotel accommodation and has been carrying out an extensive refurbishment and building programme since the late 1970s.

Dragon (¥¥¥¥) Shuguang Lu ☎ 54488 ☒ 351048. This new hotel, managed by New World Hotels International, is a 25min drive to the north of West Lake. Facilities include a swimming pool, bicycle rental, IDD and a business centre.

Friendship (¥) 53 Pinghai Lu ☎ 20639 ☒ 35068. Completed in late 1986, this is a Sino-Japanese joint venture with 200 rooms. Both Chinese and international cuisine are available. The hotel is in the city centre and has business facilities.

Hangzhou Shangri-La (¥¥¥¥) 78 Beishan Jie ☎ 22921 ☒ 35005/6 • *AE DC MC V.* The prestigious and well-appointed Shangri-La is the best hotel in Hangzhou. There are newer and more lavish hotels in town, but they do not have the same style and charm. The hotel stands on the northern shores of West Lake and commands a fine view. It consists of two wings, one built in the 1950s with many traditional architectural features, and the other in 1962 in contemporary style. The hotel offers IDD and a business centre with fax, photocopying, word processing and offset printing.

Wanghu (¥) 2 Huancheng Xilu ☎ 71024 ☒ 35003. A tourist-oriented concern run by Hangzhou Travel and Tourism Corporation, this hotel overlooks West Lake from its northeastern shore. The building was completed in 1986 and has 350 rooms.

Xihu Guesthouse (¥) 7 Xishan Lu ☎ 26867 ☒ 3500. The Xihu Guesthouse has been used as a state guesthouse since the Qing dynasty; the tradition continues. Though beautifully located on the western shores of the lake, it is small (100 rooms) and far from the city proper and its amenities.

Xinqiao (¥¥) 176 Jiefang Lu ☎ 26911 or 24991 ⓉⅩ 351028 • *AE DC MC V*. Situated in the commercial centre of Hangzhou, 300 metres from the lakeside, this is a joint venture, completed early 1987. Although it offers business services, the hotel is more for tour groups.

Restaurants

The local cuisine is excellent and you cannot go wrong entertaining in the dining rooms of the principal hotels. Local dishes include sweet and sour fish, prawns cooked in "dragon well" tea, bean curd, bamboo shoots and recipes using chicken and ham. Overlooking West Lake, *Louwailou Caiguan* (¥¥¥) Gushan Lu ☎ 21654, is the most prestigious restaurant in Hangzhou. The architecture is in traditional Chinese style. Next to the Xinqiao hotel, is *Tian Xian Lou* (¥¥) Jiefang Lu, which has good local food, and is suitable for entertaining. *Shanwaishan* (¥¥) 8 Yu Quan Lu ☎ 26621, in Jade Spring Garden, to the northwest of West Lake, has poor decor but the food is excellent.

Relaxation

Shopping Popular local products include all kinds of silk and brocade, fans, tea and scissors. Several shops specialize in each of these articles. The main shopping area is in *Hubin Lu*, along the eastern shores of West Lake, and in *Jiefang Lu* which adjoins it.

Entertainment Local opera is performed at the *Hangzhou Theatre*. Acrobatic displays and variety concerts are often put on in the *Hangzhou Shangri-La* hotel.

Sightseeing There are numerous scenic areas and historic monuments. Many of these are clustered around *West Lake*, which covers an area of 5.6 sq km/3.5 sq miles. The lake is divided into three main parts by two causeways: the *Bai Causeway*, named after the Tang poet Bai Juyi, and the

Su Causeway which recalls the Song governor and poet Su Dongpo. On the northeastern shores, one may promenade in the gardens, suggestively known as the *Listening to Orioles in the Willows Park*. From one of the several landing stages here you may take a boat trip to *Xiaoying Island*, a small artificial island built in the Ming dynasty, and containing a complex of zigzagging bridges, lotus ponds and a teahouse. Nearby are the obelisks at the *Three Pools Reflecting the Moon*.

There are several sights to the north of the lake. *Gushan* (Solitary Hill) is a group of pavilions, one of which houses the *Xiling Seal Engraving Society*, where you can obtain beautiful seals with your name carved in Chinese, another the *Provincial Museum*. *Baoshishan* (Precious Stone Hill) with its distinctive *Needle Pagoda*. *Geling Hill* and *Qixia Hill* provide a wooded backdrop. At the foot of Qixia Hill is the *Temple of Yue Fei*, a famous Song dynasty general.

To the northwest of the lake is the *Lingyin Si* (Temple of the Soul's Retreat), located at the foot of the Peak that Flew Over (*Feilai Feng*), which has fine Buddhist rock carvings and houses an impressive gilded Buddha. *Huagang Park*, on the southwestern corner of the lake, is renowned for the shoals of gold fish which fill its ponds. South, towards the Qiantang River, famous for its annual bore, you pass through beautiful, lush countryside; here are found *Tiger Well* and the *Liuhe Ta* (Six Harmonies Pagoda).

Local resources

Business services, mailing and telecommunications, and contacts with various import/export corporations and foreign trade bodies can be arranged through the business centres in the main hotels.

CAAC, 304 Tiyuchang Lu ☎ 54259 (domestic), tel 52575 (international). *CITS*, 10 Baochu Lu ☎ 27160 ⓉⅩ 35031.

HARBIN

Area code ☎ 0451

The prospect of a visit to Harbin may not be enticing, since it is one of the coldest places in China. However, there are compensations – not least the general friendliness of the local people. Harbin is the provincial capital of Heilongjiang province, China's northernmost, which borders the USSR. The average temperature in January is $-19°C/-2°F$ and can drop to $-38°C/-36°F$, and temperatures hover around freezing point from November until the end of March. In June, July and August average temperatures are around $21°C/70°F$ and can rise to over $30°C/86°F$.

At the end of the 19th century Harbin was a small fishing village on the banks of the Songhua (Sungari) river. However, after the Russians took over Dalian in 1898, Harbin was linked to the Trans-Siberian railway and became an important junction for people making their way from Japan or America into China via Manchuria. It was a refuge for many White Russians fleeing the Revolution of 1917; their influence can still be seen in its churches, and many of the hotels offer Russian cuisine. Harbin now has a population of 3m and is a centre for heavy machinery, such as turbines, boilers, power-generating equipment, tractors and precision tools. Food processing includes sugar-beet refining and flour milling. In recent years Harbin, like other provincial centres, has sought foreign partners, including the Soviet Union, particularly in heavy industry.

To the northwest of Harbin is the oil field of Daqing, which was proclaimed by Mao Zedong as a model of socialist industrial prowess and success. Today the authorities are trying to increase the recovery rate. The Economic Development Corporation of the town of Daqing, with a population of 830,000, is looking for ways to diversify. Current local plans include a brewery and factories for furniture, livestock feed and bread.

Arriving

There are daily flights from Beijing (2hr), four flights per week from Guangzhou (4hr) and five flights per week from Shanghai. There are less frequent flights from and to other cities in the northeast. The airport is 40km/25 miles from the centre.

During the winter it may prove easier to take the train. The international train to Moscow via Manzhouli and the USSR passes through once a week, on Sunday. The journey to Beijing takes 20hr.

Getting around Taxis can be hailed on the street, but it is more reliable to order them through the hotel or your host.

Hotels

Beifang Mansions (¥) 105 Huayuan Jie, Nangang District ☎ 32480. This is a massive 1,000-room, Soviet-style hotel built in the late 1950s, conveniently located close to the Exhibition Centre and Children's Palace.

International (¥) 124 Dazhi Jie ☎ 31441 ⒯ⓧ 80081. Within walking distance of the railway station, this is the most centrally located hotel, and has photocopying. It is due to be modernized.

Moderne (¥¥¥) 129 Zhongyang Dajie, ☎ 45847 ⒯ⓧ 87075. This French-built hotel dating from 1906 was re-opened in 1987 after extensive renovation. At the end of 1987 a lavish Hong Kong joint venture disco was opened. The helpful staff of Harbin International Travel Bureau on the fourth floor offer photocopying, telex, fax and interpreting.

Swan (¥) 73 Zhongshan Lu ☎ 220201 or 220219 ⊠ 87080. Harbin's newest hotel was completed in winter 1983. It has a fairly central location and is comfortably though not luxuriously appointed.

Restaurants

The Russian influence is felt here, but there is also southern cuisine. The following are all good for entertaining. *Futai Lou* (¥) 19 Shisan Dao, Daoli district ☎ 44720, specializes in Beijing and Shandong cuisine, particularly braised bear's paw and stir-fried feilong bird. *Jiang Nan Cun* (¥) 319 Fen Dou Lu, Nangang district ☎ 34860 is a vast restaurant famous for its southern-style cuisine, including *houtou* mushrooms with shredded chicken. The best exponents of Russian style cuisine are *Hua Mei* (¥) 145 Zhongyang Jie, Daoli district ☎ 47368 and the *Western* in the Moderne hotel, which also has good Japanese and Chinese restaurants.

Relaxation

Shopping Good shops include a *Friendship Store* at 93 Dazhi Jie (a principal shopping street), the *Antiques Store* at 50 Hongjun Jie, and the *Fur Shop* attached to the Harbin Fur Factory.

Sightseeing In terms of historic monuments Harbin has little to offer, but the city council and the local tourist office have gone to some lengths to exploit Harbin's natural resources with an interesting range of outdoor activities. The ice lantern and sculpture festival, held in Zhaolin Park from January 1 to mid-February is a great attraction. Coloured lights and candles illuminate delicately carved figures

from Chinese mythology or elaborate replicas of edifices such as the Great Wall.

In the summer in Harbin, the banks of the Sungari river become a focal point for the city. There are parks and promenades, sports centres, a youth palace, a zoo, and open-air cafés. On the northern banks of the river *Taiyang Dao* (Sun Island) is a popular resort with many sanatoria and swimming in the river.

Sports Harbin is a centre for winter sports and while you should not expect facilities to match those found in Western ski-resorts, at Qingyun, 240km/150 miles from Harbin, there are facilities for cross-country as well as downhill skiing with a chairlift and pommel-lift. Between September and February you may hunt or watch game in the *Taoshan* and *Pingshan* reserves, situated 230km/140 miles northeast of Harbin.

In summer, there are opportunities for hiking, cycling and fishing in the environs of the city; also for birdwatching (in the marshlands of Zhalong near Qiqihar, or at Dailing) and horse-riding in the Mongolian banner districts.

Local resources

Resources are undeveloped and you will probably be reliant on your own typewriter and the transportation and interpreters your host organization may offer you. The *Harbin Foreign Trade Bureau*, 102 Tianjiang Lu ☎ 44265 or 46661 ⊠ 87097 will liaise and refer. Otherwise contact the *Harbin International Travel Bureau* at the Moderne ☎ 44259 ⊠ 87028, not only for travel but also for business support. *CITS* is at 73 Zhongshan Lu ☎ 31088 ⊠ 87034; the *Xinhua News Agency* in the same building has a photocopier. The main post office, 51 Jianshe Lu, also has telex and fax.

CAAC 85 Zhongshan Lu ☎ 32465. *Public Security Bureau* 95 Zhongshan Lu ☎ 222172.

NANJING

Area code ☎ 025

The city of Nanjing (Nanking), pleasantly located on the southern banks of the Yangzi river at its lower reaches, is the capital of the wealthy province of Jiangsu. Nanjing means "southern capital" and it has enjoyed this status several times, most notably at the beginning of the Ming dynasty in 1368. But the leaders of the Taiping rebellion also established their capital here in 1853 and it was the capital of the Republic founded under Sun Yat-sen in 1912 and again from 1927 under Chiang Kai-shek. On the whole people here are more experienced in foreign methods of doing business than in other parts of the country.

The population of the combined city and suburbs of Nanjing is 3.6m. It is one of the leading producers of electronics; petrochemical and fertilizer plants are established here; some coal and gas are produced in the area and trucks are manufactured. The productivity of factories in Nanjing and the surrounding rural area is the highest in the country. The city is a centre for Chinese traditional medicine, with a leading hospital and research institute. The countryside is intensively farmed, producing two crops of rice annually, as well as one of wheat. Cotton is a principal cash crop.

Arriving

Flights from and to Beijing and Guangzhou take 1hr 30min and 2hr respectively. There are charter flights direct from Hong Kong, or connections on the same day via Guangzhou or Shanghai.

Nanjing is on the main Beijing–Shanghai railway: the journey from Beijing takes 20hr and from Shanghai 4hr 30min.

For novelty, rather than speed, it is also possible to travel by riverboat both upstream to Wuhan, the Three Gorges, or even on to Chongqing (five nights) and downstream to Shanghai.

Getting around Order taxis through the hotel reception desk, in advance if possible. Negotiate the fare before the journey. Bicycles may be rented through the hotel reception desks.

Hotels

First choice must undoubtedly be the Jinling, one of the earliest and best run of the new international-class hotels in China. It is also the only comfortable hotel in the centre; the rest are in the northern suburbs.

Dingshan (¥) 90 Chahar Lu
☎ 85931 ℡ 34103. The Dingshan has a "hilltop" location overlooking the Yangzi river and is close to the Qingliangshan scenic area.
Eastern Suburbs (¥) 5 Dongjiao
☎ 45181. To the northeast of the city, at the foot of Purple Mountain, this is Nanjing's "state guest house" and consists of nine villas. There is a swimming pool.
Jinling (¥¥¥) Xinjiekou
☎ 644141/641121 ℡ 34110 • AE DC MC V. The slim silhouette of the Jinling has dominated the central skyline since October 1983. Its amenities include a revolving bar with dancing on the 36th floor, a large conference hall, clinic, gymnasium, excellent shopping arcade, the World Trade Centre and office support facilities.
Nanjing (¥) 259 Zhongshan Beilu
☎ 34121 ℡ 34102. Situated in the grounds of the former International Club, some distance north, the main building was built in 1955 and refurbished in 1984.
Shuangmenlou (¥) Huju Lu
☎ 85965/85961 ℡ 34118. Again in the northern suburbs, the hotel is set

in the grounds of the former British Consulate. There is a newer main block.

Restaurants

Nanjing is a centre for the cuisine typical of the Huaiyang area (Lower Yangzi river). The kitchens of the *Jinling* can provide the most sumptuous and exotic Chinese banquets in marvellous surroundings, and the other hotels mentioned earlier also serve excellent food. Among local restaurants, *Da San Yuan* (¥) 40 Zhongshan Lu ☎ 640127 serves Cantonese cuisine and is good for entertaining. *Jiangsu Jiujia* (¥) 26 Jiankang Lu, has atmosphere and good Nanjing duck. *Meiling Palace* (¥) 9 Zhongshan Ling ☎ 46600 is located on the wooded slopes of Purple Mountain, and was owned by Song Meiling, the wife of Chiang Kai-shek.

Relaxation

Shopping The principal commercial area of Nanjing is around *Xinjiekou*, where there are good local shops and an antique shop – all close to the Jinling hotel. There is also a market in the south of the city.

Sightseeing Nanjing has a wealth of ancient and modern monuments. Close to the centre are the *Drum and Bell Towers*, dating from the early Ming dynasty. Many of the old city gates and part of the city wall can still be identified; most impressive of all is *Zhonghua Gate*.

Xuanwu (Black Dragon) Lake Park in the northeastern corner of the city offers a floating stage, tea house, small zoo, exhibition halls and boating facilities. *Mochou Park*, to the west of the city and close to Qingliang Mountain and the ancient Stone City, has a beautiful lake covered in lotus flowers and surrounded by charming galleries and pavilions. Mochou, which means "free from care," takes its name from a sad tale of a young bride who died of grief when separated from her loved one by an arranged marriage.

Her statue is to be found in one of the courtyards near the impressive *Winning-at-Chess-Pavilion*, furnished in the style of the Qing dynasty.

The *Taiping Museum* offers insight into the history of the Taiping Rebellion. It was the residence of one of its principal protagonists. The *Nanjing Museum*, situated just inside the eastern city gate, traces local history in considerable detail.

To the east of the city rise the wooded *Zijin Shan* (Purple Mountain), with the white marble tiers of *Sun Yat-sen's Mausoleum*, and the towering *Tomb of Ming Xiao Ling* (the first Ming Emperor), now in a state of picturesque decay. The *Linggu Temple* is a functioning Buddhist temple. The *Beamless Hall* is of architectural interest for that reason, and nearby is the *Linggu Pagoda*. There is a functioning *Observatory*, with an open-air exhibition of ancient astronomical instruments.

In the environs of Nanjing, the ancient city of *Yangzhou* is attractively crisscrossed by canals and is famous for its arts and crafts. The port of *Zhenjiang* at the junction of the Yangzi and the Grand Canal has many interesting monuments. *Changzhou* is a small city typical of the area and famous for its combs. The *Qixia Mountains* with a Southern Tang monastery and Buddhist grottoes are to the northeast of the city. *Suzhou*, *Wuxi* and *Shanghai* are all within reach.

Local resources

You will be best served by the *World Trade Centre Club* on the first floor of the Jinling hotel, which also has a liaison service. There is also a post office at the Jinling; the main post office is nearby on Zhongshan Lu.

CITS, 313 Bei Zhongshan Lu ☎ 686968 ⊤🗵 34119 is efficient and helpful for travel arrangements, or there is *CAAC*, 76 Dong Zhongshan Lu ☎ 643378, or the reception desk at the Jinling. The Jinling has a medical clinic.

QINGDAO

Area code ☎ 0532

The major port of Qingdao is situated on a promontory on the southern side of the Shandong Peninsula, facing the Yellow Sea. Although the provincial capital is inland at Ji'nan, Qingdao is the larger city with a population of 4.1m. While the residential, commercial and recreational areas are to be found on the southern side of the promontory, the port is to the west on Jiaozhou Bay at Dagang. The port is ice-free and in the late 19th century was annexed by the Germans as a naval base; the town still shows many signs of their influence. The city has recently benefited from decentralization policies: under an autonomous authority it is now expanding. Qingdao generally enjoys a favourable climate, with warm summers and mild winters. Local industries include electronics, machine tools, vehicles and precision instruments. The town can also exploit the oil fields at Shengli in the north of the province.

Arriving

Qingdao airport has international facilities, but so far there are no scheduled international flights which land here. There are three flights weekly from Beijing, Shanghai and Nanjing (1hr 30min each), and daily flights, except Wednesday, from Guangzhou (3hr). There are twice-weekly flights to and from other cities in the northeast and also Xian. The airport is 30km/19 miles from the city centre and taxis are available at the terminal.

Qingdao is linked by rail to Yantai (6hr), an important port on the north of the Shandong Peninsula, as well as to Ji'nan (13hr), where it joins the main Beijing-Shanghai line. The journey to Beijing takes a further 9hr, to Shanghai 14hr. The railway station is in the city centre (taxis available). Several major international cruise companies dock here and there are local ferry services to Shanghai (minimum travel time 24hr).

Getting around You are recommended to make reservations for taxis with your hotel and to keep the taxi waiting for you for the duration of your meeting, even if it is a long one. If you are not at your hotel and need a cab, you will probably need a Chinese colleague to phone the local taxi companies ☎ 286302 or 332816.

Hotels

A longstanding seaside and health resort, Qingdao has recently made some investment in new accommodation.

Badaguan Guesthouse (¥) 15 Shanhai Guan ☎ 362800 ☎ 32224. This is an older hotel, set in the sanatorium area, consisting of a main building and attractive villas, with several restaurants. It has 100 rooms and through CITS offers telex, photocopying, translating and interpreting.

Beihai Fandian (North Sea) (¥) 7 Zhanliguan Lu ☎ 363500 ☎ 32244. Completed in 1985, the hotel has 100 rooms and two restaurants and offers business services including photocopying, telex, translating, interpreting and limited secretarial support which must, however, be pre-arranged.

Huanghai Fandian (Yellow Sea) (¥) 75 Yenanyi Lu ☎ 284215 ☎ 32151. Completed in 1983, the hotel overlooks No. 1 Beach. It has 175 rooms and offers business services including telex, photocopying, translating, and interpreting.

Huiquan Dynasty (¥) 9 Nanhai Road ☎ 285215 ☎ 32272. This slightly older and smaller hotel (completed 1979) also overlooks No. 1 Beach. It has business services like those of the Huanghai.

Restaurants

Shandong cuisine is popular throughout China and the seafood is particularly good in Qingdao. For entertaining, two local restaurants are recommended: *Chun He Lou* (¥) 146 Zhongshan Lu ☎ 228482 and *Bailanghua* (¥) Nanhai Lu ☎ 283021. For more informal dining local people recommend *Nanhai Fandian* (¥) 14 Nanhai Lu ☎ 285683 and *Lianyi Canting* (¥) Guangxi Lu ☎ 284293.

Cuisine

Information and guidance on Chinese food, including an explanation of the various regional cuisines and advice about restaurants, is given in the *Planning and Reference* section.

Relaxation

Shopping *Zhongshan Lu* is the main commercial and shopping area. Here you will find the *No. 1 Department Store* for Chinese goods, the *Friendship Store*, an antique store and an arts and crafts shop – local crafts include intricately carved shells and woven straw. Qingdao beer, brewed in the fashion of good German lagers, is one of the best in China, and is not only drunk throughout the country but exported to South-East Asia. At the northern end of Zhongshan Lu is a thronging market.

Sightseeing Qingdao has many pleasing aspects – not only the beaches and sea-front, but a hilly situation and attractive tree-lined streets. Much of the layout is due to the former German influence and if you arrive in Qingdao by rail you could be forgiven for thinking that you had come to a small German town. The station, in particular, is exactly in the style of small-town stations in Germany.

The main *Qingdao Pier*, opposite the southern end of Zhongshan Lu, extends some 400 metres/1,300ft into the sea to the Huilan Pavilion, with views across to *Little Qingdao Island*, which is connected to the land by a causeway. *Luxun Park* to the east of the pier is an attractive ensemble of wooded hillsides and pavilions where temporary exhibitions and concerts are held in the summer. *Qingdao Aquarium* is also here, housed in fort-like premises. *Zhongshan Park*, the most extensive of Qingdao's parks, includes a plant nursery and the *Zhan Shan Temple*.

Qingdao is a popular health resort and in a grid of attractive streets to the east of the main beach, in the area known as the *Badaguan* (Eight Great Passes), there are many sanatoria. As witness to the town's previous history there is still a functioning Catholic church.

Lao Shan, 75km/47 miles to the east of Qingdao, is a scenic spot with several Daoist temples. It is also the source of the mineral water (Laoshan Shui) which is sold in most hotel dining rooms in China.

If possible you should visit *Qufu*, the birthplace of Confucius, and *Mt Tai*, the most important sacred mountain in China. You will need a couple of days to visit the two sites. The journey by train reveals an almost unchanging rural life. *Weifang* is famous for its kite festival.

Local resources

The best business support services are to be found in the Huiquan Dynasty and the Huanghai hotels, but even these are fairly basic. The main post office is on Zhanshan Lu ☎ 364577.

For local business contacts the *Foreign Economic Commission*, 17 Hubei Lu ☎ 286968 and the *Shandong Foreign Trade Corporation and Trade Centre*, 11 Nanhai Lu ☎ 284011 may be useful. Next door is CITS, 9 Nanhai Lu ☎ 283876 for travel arrangements and interpreters. For flight information and reservations: CAAC, 29 Zhongshan Lu ☎ 286047. The *Public Security Bureau* (*Gongan Ju*) is at 5 Xinjiang Lu ☎ 225973.

SHANGHAI
Area code ☎ 021

Shanghai has the appearance of an untouched and neglected Western metropolis of the 1930s. A New Yorker would feel at home with the solidly built Art Deco skyscrapers. A Continental European would regret the lack of street-side cafés while finding familiar the wide tree-lined boulevards. But Shanghai is a very different place from its heyday in the 1930s when it was reputed to be the most sinful city on earth, and its name was a byword for adventure, entrepreneurship and corruption.

Shanghai was virtually created by foreigners. It was a small but flourishing port until towards the end of the First Opium War, when the Europeans imposed the 1842 Treaty of Nanking on the Chinese, formally opening Shanghai, along with Guangzhou (Canton), Ningbo, Fuzhou and Xiamen, to foreign trade and residence. Each of the major Western powers developed its own sector of the city, creating the French, British and American concessions, the latter two being merged later to create the International Settlement. Within these districts, foreigners were exempt from the law, and locals were excluded by the infamous "No Chinese, No Dogs" notice. The Shanghai waterfront or Bund (an Anglo-Indian word meaning embankment), now called Zhongshan Dong-1 Lu, is a legacy of this period. Along its length stand the imposing temples of foreign power, that once housed the Hongkong and Shanghai Banking Corporation, the British Consulate, Jardine Matheson, the Bank of Indo-China and other Western concerns. The old Customs House still serves its original function; and so, too, does the legendary Cathay Hotel – now renamed the Heping (Peace) – if somewhat less glamorously than in its prewar days.

The idyll ended with the Japanese invasion of 1941. When the Communists achieved power in 1949, foreigners were expelled and mighty trading houses such as Jardine Matheson – not to mention hundreds of Shanghainese middlemen – lost all their assets. The former wheelers and dealers fled to Hong Kong, some to create new and even bigger empires. The post-Revolutionary government set about rounding up the former pimps, prostitutes and opium addicts and clearing Shanghai's notorious slums. Today, people no longer die of starvation in the streets, but crowding and poverty are still in evidence.

Shanghai is one of the world's most populous cities, with more than 13m inhabitants. It also has an acute pollution problem, the result of its concentration of smokestack industries – steel and chemicals, heavy machinery and shipbuilding. Beijing is the political and administrative capital of China, but Shanghai is the industrial capital. Its factories account for some 30% of China's exports, which is nearly equivalent to the total exports of Taiwan. Almost 50% of China's domestic product passes through Shanghai for redistribution by rail or water. Shanghai is at the hub of China's rail network, and from its location on the Huangpu River it has access to the Yangzi River, some 16km/10 miles downstream, which flows into the Pacific and is navigable for several hundred kilometres inland.

Some of the most successful joint ventures were started here, including the first ever, the Jardine Schindler Elevator Company, which has equipped many of China's new hotels and office blocks. The Volkswagen Automobile Plant produces the Santana for sale to foreigners and other joint-venture companies; the McDonnell Douglas plant is building jets to modernize the CAAC fleet, and Pilkington's has a major industrial glass factory.

It was at first thought by many that of all China's cities Shanghai would benefit most from the government's new open-door policy, and had the potential to become, once again, the major trade capital of the East, rivalling Tokyo and Hong Kong. An uneasy relationship with the central government in Beijing, which retains its control over spending in Shanghai (Guangzhou, in contrast, is largely autonomous), is often suggested as the reason why this has not happened. Nevertheless, the municipality has been pushing on with several much needed developments: a new housing programme in the southwest of the city; a subway and new deep-water dock facilities. The Caohejing Microelectronics Industrial Area, 7km/4 miles from the city centre, produces a fifth of China's integrated circuits and is leading the country in optical fibre and laser technology. Foreign confidence in Shanghai's future is shown by US and Japanese investment in a new business and commercial centre being built in Nanjing Road, and the Shanghai Stock Exchange began trading again in 1986, albeit at a basic level. It is too soon to dismiss Shanghai's renaissance as wishful thinking; the city may yet become again the most cosmopolitan and go-ahead in the East.

Arriving

Shanghai has direct international flights from Hong Kong (CAAC and Cathay Pacific); Tokyo, Osaka and Nagasaki (JAL); San Francisco (Northwest Orient); Singapore (Singapore Airlines); and Vancouver (Canadian Pacific). There are direct flights from most Chinese cities, and connections to all that have an airport. Rail travellers from Beijing or Guangzhou have a long, but pleasant enough, journey (22hr and 36hr respectively).

Shanghai (Hongqiao) airport
The airport terminal, which was rebuilt in 1984, is the most up-to-date in China. Modern air-conditioned buses carry passengers between plane and terminal, and automated carousels make baggage reclaim more orderly than at other Chinese airports. Visitors entering on an international flight have only a short walk from the arrival hall through immigration, baggage reclaim and customs to the exit, where the taxi rank is located. Those on internal flights are taken to a separate building, south of the main terminal, where there is a 20min wait for baggage before exiting to the taxi rank. It rarely takes more than 30min to clear the airport.

Despite the rebuilding, facilities are spartan by Western standards. There are the usual long lines at the check-in desks, and the departure lounge is always crowded, although there is a quieter first-class lounge on a separate floor by Gates 1 and 2. Services consist of a bank, a snack bar and a Chinese restaurant. The duty-free shop sells a limited range of imported liquors (the choice is much greater in hotel lobbies and only marginally more expensive). Flight inquiries ☎ 537664.

City link Shanghai airport is 8km/5 miles west of the city centre. Visitors who are not being met should take a taxi. Few hotels provide their own transport. If you are being met, be sure to specify whether your flight is international or domestic, since the two terminals are some distance apart. Taxis are plentiful at both, except sometimes at night, when sharing may be necessary.

The major hotels are either on the airport road or in the city centre. It is about a 15min drive (fare ¥12) to those on the airport road. The farther into the city you go, the narrower and more congested the streets become. It can take 45min to reach hotels on the Bund (fare ¥20).

Railway station
Shanghai station is just to the north of the city centre. There is a separate foreigners' exit at the end of the platform for trains arriving from Guangzhou and Beijing, and taxi ranks just outside the station. The facilities are rudimentary. Inquiries ☎ 253030.

Getting around
Granted suitable weather Shanghai can be a pleasant city to walk in, and in the congested streets of the commercial district walking may be faster than a taxi ride. The city is laid out in a grid pattern, road names are also in English and so, armed with a map, it should be possible to avoid getting lost.

Taxis Taxis will, in theory, stop anywhere when hailed, but they are not so plentiful as to make this a

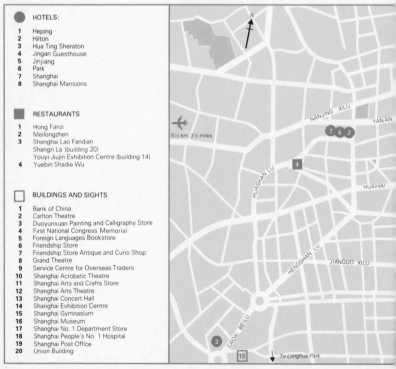

HOTELS:

1 Heping
2 Hilton
3 Hua Ting Sheraton
4 Jingan Guesthouse
5 Jinjiang
6 Park
7 Shanghai
8 Shanghai Mansions

RESTAURANTS

1 Hong Fanzi
2 Meilongzhen
3 Shanghai Lao Fandian
  Shangri La (building 20)
  Youyi Jiujin Exhibition Centre (building 14)
4 Yuebin Shadie Wu

BUILDINGS AND SIGHTS

1 Bank of China
2 Carlton Theatre
3 Duoyunxuan Painting and Calligraphy Store
4 First National Congress Memorial
5 Foreign Languages Bookstore
6 Friendship Store
7 Friendship Store Antique and Curio Shop
8 Grand Theatre
9 Service Centre for Overseas Traders
10 Shanghai Acrobatic Theatre
11 Shanghai Arts and Crafts Store
12 Shanghai Arts Theatre
13 Shanghai Concert Hall
14 Shanghai Exhibition Centre
15 Shanghai Gymnasium
16 Shanghai Museum
17 Shanghai No. 1 Department Store
18 Shanghai People's No. 1 Hospital
19 Shanghai Post Office
20 Union Building

5½ km 3½ miles

NANJING XILU
YAN'AN
HUASHAN LU
HUAIHAI
HENGSHAN LU
JIANGUO XILU
CAOXI BEILU
To Longhua Park

practical proposition. It is always quicker to arrange a taxi at the taxi service counter of a hotel. The *Shanghai Taxi Company* ☎ 222999 or 223792 and the *Shanghai Friendship Taxi Service* ☎ 586732 or 584584 both operate around the clock, but you will need someone who speaks Chinese to call them for you.

Taxis come in every colour and model available, from tiny Fiats to the stately old Red Flag limousines with fans on the dashboard and lace-curtained windows; the majority, though, are Japanese imports, kept clean and well maintained. All have a taxi sign on the roof, but not all have a "for hire" flag to indicate whether they are free. Nor do all have meters, but this is nothing to worry about since fares are fixed according to vehicle model at between ¥.06 and

¥.08 per km and can be worked out from the odometer reading.

Hotel transport The Hua Ting Sheraton has its own fleet of Volvo taxis which are available at the rate of ¥70 a day, plus ¥0.7 per km after the first 80km/50 miles. All the out-of-town hotels have minibuses which operate a regular shuttle service to the airport and commercial district and can be hired for independent travel.

Minibuses Both the *Shanghai Taxi Company* ☎ 222999 or 223792 and the *Shanghai Friendship Taxi Service* ☎ 586732 and 584584 have 12-seater minibuses for hire by the hour – useful for group excursions out of town.

Buses and trolley buses The locals call the buses sardine tins because of their shape and the crush. Avoid them.

Area by area

One link between old and new Shanghai is that the former foreign concessions now form the city's commercial heart. The British and American International Settlement was located north of what is now Yan'an Road (once Avenue Edward VII), and the French concession lay immediately to the south. To the east are the Bund and the River Huangpu, constituting one boundary of the modern city centre. The River Wusong (also called Suzhou Creek) to the north, the Renmin (People's) Park to the west and Jinling Road to the south form the others. Within this area, which is roughly a mile square, are the offices of nearly all the state and regional trading corporations.

Until recently most Western and Japanese companies based here had their offices in the smart Union Building, 100 Yan'an Donglu, with Japanese banks, investment houses and trading companies far outnumbering those from the USA, Hong Kong and Europe. Meetings were generally held in this building, although the presentations, seminars and product exhibitions that form an important part of the ritual of selling to China are usually held on the premises of Chinese corporations housed in the grand, formerly foreign-owned buildings of the Bund. The commercial geography has lately changed with the completion of the Shanghai Centre on Yan'an Donglu. This consists of a 50-floor office block and two residential towers and may in the future house the foreign firms currently operating from the Union Building and from various hotels.

Also in this central district are Shanghai's two main shopping streets, Nanjing Donglu and Yan'an Donglu. Uniquely for a Chinese city, the many shops and department stores along these avenues have Western-style shop fronts, and an effort is made to fill the windows with attractive displays.

The Old Town lies immediately to the south of the centre, in the area encircled by the Renmin and Zhonghua Roads. The contrast between Western-built and Chinese Shanghai is telling, as wide streets suddenly give way to a warren of narrow alleys, but visitors can now wander freely and unmolested through what was once a notoriously crime-ridden slum. The Old Town has a medieval atmosphere: the lanes are too narrow for cars, and lines stretched between the overhanging balconies are strung with drying fish and washing. Life is lived mainly in the streets, and the visitor can watch food being prepared and the local craftsmen at work, making furniture and clothing. Street markets abound, with their tubs full of live fish, nets of frogs and snakes, cages full of ducks and chickens, and vegetables piled on mats on the ground.

Western districts Renmin Park, on the western boundary of the commercial district, was once the Shanghai racetrack, and here bandits hid vehicles and furniture looted from the foreigners' houses during World War II. Today it is a favourite rendezvous for courting couples, and the former racing club building houses the Shanghai Municipal Library. The large square immediately to the south is used for parades on public holidays.

Immediately to the west of the park is an area which bears no sign today that it was once the heart of the brothel district and housed thousands of prostitutes and opium addicts. Here were the infamous "Meet with Happiness Lane" and "Blood Alley," where powerful secret societies like the Green Gang controlled professional beggars, the night-soil trade, protection rackets and illegal gambling dens. All this has now disappeared, to be replaced by the postwar broadcasting complex. Between this complex and the newly developed suburbs are many wide, shady streets lined with the decaying mansions of the prewar British colony, all built in the style of suburban England in the 1930s. A group of these around the intersection of Huaihai Donglu and Hengshan Lu house the foreign embassies; others are now schools, kindergartens and clinics.

Southwest of this district is the focus of all Shanghai's modern development. The view from the Hua Ting Sheraton, located in the middle of it, is quite different from that of the older, central hotels: rows of neat apartment blocks stretch to the horizon. Beyond these are the Caohejing Microelectronics Park to the west and the Minhang Industrial District to the south, centre of Shanghai's power-generating equipment industries.

Hotels

Disappointment awaits the visitor who expects Shanghai's hotels to offer the kind of sophisticated high living that allegedly inspired Noel Coward's *Private Lives*. Visitors do still stay at the Heping (Peace), formerly the Cathay, or at the Park or Shanghai Mansions for the sake of their associations and decayed grandeur. The Hua Ting Sheraton and the Hilton are the only hotels in Shanghai that could stand comparison with the best international hotels outside China.

In general the lack of services, such as business centres and health facilities, and the unhelpful attitude of hotel staff, make Shanghai the least comfortable city of China's big three to stay in. There is no sign of the intense rivalry for business trade that characterizes hotels in Guangzhou and Beijing. However, a major hotel building boom is under way, with an estimated 60 hotels projected for the early 1990's. Most of these, however, will be out of town, in the Hongqiao Development Zone near the airport.

Heping (Peace) ~~¥¥¥¥¥~~
20 Nanjing Donglu ☎ 211244 • AE DC MC V • 387 rooms and suites, 4 restaurants, 1 coffee shop/bar
Before World War II, the Cathay, as the Heping was then called, was far and away the most fashionable hotel in Shanghai. The sounds of jazz and cocktail chatter were loud enough to entertain the waiting chauffeurs in the street, and armies of servants awaited guests' every beck and call. Today the staff are abrupt and the hotel is rather seedy, though a sense of grandeur remains in its splendid architecture. Refurbishment is much needed, and in fact is planned. The solid granite building was built in 1906 and has a magnificent site on the Bund. The best suites, furnished in different styles, overlook the Huangpu River. The ordinary rooms are spacious but plain and either look into the well of the hotel, where the sun rarely penetrates, or are in the southern annex on the opposite side of the road. The architecture is particularly fine, however, in the hotel's restaurants, which serve Shanghainese, Cantonese and French cuisine. Anyone wanting a table with a river view must arrive by 7pm. The coffee shop on the ground floor of the hotel doubles as a bar; there is a cover charge in the evening after 8pm, when the jazz band begins to play. Business services are limited. CITS travel desk, hairdresser.

Hilton ~~¥¥¥¥¥~~
250 Huashan Lu ☎ 563343 ⊠ 33612 • AE DC MC V • 800 rooms and suites, 5 restaurants, 3 bars
The Shanghai Hilton opened at the end of 1987. It is closer to the town centre than the Hua Ting Sheraton, with which it is intended to compete. Its rooms, including luxurious

executive suites with private facilities on the top floors of its 40-floor tower, are blandly decorated in Western style. It has three Chinese restaurants, one of which, the Shanghai Express, sets out to be informal; the Teppan Grill serves both Western and Japanese food. There are bars in the lobby, by the swimming pool and on the roof. Shopping arcade, travel desk, medical clinic, shuttle service to centre • gym, tennis court, squash courts, pool, ballroom • business centre with 24hr communications service, 5 meeting rooms.

Hua Ting Sheraton ¥¥¥¥¥
1200 Caoxi Beilu ☎ *386000* ⊤ˣ *33589 • AE DC MC V • 1,008 rooms and suites, 5 restaurants, 2 bars*
The Sheraton was the first *de luxe* international hotel in Shanghai. It has a range of features which amply justify its high rates. In particular, the service is outstanding and staff eagerly volunteer help and information. It is much in demand, and reservations must be made as much as a month in advance. Guests enter the 26-floor building through a large lobby, full of light from the overhead windows, clad in rose and black granite. Gilded wooden reliefs of dancing maidens, based on Tang dynasty carvings from the Dun Huang caves in Guangsu Province, decorate the ceilings. Two exterior glass elevators provide views eastwards over Shanghai, and most of the rooms have equally panoramic views to the distant horizon. Rooms are decorated with specially commissioned carpets, contemporary paintings and Japanese-inspired furniture with raw silk upholstery. The English Grill Room, Anton's French restaurant and the Guan Yue Tai Chinese restaurant (see *Restaurants*) are so popular that even hotel guests must make reservations well in advance. The 24hr Ka Fei Ting serves a fixed-price buffet breakfast, lunch and dinner, and excellent espresso. Recently released

international films are available, and minibars are well stocked. There is a video disco (see *Entertainment*) and live piano music all evening in both bars. Shopping arcade, hairdresser and beautician, travel desk, medical clinic, hotel taxis, shuttle service to centre • pool, bowling alley, health club, billiards, tennis • well-equipped business centre, 4 offices, 14 meeting rooms (capacity up to 350), auditorium (seating 850) with audiovisual and simultaneous translation facilities.

Jingan Guesthouse ¥
370 Huashan Lu ☎ *551888 • AE DC MC V • 211 rooms and suites, 2 restaurants, 1 coffee shop/bar*
The Jingan is a refreshingly friendly hotel with prices that are fair for the level of service provided, unlike those of its more pretentious rivals. Rooms in the white 9-floor building built in the 1930s but refurbished in 1969 are preferable to those in the new west wing. The hotel is set well back from the street, behind a spacious, well-tended garden, with large trees, and hollyhocks and snapdragons growing among the shrubbery. The restaurant in the old building overlooks the gardens and serves Chinese, particularly Sichuan, and Western food.

Jinjiang ¥¥
59 Maoming Nanlu ☎ *534242 or 582582* ⊤ˣ *33380 • AE DC MC V • 720 rooms and suites, 5 restaurants, 1 bar*
The Jinjiang is like a campus, with several independent residential buildings, each of which has its own dining room, set around two spacious gardens and a large shopping arcade running the length of the western part of the grounds. Rooms in the 18-floor north block are generally reserved for short-stay visitors, whereas the other blocks house long-term residents in apartment-style suites. The best rooms in the north block look inwards to the gardens, and the wide leaded bay windows impart the feel of an English country

house. The dining halls offer a choice of Cantonese, Sichuan and Western cuisine; there is also the elegant Café de Rêve (see *Restaurants*). A British-style bar serves imported lagers and there is a nightclub, the Club d'Elégance (see *Entertainment*). The hotel scores highly for its comprehensive range of shops, including a supermarket, book shop, hair and beauty salon, and several boutiques. Its services are open later than most. A circular tower-block extension features a revolving restaurant, swimming pool, health club and business centre.

Park ¥¥¥¥
170 Nanjing Zhonglu ☎ 225225 • AE MC V • 170 rooms and suites, 7 restaurants, 1 coffee shop/bar
The 24-floor Park, also known as the International (Guoji), is a less grand version of the Heping. Built in 1934, it is situated at the western end of the commercial centre. Although the staff can be brusque, the hotel has a comfortable, old-fashioned atmosphere. The best rooms are those at the front of the hotel overlooking Renmin Park, and these all have solid, if rather antiquated, furniture and modern bathrooms. Like the Heping, the Park has resurrected its jazz orchestra, which plays in the lounge in the evening, though not its once-fashionable tea dance orchestra. The choice of restaurants ranges from simple café style, where smaller portions are served for solitary diners, to elegant banqueting rooms. The hotel has standard services but no business facilities.

Shanghai ¥
505 Wulumuqi Beilu ☎ 312312 ⊤⨉ 33022 • AE DC MC V • 600 rooms and suites, 6 restaurants, 1 bar
The Shanghai was the city's first modern hotel, opened in 1983 but built in an antiseptic, featureless style which was already 15 years out of date in the West: functional glass and steel outside and much use of plastics

and cheap wood veneers inside. It is 30min from the centre. Nevertheless, the hotel is reasonably priced and nearly always full of tourists and cost-conscious business travellers who are still able to enjoy greater choice of menus than is usual for Shanghai, with a grill room and a Japanese restaurant in addition to the flagship Chinese restaurant, the Wang Haihou, which specializes in seafood. There is a 24hr coffee shop serving snacks, and a pianist entertains guests in the lobby bar during the evening. The banqueting room seats up to 450 and is often used by foreign businesses for conferences and seminars. Big shopping arcade, hairdresser, travel desk, hotel taxis, shuttle bus to centre • telex.

Shanghai Mansions ¥¥¥¥
20 Suzhou Nanlu ☎ 246260 ⊤⨉ 33007 • AE DC MC V • 254 rooms and suites, 3 restaurants, 1 bar
Originally named Broadway Mansions, this hotel was built in 1934 to house British residents of Shanghai and has recently been refurbished. It is a huge yellow-brick monstrosity with a central 22-floor tower and buttressing wings of 17 floors. Except for the Heping, it is the most central hotel, situated on the curve of the Huangpu River. The rooms vary greatly in size and the sophistication of their decor; standard rooms are small. The restaurants specialize in elaborately decorated freshwater fish creations and have extensive menus, including many Western dishes. Disco • billiards • telex, fax.

OTHER HOTELS
JC Mandarin (¥¥¥¥¥) *1225 Nanjing Xilu ☎ 324960 ⊤⨉ 33346,* **Jinjiang Tower** (¥¥) *161 Changle Lu ☎ 582582 ⊤⨉ 30040* and the **Nikko Longbai** (¥¥¥¥¥) *2451 Hongqiao Lu ☎ 593636 ⊤⨉ 30138* are all recently opened hotels with business and convention facilities.

Restaurants

For formal banquets the Banquet Room at the Jinjiang is considered one of Shanghai's best, because of the trouble its chefs take in the visual appearance of their dishes, arranging the food in various shapes to resemble a cockerel, butterfly, crab or fish. The Peace Hall at the Heping offers the most impressive surroundings: Italianate in style with splendid chandeliers and Venetian windows.

In Shanghai most restaurants are fully booked by the time they open at around 5.30pm and they have only one sitting. Independent restaurants do not accept orders after 8pm, and few hotel kitchens remain open after 9pm. Arriving early is the only way to ensure a table with a view. Although the choice of restaurants is limited, all have extensive menus. Most of the hotel restaurants accept major credit cards, the local, non-hotel restaurants almost always do not.

HOTEL RESTAURANTS

Western food For formal, stylish dining there are only two choices, both at the Hua Ting Sheraton. *Anton's* (¥¥¥) which is open only for dinner, serves fine French-inspired food in a candlelit atmosphere. The *English Grill Room* (¥¥¥) serves roast beef, charcoal-grilled steaks and seafood. Both have a limited range of French wines, including champagnes.

Chinese food Also at the Sheraton, the *Guan Yue Tai* (¥¥) is top of the list of most favoured Chinese restaurants. It has 15 tables on the top floor of the hotel, where big windows give uninterrupted views of the often spectacular Shanghai sunset. It is essentially Cantonese but also serves characteristic Shanghainese dishes such as prawns in chili, eel and sautéed eggplant. The *Friendship* (¥¥) at the Jinjiang is larger, though equally busy; its leaded glass windows, parquet floors and stags' heads on the walls are an incongruous accompaniment to rich Shanghainese and Cantonese dishes. The same hotel's *Sichuan* restaurant (¥¥) stays open later than most – until 10pm – and its *Seafood Restaurant* (¥¥) specializes in the local hairy freshwater crabs in season (Oct–Dec).

Among the others the *Peacock* (¥¥) and the *Fengze* (¥¥) at the Park are sought out for their Beijing duck; the Shanghai has a *Japanese Bistro* (¥¥); the Heping's *Dragon-Phoenix* and *Crane Longevity* halls (both ¥¥) have tables with the best river views for those who arrive early for a meal.

Informal dining The 24hr *Kai Fei Ting* at the Sheraton (¥) serves an extensive fixed-price breakfast, lunch and dinner buffet, including roast rib of beef, Chinese hot dishes and cold meat salads. The more expensive *Café de Rêve* (¥¥) at the Jinjiang serves Western foods, including very good sandwiches and desserts, and has a limited number of French wines. The Heping's newly opened *Peace Café* (¥), on the ground floor of the south building, has already established a reputation for its generous pizza and apple tart; it also serves pasta, beefburgers and a range of imported Continental beers.

Reservations Heping ☎ 211244, Hua Ting Sheraton ☎ 386000, Jinjiang ☎ 582582, Park ☎ 225225, Shanghai ☎ 312312.

LOCAL RESTAURANTS
Hong Fanzi (Red House) ¥¥
37 Shaanxi Nanlu ☎ 565220
Known before World War II as Chez Louis, the Red House is an unlikely survival, since it has continued to serve exclusively European food throughout the postwar period. It is

particularly noted for its snails, tournedos and crêpes Suzette.

Meilongzhen ¥
22 Nanjing Zhonglu ☎ 535353
The three floors of this traditional Chinese-style, pre-World War II building are always full of old Shanghai hands and tourists. The manager speaks good English and extends a warm welcome, especially to regulars. Guests are encouraged to order a meal that contrasts the five distinct flavours of Sichuan cuisine: sweet, sour, fragrant, peppery and hot. Its celebrated dishes include crisp-fried duck, Imperial Concubine's chicken (with peanuts and chili), and bean curd braised with minced beef and chili.

Shanghai Lao Fandian (Old Shanghai) ¥
242 Fuyou Lu ☎ 282782
Located opposite the entrance to the Yu Yuan Garden in the Old Town, this is by no means a smart restaurant, but the century-old building and authentic Shanghainese cuisine reward a visit. Dishes include stuffed duck, sizzling shrimps and stewed turtle. With the aid of one's Chinese host organization, it is possible to arrange a banquet for up to 25 guests in the Yu Yuan Garden, which offers a memorable setting.

Shangri La ¥¥
Union Building, 100 Yan'an Donglu ☎ 265230
The Shangri La has a captive market in the large number of staff working for foreign firms in the Union Building and is consequently busy at lunch time, though less so in the evenings. It serves standard Western food, pasta and Singapore-style noodle dishes.

Youyi Jiujia (Friendship) ¥
Shanghai Exhibition Centre, 1000 Yan'an Zhonglu ☎ 534078 •
AE DC MC V
This large and busy restaurant serves the best Cantonese *dim sum* in Shanghai. It is convenient for trade fair visitors and popular with expatriate families.

Yuebin Shadie Wu (VIP Satay House) ¥¥
849 Huashan Lu ☎ 312211 •
AE DC MC V
Run by an overseas Chinese, this is a welcome new arrival, also offering Indonesian food, including succulent pork, chicken, beef and prawn satay.

Bars
The two cocktail lounges at the *Hua Ting Sheraton* bustle with visiting American and European business travellers every evening of the week and often late into the night, but they have the disadvantage of being some distance from the centre. The only other bar that could truthfully be described as a popular meeting point is the one on the ground floor of the central block of the *Jinjiang*, which serves so many of Shanghai's expatriate community living in the hotel. It stocks imported draught beers, wines and spirits.

Entertainment
Acrobatic displays Every visitor should see the show at the *Shanghai Acrobatic Theatre*, 400 Nanjing Xilu. There are performances every night except Tuesday. The troupe, regarded as the best in China, puts on a dazzling display of juggling, acrobatics, dance and mime. Hotel travel desks keep details of the times of shows and will arrange tickets and transport, or visitors can pay at the door.
Music The Shanghai Orchestra regularly performs concerts of popular Western classical music at the *Shanghai Concert Hall*, 523 Yan'an Donglu ☎ 281714. Jazz bands play every evening 8–11 at the *Heping* and the *Park*. A seven-piece ballroom dance orchestra plays between 8.30 and 11.30 every night in the Souding Room of the Heping southern annex. Even those who do

not know the steps go to watch dignified Shanghainese couples waltz around the floor.

Nightclubs *Nicole's* at the Hua Ting Sheraton is a lively video disco with a British DJ, and the Jinjiang's expensive *Club d'Elégance* has both a Japanese *karaoke* bar and a separate disco.

Shopping

Shanghai's shops are the most attractive in China, although their stock is not necessarily greater than elsewhere. The neat, well-kept stores along Nanjing Donglu – more than 330 in all along both sides of its 5km/3 mile length – provide ample browsing. There is surprisingly little demarcation between domestic and industrial goods, and a shop selling agricultural implements will be found next to one selling cooked meats, cakes or children's clothing.

Nanjing Road Proceeding westwards along Nanjing Donglu, notable shops include the *Shanghai Theatrical Costumes and Miscellany Factory Sales Department* at no. 279, with the *Stage Weapons Factory* upstairs. This not only sells elaborate masks and rich clothing for the Chinese opera but is popular also with engaged couples for wedding attire. At no. 329 is the large *Xinhua* bookshop, which has a foreigners' section, selling English-language books on Chinese art and architecture, good-quality posters, and Chinese novels and folk tales in translation. The *Duoyunxuan Painting and Calligraphy Store*, at no. 422, is notable for its beautiful 80-year-old interior.

Farther along on the right is the *Shanghai No. 1 Department Store*, which is good for silks and inexpensive arts and crafts. At nos. 190–208 Nanjing Xilu, next to the Park Hotel, is the *Shanghai Arts and Crafts Store*. This has fine embroidered and hand-painted ladies' silk blouses and bathrobes; and a wide selection of hand-made silk carpets. Finally, at no. 649

Nanjing Xilu, just before the intersection with Shimen Lu, is the *Antique and Curio* branch of the *Shanghai Friendship Store*. There visitors can buy anything from a mother-of-pearl inlaid clock to a four-poster bed. One small section of the store specializes in the former possessions of Shanghai's foreign community: Art Deco cutlery, dressing table sets, pocket watches and bits of garden statuary. Credit cards are accepted, and the store is open until 10pm every day.

Bookshops Three blocks south of Nanjing Donglu where the *Xinhua* bookshop (see above) is located, there is a concentration of shops selling books and artists' materials, haunted by young Chinese intellectuals and students. One of these, the *Foreign Language Bookstore*, no. 380, stocks a good range of novels, magazines and guidebooks in English, French, German and Spanish.

Friendship Stores The main *Friendship Store* is on Zhongshan Dong I-Lu (the Bund), north of the Heping and just before the Waibaidu Bridge. It is located in the garden of the former British Consulate, now the International Seamen's Club, on the left inside the main gates. The store has a café and maintains a comprehensive stock of silks, clothing, antiques and reproductions, traditional writing instruments, woodblock prints, embroidery, and jewellery boxes. The shipping and credit card sales offices are on the top floor.

Sightseeing

The Bund The Shanghai waterfront, the famous Bund, is one of the most impressive in the world. Once, in this foreigners' city on Chinese soil, the Bund represented all that the postwar revolutionary government most hated about the arrogant and intrusive capitalist West, and even to call it the Bund was temporarily frowned upon. But fortunately the Chinese authorities did not demolish its buildings when they expelled their occupants. One can get an uninterrupted view of the Bund from the footbridge over the Huangpu at its southern end, at the intersection with Yan'an Donglu. Immediately to the left is the Dong Feng Hotel, formerly the male-only Shanghai Club; it has what was once claimed to be the longest bar in the world, measuring 30 metres/110 feet, though drinks are no longer served there. Looking north, the eye is drawn to the clock tower of the Customs House. Every quarter hour the Big Ben chimes of the clock tower can just be heard above the Shanghai traffic, but on the hour the peal changes to "The East is Red."

To the left of the Customs House is the domed building that once housed the head office of the Hongkong and Shanghai Banking Corporation, familiarly known as the Honkers and Shankers. Now it houses the offices of the Shanghai city government. In the distance is the green copper-clad pyramidal roof of the Heping (ex-Cathay), built and owned by the Sassoon family, once the foremost merchant bankers in the region. The other building of note is the blue-roofed Bank of China headquarters, while to the north, at no. 1 is the former headquarters of Jardine Matheson, the mighty trading house once known as "the Princely Hong."

First National Congress Memorial
Shanghai has several monuments to recent history in the district south of Huaihai Road, including the hall where the Communist Party constitution was approved on July 1 1921 at the First National Congress of the Party.

Jade Buddha Temple
In the northwestern suburbs, the temple contains two *Buddhas* brought from Burma in 1890, each carved from a block of white jade, and also several smaller *Buddhas* dating from the Northern Wei (386–543) and Tang (618–907) dynasties. It is still a place of worship, and the monks run a vegetarian restaurant next door.

Longhua Pagoda and Temple
Shanghai's only ancient building is in the Longhua Park in the southern suburbs. It was founded in 247, rebuilt in 977 and restored in 1954.

Shanghai Botanical Gardens
The bonsai trees (of which there are more than 100 species) are sometimes several centuries old, and still in their original pots. *Longhua Lu (southern suburbs). Open 8.30–4.30.*

Shanghai Museum
This has one of the few good collections of ancient Chinese art left in the country. One floor is devoted to sculpture and paintings, with some delightful Ming scrolls illustrating rural life; another floor houses the ceramics collection and a good museum shop; the ground floor has a modern display of bronze-casting technology and a renowned collection of ritual vessels, musical instruments and weaponry dating from the 14th to the 1st centuries BC. *Henan Nanlu. Open 9–4.45 (last admissions 3.30).*

Shanghai Zoo
This zoo has indigenous wildlife kept in a natural environment, including the giant panda, golden-haired monkey, tigers from northeast China and crocodiles from the nearby Yangzi. *In Xijiao Park (western suburbs). Open 7–5.*

Yu Yuan Garden
A short walk from the Bund, through the narrow alleys of the Old Town, takes one to the Yu Yuan Garden. This fine example of the landscape art practised during the Ming and Qing dynasties was begun during the years 1559–77 by a local government official, Pan Yunduan, and added to over the centuries; it was restored in 1956. It is reputedly the source of the famous Willow Pattern of Chinese export porcelain. High brick walls decorated with dragons divide the park into its three main parts, and narrow paths lead visitors around the pools and rockeries to teahouses and pavilions with evocative names, such as the Tower for Appreciating the Moon and the Temple of Tranquillity. Unfortunately tranquillity is not easily found,

because the garden is always crowded.
Open 8–10, 2–5.

Harbour trip
For a view of the Bund from the river,
and of much else besides, you can take
a trip on the triple-decker Pujiang
pleasure boat. Hotel travel desks
arrange group excursions, or tickets
can be bought at the embarkation
wharf opposite the Heping ☎ 211098.
The cruise takes 3hr 30min, departing
at 8.30am and 1.30pm, with an
additional 7.30pm sailing in the
summer. First-class tickets, including
refreshments, cost ¥15. The trip takes
passengers down the Huangpu
through busy shipping lanes and past
bustling warehouses to the point where
the river joins the huge Yangzi, but
the high point of the journey is
probably the return trip to the
harbour, as the imposing buildings of
the Bund come slowly into view.

Out of town
Suzhou One of China's most beautiful
cities, Suzhou is known as the "Venice
of the East" because of its extensive
network of ancient waterways,
teeming with small craft, which feeds
off the main artery, the Grand Canal.
It is on the Shanghai to Beijing railway
and can be reached in 3hr. The travel
desk at the Hua Ting Sheraton
organizes day trips by taxi (journey
time is 2hr each way) at ¥200 per
person. The city has two tourist-
oriented hotels: the *Suzhou*, 115 Youyi
Lu ☎ 4646, and the *Nanlin*, 19
Gunxiu Fang ☎ 4441.

A loop in the Grand Canal
surrounds the city, and it is pleasant to
walk along its masonry towpath and
under graceful stone bridges, watching
the local people travelling to work and
carrying produce to the markets on
simple rowing barges. Suzhou also has
several beautiful gardens and is an
important centre for silk production
and embroidery.

Spectator sports
The *Shanghai Gymnasium* ☎ 385200
is China's largest, with seating for

18,000, air conditioning and
computerized scoreboards. It is used
largely for regional athletics,
gymnastics, volleyball, basketball and
table tennis, and occasionally hosts
All Asia championships.

Keeping fit
The only hotels with sports facilities
are the Hua Ting Sheraton, which
has a swimming pool, tennis court
and health club and the Hilton with a
gymnasium, tennis court and squash
courts. Residents are allowed to take
in one non-resident guest each. The
International Club, 63 Yan'an Xilu
☎ 581700, is currently where local
expatriates go in search of recreation,
and the open-air swimming pool is
often crowded. The tennis,
badminton and basketball courts must
be booked well in advance to avoid
disappointment.

Jogging in Shanghai is difficult
because the streets are congested from
dawn until well after dusk. The least
crowded place is Renmin Park (open
7.30am–8pm; ¥0.5 admission). The
Shanghai Marathon, China's premier
event of the kind, is run in Shanghai
every March.

Local resources
Business services
The *Hua Ting Sheraton Business
Centre* ☎ 386000 is open to non-
residents and provides typing from
manuscript, shorthand or
dictaphone; translation from English,
Japanese, German, Italian, French
and Spanish into Chinese and *vice
versa*; photocopying; local and
international delivery services; telex
and fax; office and meeting room
rental; and equipment rental,
including slide and overhead
projector and video player.

Alternatively there is the *Shanghai
Jinjiang Service Centre for Overseas
Traders* (SCOT), 58 Maoming Nanlu,
opposite the Jinjiang, ☎ 375334.
Temporary membership is obtained
with an introduction by the
sponsoring party in Shanghai and
upon making a payment of ¥100.

Rates are slightly lower than at the Hua Ting Sheraton.

Communications
The *Hua Ting Sheraton Business Centre* provides local and international courier services. All hotels have post offices for letters and parcels, and the *Shanghai Post Office*, 267 Suzhou Beilu ☎ 245025, has an international express mail section. The Hua Ting Sheraton, the Hilton and the Jinjiang all have fax.

IDD telephone calls can be made from many hotels listed above to Hong Kong, Japan and the USA. Calls in other hotels or to other destinations have to be arranged in advance at the hotel service desk and can be made collect or they can be paid for in cash at the end of the call if so wished.

Conference/exhibition centres
The *Shanghai Exhibition Centre* is on Yan'an Zhonglu, its high steel tower being one of the city's major landmarks. It has a permanent display of industrial products and arts and crafts open every day 8.30–11 and 1–5, and temporary regional trade promotions. The best equipped hotel conference centre is at the Hua Ting Sheraton (see *Hotels*).

Emergencies
Bureaux de change Desks at the Jinjiang ☎ 582582 and Hua Ting Sheraton ☎ 386000 are both open to 10pm; the desk at the Hilton ☎ 563343 is open 24hr.
Hospitals The *Shanghai People's No. 1 (Red Cross) Hospital*, 190 Suzhou Beilu ☎ 240100, has a 24hr emergency section and is able to treat foreigners.
Pharmacies A limited range of basic pharmaceuticals is stocked by the Jessica Supermarket in the Jinjiang shopping complex and they can also be obtained at the bookstore at the Hua Ting Sheraton.
Police The Public Security Bureau, Foreigners' Section, is at 210 Hankou Lu ☎ 215380.

Government offices
The *China Council for the Promotion of International Trade* (CCPIT), which has a national role in disseminating trade information, is at 27 Zhongshan Dong-I Lu (the Bund) ☎ 210722. In the same building is the *Shanghai Foreign Trade Centre* (and its subsidiary the *Shanghai Computer Centre*), a useful starting point for finding goods, buyers and investment partners. The *Shanghai Investment and Trust Corporation* (SITCO), 33 Zhongshan Dong-I Lu (the Bund) ☎ 232200, coordinates foreign investment, imports and exports and arranges loans for local firms through bond issues on the international markets.

Information sources
Business information The *Shanghai Jinjiang Service Centre for Overseas Traders*, 58 Maoming Xilu ☎ 375334, provides a liaison service for foreign traders who are seeking suitable local partners. Otherwise, visitors with no local representative would be well advised to seek the help of the resident foreign banks, such as the *Bank of America* ☎ 262933, *Banque Indosuez* ☎ 311753, *Hong Kong and Shanghai* ☎ 216030, *Société Générale* ☎ 582582 ext. 58136 and *Standard Chartered* ☎ 264820.
Tourist information CITS is at 33 Zhongshan Dong-1 Lu (the Bund) ☎ 217200, though most visitors use the branch office in the lobby of the Heping ☎ 211244, for ticketing and confirming flights, or the travel desks at the Jinjiang ☎ 582582, the Hilton ☎ 563343 and the Hua Ting Sheraton ☎ 386000, for information on excursions and tours.

Thank-yous
Imported spirits and cigarettes can be bought in all hotel lobbies. The Jessica Supermarket at the Jinjiang has the widest selections. Fancy cakes can be bought in the Jinjiang shopping complex. There is a florist in the Hua Ting Sheraton arcade.

SHANTOU
Area code ☎ 0754

Shantou, also known as Swatow, was one of the original four Special Economic Zones. It is situated close to the mouth of the Han river in the northeast of Guangdong province, and is Guangdong's second largest city. Since many of its people emigrated in the 19th century, Shantou has strong overseas ties. After a dull period in 1986, foreign investment quadrupled to US$11m in the first half of 1987. Shantou has worked hard to provide the necessary infrastructure: the airport has been expanded, there are new docks and a digital telephone exchange has been installed. The city has a strong, young, reasonably educated workforce of 100,000. Its joint venture priorities are in electronics and new technology, textiles and food processing.

Arriving
There are daily connections to Guangzhou, and thence to Hong Kong, as well as frequent flights to Xiamen, but only one flight per week to Beijing. There is no rail link to Shantou, although you may travel by sea from Guangzhou or from Xiamen and Fuzhou.

Hotels
The best hotel in Shantou is the *Long Hu* (¥) Yingbin Lu ☎ 60703 ⓉⓍ 45458, fax 60708. Though rather less than international standard, it provides the essential minimum in communication facilities.

Local resources
The principal offices which can assist you are to be found in the new Longhu industrial area, notably: *Special Economic Zone Administrative Committee*, Dong Jiao, Longhu ☎ 4806; *Shantou International Trust Service Corporation*, Dong Jiao, Longhu ⓉⓍ 45411. You would be well advised to take an interpreter from Hong Kong with you, one familiar with the local dialects as well as Putonghua.

CITS, 1st Fl, Peninsula Hotel ☎ 35226, fax 50033.

SHENYANG
Area code ☎ 024

The normally rather staid city of Shenyang took many people by surprise in spring 1986, when it was the first city in China since 1949 to open a public bond market, enthusiastically subscribed by the citizens. No less controversial was the decision in July 1986 to allow a Shenyang company to be declared bankrupt, when guaranteed jobs had so long been the norm. A modernization programme to the value of ¥240m was begun as early as 1982.

Shenyang is the provincial capital of Liaoning Province, with a population of 4m. Principal industries are heavy machinery, such as railway equipment and agricultural machinery, and there are steel mills. Light industry includes flour milling, textiles and a wide range of household and consumer goods. Anshan, 90km/56 miles southwest of Shenyang, is one of the country's leading iron and steel works.

While temperatures of around 28°C/82°F are reached in the summer months, winters are long and bitterly cold: there is snowfall from late October and temperatures of -18°C/0°F are not uncommon.

Arriving

There are daily flights to and from Beijing (1hr 15min), Guangzhou (3hr 45min) and Shanghai (2hr), as well as regular flights to more cities in the northeast and other parts of China. There are no international flights. The airport is 16km/10 miles from the city centre. There are few taxis; you should arrange to be met.

Shenyang is connected by rail with most cities in northeastern China; Beijing is 10hr away. The railway station is centrally located.

Hotels

The hotel stock of Shenyang has been improved in the last few years. The joint venture Youyuan is the newest of those listed.

Dongbei (¥) 1 Qi Li, Taiyuan 7-Jie ☎ 32031. Prewar hotel close to the railway station and city centre.

Friendship Guesthouse (¥) 1 Huanghe 7-Dajie ☎ 62822. Low-rise resort hotel, built in 1950 in pleasant grounds, with an indoor pool.

Hua Xia (¥) 3 Zhongshan 1-Lu ☎ 735170 ⊠ 80088. This has 70 rooms, two restaurants, photocopying and telex.

Liaoning (¥) 1 Huanghe 1-Dajie ☎ 62536. Dates from the late 1950s and has over 500 rooms.

Liaoning Guesthouse (¥) 27 Zhongshan 2-Guangchang ☎ 732205 or 733644 ⊠ 80083. Centrally situated overlooking Zhongshan Square; photocopying and fax available.

Phoenix (¥) 3 Huanghe 6-Dajie ☎ 64854/64069 ⊠ 80045. Opened in 1984 and pleasantly situated in the northern part of the city; the building also houses the offices of several overseas companies. Some sporting facilities and photocopying.

Youyuan (¥¥) 4 Taishan 2-Lu ☎ 66616 ⊠ 80019. Completed in 1986, with 100 rooms, this joint-venture hotel is in the northern part of the city. There are four restaurants. Photocopying and interpreters can be obtained through the reception desk.

Restaurants

The hotels offer the most comfortable surroundings for business entertaining. For novelty you should try the Korean-style restaurants, for instance the *Korean Nationality* (¥) at Xi Ta ☎ 22903. Also worth trying is the *Imperial Food* (¥) on Wuna Nanlu ☎ 36046, which offers Chinese "imperial" cuisine.

Relaxation

Shopping The principal commercial area is on *Taiyuan Jie*, where there is an antique store, bookshop and department store. The *Friendship Store* is on Zhongshan Xilu. The food market at *Peihang* is also interesting.

Entertainment The Shenyang acrobatics troupe are highly professional and have performed abroad.

Sightseeing The few sites of historical interest in Shenyang date from the Manchu period. The *Imperial Palace*, reminiscent of the Palace in Beijing, dominates the old city of Shenyang, and the climb to the top of Phoenix Tower gives a good view of the city. It was begun by Nurhachi, leader of the Manchus in 1625, who is buried 20km/13 miles to the east of the city at *Dong Ling* (The Eastern Tombs), built in 1629.

Some 10km/6 miles to the north of the city is *Bei Ling* (The Northern Tombs), where the Qing Emperor Tai Zong is buried. The harmonious surroundings are those dictated by the requirements of geomancy. The tomb is approached along a "sacred way" with its usual guard of stone-carved animals and officials.

Local resources

Business services for travellers or residents are limited. Hotels will offer telex services. Interpreters may be found through *CITS*, 3 Zhongshan 1-Lu, Heping ☎ 66953/66039. The *CAAC* office is at 31 Zhongshan 3-Lu ☎ 34089. *Bureau of Foreign Economic Relations and Trade*, Zhongshan Lu ☎ 28050 ⊠ 80034.

SHENZHEN

Area code ☎ 0755

For many years Shenzhen, on the border between Hong Kong and mainland China, was the world's window on Communist China and *vice versa*. A huddle of uninspiring buildings, a Friendship Store with a neon sign, a restaurant and a small station with a corrugated iron roof – the contrast between Hong Kong and Shenzhen could hardly have been greater. Things have changed since then.

Shenzhen, total population 400,000, is on the Shenzhen river in Guangdong province, an hour's journey from the centre of Hong Kong. In 1979 it was designated a Special Economic Zone, and it is the largest of them, producing US$726m worth of exports, over 75% of the total for the four Special Economic Zones. Shenzhen may well provide a good starting point for those seeking to establish commercial relations in China. It is a centre for the electronics industry, and an entrepôt for exports from other parts of the country.

Shekou, situated some 30km/19 miles west of the city, is the major passenger and cargo port for Shenzhen and has recently built Chiwan dock to service oil exploration in the South China Sea. At Daya Bay work has started on a nuclear power station, a joint venture involving British, US, French and Japanese companies.

Arriving

Shenzhen has no airport yet, although CAAC has a booking office at the Baiyun Air bureau, 618 Bagualing Industrial Estate, Jungang Lu ☎ 26661 and runs a shuttle service to Guangzhou airport.

The railway station, situated in a crook of the Shenzhen river, has long been the hub of Shenzhen's economic life, and is busy to the point of chaos (plenty of taxis available). There are several trains daily to and from Hong Kong and the journey takes 1hr 30min.

Hotels

There is no shortage of good new hotels in Shenzhen, both resort hotels and some designed for business travellers. All mentioned here have IDD.
Bamboo Garden (¥¥¥) Dongmen Lu (Tong Moon Rd) ☎ 22934 or 21848; no ℡ • AE DC MC V. This is a new low-rise hotel combining traditional Chinese architectural features with international interior decor, and there is a landscaped garden. The hotel has 180 well-appointed rooms with balconies. Shuttle bus

to station and to Hong Kong; shopping arcade, disco. Sports facilities include a games centre, snooker and bowling. Business services include photocopying and interpreting.
Century Plaza (¥¥¥¥) Jianshe Lu (Kin Chit Rd) ☎ 20888 (Hong Kong reservations ☎ 5-8680638) ℡ 81320 • AE DC MC V. Opened at the end of 1987, with 425 rooms, this hotel is a rival to the International. It is 5min from the railway station, and its restaurants have earned praise. It also offers a gym, swimming pool and billiards as well as a comprehensive business centre.
Dong Hu Binguan (East Lake) (¥¥¥) Shenzhen Reservoir ☎ 22727 or 22728 ℡ 42236 • AE DC MC V. This low-rise resort hotel with 136 rooms is set in an attractive landscape and offers a bus service to the railway station. Sports facilities include tennis, billiards, squash, tennis, sauna and gym. There is a wide ranges of business services (though no fax). Conference centre (capacity up to 300).
International (¥¥¥¥) Dongmen

Lu (Tung Moon Rd) ☎ 22763 or 22773 🆃🆇 42029. Hong Kong booking office ☎ 3-7211555 🆃🆇 54228 • AE DC MC V. Located in the northeast of town, 10min from the railway station, the International is the most prestigious hotel. Its 96 rooms have minibars, TV and in-house films. There are 12 suites. Sports facilities include sauna, gym and swimming pool. It has full business support services, and conference rooms with audiovisual equipment.

Nanyang (¥¥¥) Jianshe Lu ☎ 24968 • AE DC MC V. This is a middle-range hotel with 200 rooms on 28 floors. It is centrally located with a business centre and secretarial support, but no telex or telephones in the rooms.

Xin Yuan Da Jiudian (New Garden) (¥¥) Xinyuan Lu (Sunyuen Rd) ☎ 26333 • AE DC MC V. A new and moderately priced hotel owned by the Shenzhen Economic Trade Group, it has a restaurant on the 14th floor with panoramic views and a swimming pool for use in summer. Bus service to Hong Kong. No telex or business facilities.

Restaurants

The principal style of cuisine in Shenzhen is naturally the varied and exotic fare of Guangdong, served by several choice restaurants. For entertaining, the revolving *Rooftop Cantonese Restaurant* (¥) 53rd floor, International Trade Centre, AE DC MC V, is highly recommended. Opening hours are 7.30–11pm. The *Hong Kong Restaurant* (¥) Jiabin Lu, AE DC MC V, has a pleasant decor, an extensive Chinese menu and a receptive staff. Also recommended are the Chinese restaurants in the *International* and the *Bamboo Garden*.

For more informal dining try the *Pan Xi Jiujia* (Riverside Restaurant) (¥) Jiabin Lu, where the Cantonese cuisine is excellent. *Jimmy's Café* (¥) (Ground floor, International Trade Centre) has a coffee shop atmosphere with good value Western *table d'hôte* meals.

Relaxation

Shopping The *International Trade Centre*, Renmin Lu, has imported goods as well as local products. *The Bo Ya (Pok) Gallery*, Jiefang Lu, has attractive examples of the folk arts.

Entertainment Shenzhen has its own theatre on Dongmen Lu, where Chinese shows are performed.

Sightseeing Most of the new hotels offer tours of the area, which can be reserved through the reception desk. These tours usually take in the *Lychee Garden* and *People's Park* and the *Reservoir*, the *Observatory* and *Honey Lake Amusement Park*. Several areas in the vicinity are being developed as beachside or lake resorts.

Local resources

Many of China's provinces and large cities have representative offices, where preliminary contacts can be made. For liaison, an established organization is *Shenzhen International Management Services*, at the International Exhibition Centre, 50 Heping Lu ☎ 25900 🆃🆇 420221, a subsidiary of the Shenzhen Special Economic Zone Development Co. The same building also houses the *Shenzhen Exchange Centre for Modern Medical Science and Technology* ☎ 25983 and 25984 🆃🆇 420211.

Alternatively, for direct contacts, try the *Shenzhen Special Economic Zone Import and Export Corporation*, Shen Nan Donglu ☎ 38848 🆃🆇 4223952. or *The Shenzhen Exhibition Centre*, 5 Hongling Bldg, Hongling Nanlu ☎ 43260 🆃🆇 420317. Several overseas banks and companies have offices at the *International Trade Centre*, which has a large, air-conditioned exhibition hall.

For post and telecommunications, use the facilities provided by your hotel. *CITS* is at Heping Lu ☎ 38401 🆃🆇 420250. For *CAAC* see *Arriving*. For visas contact the *Bureau of Public Security* office on the fourth floor of the railway station. The police are at Shen Nan Zhonglu.

TIANJIN
Area code ☎ 022

In the past Tianjin (Tientsin) may have suffered from being in the shadow of Beijing, but the city took on a new businesslike vibrancy with the injection of funds from the capital and the arrival of Li Ruihuan in 1981. As mayor, Li Ruihuan, elected in 1987 to the national Central Committee, was not only been responsible for sprucing up the city, which was badly affected by the earthquake of 1976, but presided over several major economic developments.

Further, the Foreign Economic Relations and Trade Commission in Tianjin, usually a cautious and bureaucratic body, has under its director Zhang Zhaoruo earned a reputation for decision-making. A vital criterion for approval is that projects should be self-supporting in foreign currency and in the first half of 1986, when in the rest of China joint ventures were suffering from a shortage of foreign exchange, Tianjin's projects had a balance of US$11m with the Bank of China. The city has looked for ventures in the production of wine, cosmetics, lift machinery, plastic rainwear, lightbulbs, feather articles and electronics, but also in hotels, taxi companies and restaurants. In summer 1987, Tianjin was estimated to have 244 arrangements with companies from Japan, West Germany, USA, Australia and Hong Kong. A favoured form of agreement has been compensation trading.

At Tanggu, near the port of Xingang, the Tianjin Economic and Technological Development Zone has been established, offering various tax incentives to overseas investors particularly in areas of advanced technology. The local office of the China Council for the Promotion of International Trade is actively carrying out its liaison and promotion role, constructing a new exhibition centre, which makes Tianjin an ideal venue for international trade exhibitions, conferences and seminars. From Tianjin, there is ready access to Beijing and the rest of the country, without the pressure that organizing such events in the capital means for everyone involved. Also, it has many colonial buildings dating from the first half of the century, which may make it less disorientating to the Western visitor than Beijing.

Tianjin is China's third municipality and, like Beijing and Shanghai, enjoys the status and powers of a province. It has a total population of 8m and covers an area of 11,000 sq km/6,830 sq miles. Its port at Xinggang, 35km/22 miles from the city centre, is China's second largest. Tianjin has every kind of industry: small trucks, iron and steel, ship-building, petrochemicals and machinery. There is oil and gas at Dagang and prospecting in the Bohai Gulf. One of the oldest industries of all is salt-panning and soda ash production along the Gulf. Light industry includes textiles, electronics, food processing and clothing. Cultural traditions are strong: Nankai University is one of the most prestigious in China – the more so as Zhou Enlai studied there.

Arriving

Tianjin is 137km/85 miles from Beijing, and its airport is almost a second airport for the capital and an immediate alternative in emergency. There are daily flights to and from Hong Kong, Guangzhou and Beijing. There is a taxi rank at the airport and the journey to town takes 30min.

Travelling to or from Beijing by rail takes a little under 2hr; Tianjin is also on the main northeast–south line to Ji'nan (7hr) and Shanghai (18hr).

Hotels

Tianjin already had a reasonable hotel stock, some of it dating from colonial days, but to cope with increased demand from business and tourist traffic in the last few years it has been investing heavily in new international-standard hotels, and now offers a good choice of accommodation. A major advantage of the newer properties is the direct dial facilities to Hong Kong and overseas. The local tourist corporation has categorized four hotels as "deluxe:" the Astor, Crystal Palace, Hyatt Palace and the Sheraton Tianjin.

Astor (¥¥) 33 Taier Zhuang Lu ☎ 311112 ⊠ 23266. Known as the Tianjin until 1985, this joint-venture hotel consists of an old wing dating from 1901 which has recently been refurbished, and a new wing overlooking the Hai River. Situated in the city centre, 2km/1 mile from the railway station, it offers all the usual amenities together with a health club, limousine service and business centre.

Bohai (¥¥) Gongnong Xicun, Tanggu district ☎ 1732596. This is a new project in conjunction with a Japanese consortium. Close to the economic development area, it is a comfortable, medium-sized standard hotel.

Crystal Palace (¥¥¥) Binshui Dao, Hexi District ☎ 310567 ⊠ 23277 • AE DC MC V. A 350-room hotel, completed in early 1987 for Tianjin Tourism Administration and managed by Swissotel. Set in attractive lakeside surroundings, 10min from the city centre, its amenities include a Japanese

restaurant, a swimming pool and a sauna. Business centre, banqueting rooms and a conference hall (capacity up to 600).

Hyatt Palace (¥¥¥¥) Jiefang Beilu ☎ 318888 ⊠ 23270, fax 310021. A sleek modern building incorporating features of Chinese traditional architecture, the hotel is conveniently situated overlooking the Hai River and close to the Foreign Trade Bureau and other government offices. It is now well established and probably offers the best services to the business traveller. The hotel has three Chinese restaurants, a Japanese restaurant and a Western-style one. Health spa, riverside jogging, use of tennis courts. Its 24hr business centre offers a comprehensive range of services, with translation, word processing, fax and courier service.

Sheraton Tianjin (¥¥¥¥) Zi Jin Shan Rd, Hexi district ☎ 333388 ⊠ 23353 fax 318740. This sophisticated link in the Sheraton chain has 282 rooms and is located close to the waterfront and the business area. Swimming pool and health club. Business centre and meeting rooms; facilities for simultaneous translation.

Victory (¥¥) Jintang Lu, Tanggu district ☎ 985833/984984 ⊠ 23375. Offering standard facilities, this hotel is convenient for the port area.

Other hotels These hotels are rather cheaper; all have standard facilities.

Friendship (¥) Nanjing Lu, Heping district ☎ 310732 ⊠ 23264. Completed in 1975 and located in the city centre.

Park (¥) Leyuan Lu, Hexi district ☎ 285252 ⊠ 23381.

Tianjin Grand (¥) Youyi Lu, Hexi district ☎ 319000 ⊠ 23276. This massive 750-room hotel, completed in 1960, in the southern part of the city, has a water supply from local hot springs. There are two conference halls (capacity 1,000).

Restaurants

Although you cannot do better than use the banqueting facilities of the new hotels, there are some interesting and charming restaurants in Tianjin which are worth a visit. Local dishes are seafood, dumplings and *ma hua*, a kind of doughnut. One of Tianjin's exciting recent ventures is the massive arcade called *Nanshi Food Street*, where more than 100 restaurants and snack bars offer delicacies from every part of China. The *Goubuli Restaurant* (¥) Nanshi Food Street ☎ 223277, which serves dumplings, is famous throughout China and is suitable both for entertaining and for informal dining. At the *Tian Fei Lou* (House of the Heavenly Concubine) (¥) Ancient Cultural Street ☎ 255275, you may sample Sichuanese and Cantonese cuisine. The *Huaxia Restaurant* (¥) Dongma Lu ☎ 223942, serves local cuisine. For informal dining try *Qisiling Canting* (Kiesling's Café) (¥) 33 Zhejiang Lu. Named after its original Austrian owner, it offers Western-style dishes, pastries and coffee in a faded Art Deco setting. A branch is also in Nanshi Food Street.

Relaxation

Shopping Tianjin is noted for several traditional crafts and arrangements can be made to visit the ateliers. The crafts include wool and silk carpet-weaving, Yangliuqing New Year woodblock pictures, cloisonné and paper kites – kite festivals are held in the spring and autumn.

Sightseeing Although Tianjin has few historic sights, there are places to visit in the environs of the city and, of course, Beijing is readily accessible.

Within the city your exploration may take in the various concession areas, which contain several examples of colonial architecture newly smartened up as part of Mayor Li Ruihuan's refurbishment programme. The *City Art Gallery* is housed in a former French Bank, while the *Municipal People's Congress* occupies the former British Club. The old Tianjin Country Club, situated on Machang Dao

(Racecourse Street) has been renamed the *Friendship Club* – a period piece of panelled billiard and skittle rooms. These are all in the southern part of the city.

In the northeast of the city, just south of the confluence of the Hai River and the Canal, is the old city. Here *Ancient Cultural Street* is a reconstruction of a typical Chinese street, with the traditional carved *pailou* entrance and numerous craft studios. Here, too, is the oldest building in Tianjin, the *Confucian Temple of the Marine Goddess*. There is also a Ming dynasty mosque.

Outside Tianjin one of the most popular sites is the recently renovated part of the *Great Wall* at Huangya Pass in the northern part of Jixian county, a 2hr 30min trip by rail or road. *Pan Shan*, in the same county, 12km/8 miles to the northwest of the town of Jixian, is a scenic area including the 1,000-year-old wooden *Temple of Solitary Joy*, one of the oldest in China. There is reasonable accommodation in the area.

The *Eastern Qing Tombs*, where Emperors Kang Xi and Qian Long, and the Dowager Empress Ci Xi, are buried, are to the northeast of Tianjin, adjoining Hebei province (journey time 3hr). In summer, you can visit the seaside resort of *Beidaihe* on the Bohai Gulf.

Sports Opportunities are now expanding with an International Golf Club recently opened near the airport; a marathon is held every October. There are swimming pools and health clubs in some of the new hotels.

Local resources

Comprehensive business and communication services are available in the new hotels. *Tianjin Foreign Trade Corporation*, 59 Nanjing Lu ☎ 316551 ⓣ 23206. *Foreign Trade Bureau*, Qufu Dao ☎ 310225. *CITS*, 20 Youyi Lu ☎ 312619 ⓣ 23281. *CAAC*, Heping Lu ☎ 706513. *Public Security Bureau*, Tangshan Dao ☎ 223613.

WUHAN

Area code ☎ 027

Wuhan (Hankow), known in Chinese as "the cross-roads of nine provinces," is the largest and most important city in central China, with a total population of 6.8m. It stands on the middle reaches of the Yangzi river, and is the capital of fertile Hubei province. As a foreign concession port and later the capital during the war with Japan, it was known as Hankow, and Hankou is in fact one of the three cities of which modern Wuhan is a conglomerate. On the northern bank of the Yangzi, Hankou is the commercial centre of Wuhan and has a Bund (like Shanghai) and a skyline of Western-style buildings. Hanyang, also on the northern bank, is separated from it by the Han river and is a predominately industrial area. In the third of the cities, Wuchang, on the south bank, you will find traces of the old Chinese city, the East Lake, the University, and one of China's major iron and steel works.

Wuhan has been encouraged to engage directly in foreign trade since 1984, yet rather a small number of joint-venture agreements have so far been made. However, the city has brought in foreign "troubleshooters" to improve efficiency and production in its factories: the West German Werner Gerich made some startling changes in the management structure of a diesel engine factory and was proclaimed a national hero! Wuhan and the province of Hubei are fertile, producing 6% of the country's rice, cotton and ramie. Pig, duck and chicken-breeding are all important and aquaculture and fish farming are rapidly developing.

The further development of Wuhan will be closely linked with the exploitation of the Yangzi river as a transportation link and a source of hydro-electric power. Upstream, close to the city of Yichang, the Gezhouba dam was recently completed, and a yet more ambitious dam is being built at the Three Gorges. In the northern part of Hubei province, Shiyan is China's second most important centre for the motor industry. It has imported machinery from West Germany, Japan and Britain and now has the autonomy to set up direct overseas contacts, as China is poised to develop its domestic car market. South of the Yangzi, Huangshi is a leading producer of special steels.

In Wuhan and Hubei province the winter climate is mild; the coldest period of the year is in early February when Siberian winds blow. High summer is extremely hot and humid, with average temperatures around 35°C/95°F. People take to the streets, typically one sees them lying out on bamboo *chaises longues*.

Arriving

The flight network to Wuhan increased considerably in the mid-1980s, with daily domestic flights from and to Beijing, Guangzhou, Shanghai, Fuzhou, Yichang, Chongqing (except Saturdays) and less frequent but regular flights to other cities throughout China. The airport is 25km/11 miles to the south of the city and travel by taxi is recommended.

Wuhan is on the main Beijing-Guangzhou line. Passengers usually alight at Hankou, a large, busy and relatively modern station, where you should take the "soft class" exit and seek assistance with taxis there.

The time-honoured way to travel to and from Wuhan is along the Yangzi. On scheduled passenger ferries the journey upstream to Chongqing will take four nights, while from Yichang and Shashi it takes 24hr. These vessels are crowded and busy, with a limited number of twin cabins. But there is an increasing number of well-equipped cruisers, designed for the tourist market.

Getting around Taxis should be arranged through the hotel reception desk and kept waiting for you while you attend meetings.

Hotels

Wuhan relies largely on its existing hotel stock, some of which is pre-1949. The exceptions are the Qingchuan, completed in 1984, and the Yangtze. Most hotels are situated in Hankou.

Jianghan (¥) 245 Shengli Jie ☎ 21253 ☎ 40150. Built in the former French concession in 1917, but the rooms have been refurbished. It has limited office support facilities but a good location for trade offices in the city centre.

Qingchuan (¥) 1 Ximachang Jie, Hanyang ☎ 441141 ☎ 40134. This modern 24-floor building is appointed in modern Chinese style and overlooks the Yangzi. It has limited business facilities.

Yangtze (¥¥) Jiefang Dadao, Hankou ☎ 562828 ☎ 40204 • AE DC MC V. A joint-venture hotel with small but comfortable rooms and friendly service. It is the best choice for the business traveller, with fax and photocopying.

Restaurants

Local delicacies include fish, steamed dumplings made from wheat flour known as *shao mai*, a filling soup served in earthenware dishes and with pancakes called *weitang*, "eight treasure rice" and *sanxian doupi* (fresh bean curd skin). The Western or Chinese restaurants of the *Yangtze* (¥¥) are best for entertaining.

Laotongcheng (¥) 1 Daxi Lu ☎ 24559 is famous for dumplings and *doupi* (bean curd skin) and has good banqueting facilities.

Relaxation

Shopping Local products include carved bamboo artifacts, cotton, silk and embroidery. Hankou's commercial area is on *Zhongshan Dajie* and *Jiefang Lu*.

Entertainment The best available evening entertainment is the Wuhan acrobatics troupe.

Sightseeing Principal sights start from the first bridge to be built across the Yangzi and continue to several monuments relating to Wuhan's revolutionary history. Two traditional landmarks are *Tortoise Hill* and *Snake Hill*, in Hanyang and Wuchang respectively, now laid out as parks, facing each other. Both are redolent with ancient legends and stories. Snake Hill used to stand in the middle of the old city and was surrounded by a wall, and in it the historic *Yellow Crane Pagoda* has recently been rebuilt. In Wuchang, *East Lake* has boating and swimming facilities, the University, the Museum of History, a botanical garden and the Reciting Poetry Pavilion, which commemorates the early poet Qu Yuan.

In Hanyang the *Guiyuan Temple*, which is built in the elaborate style of southern China, has a hall of 500 *arhats* (disciples).

In the vicinity of Wuhan you may travel upstream to Yichang and also visit the *Three Gorges* or travel southwards to *Yueyang* and *Dongting Lake*.

Local resources

There is little specialized business support beyond what is available in the hotels. *Department of Foreign Economic Relations and Trade* (*Hubei*), Yanjiang Dadao ☎ 21145. *CITS*, Jianghan Lu, Hankou ☎ 511891. *CAAC* Hankou Liji Beilu ☎ 54597. *Bureau of Public Security* ☎ 25349.

XIAMEN
Area code ☎ 0592

Xiamen (Amoy) is a coastal city, built on a series of islands in southern Fujian province. Taiwan is 161km/100 miles away and many people from Fujian province emigrated to Taiwan when the Communists came to power. Visitors from Taiwan have been rare, but considerable investment has come from there via Hong Kong or Singapore. Xiamen was given the status of Special Economic Zone in 1979 and has set up around 165 joint ventures since then. It has an excellent natural harbour with a container terminal and at Dongdu four 10,000 tonne/11,025 US ton berths have been constructed. The industrial output value of foreign-funded enterprises reached ¥300m in 1987, a quarter of Xiamen's total. Two-thirds of these ventures are productive.

Arriving
Thanks to the completion of the new airport in 1986, Xiamen is now within easy reach of China's major cities, with six flights a week from Beijing and Shanghai, daily flights from Guangzhou, and also flights from Fuzhou, Xian and Hangzhou.

Travel by rail or sea from Fuzhou, Guangzhou or Shanghai is lengthy.

Hotels
Xiamen has newly built or renovated several hotels, but standards are still generally short of international.
Jinbao (¥) Dongdu Xingang Lu ☎ 26888 TX 93034. This well-appointed hotel with a sea view is close to the trade offices of Xiamen.
Lujiang (¥) 54 Lujiang Dao, Siming ☎ 24622 TX 93024 • AE DC MC V. A seafront hotel, near the ferry for Gulangyu, the customs and foreign trade corporations.
Xiamen Guesthouse (¥) 16 Huyuan Lu ☎ 22265 TX 93065. This centrally placed state guest house has a newly completed wing and its facilities include a swimming pool, billiards, disco, photocopying and IDD.
Xiamen Mandarin (¥) Huli Foreigners Residential Area ☎ 43333 TX 93028. This small hotel (130 rooms) has an attractive seafront location and also adjoins the Huli industrial development zone. Limousine service, swimming pool. Business centre.

Restaurants
Seafood is good in Xiamen, and the local cooking has a certain sweetness and succulence not found elsewhere. For entertaining and informal dining, try the Western and Chinese restaurants at the *Xiamen Guesthouse* or the Cantonese and local cuisines at the *Lujiang* or the *Fuhao Seafood* (¥) 14 Huyuan Lu ☎ 24127.

Relaxation
Sightseeing Xiamen has a delightfully faded charm, and all the attractions of its location on the sea, above all the little offshore island of *Gulangyu* with its colonial villas nestling among lush vegetation.

Local resources
While photocopying, telex and even fax may be found in hotels, there is no comprehensive business support service in Xiamen. The main post office is on Xinhua Lu.

The principal bodies for trade contacts are the *Foreign Affairs Office of Xiamen Government* ☎ 20442; *Head Office for Foreign Trade, Xiamen Special Economic Zone*, Foreign Trade Bldg, 38 Haihou Lu ☎ 24612; *International Trade and Trust Corporation of Xiamen Special Economic Zone*, 52 Huaxin Lu ☎ 26673.

CITS, 7 Haihou Lu ☎ 25277. *CAAC*, airport inquiries ☎ 20630, reservations ☎ 20497. *Public Security Bureau*, Xinhua Lu ☎ 25502.

ZHUHAI

Area code ☎ 0756

Zhuhai, one of the four Special Economic Zones, is conveniently located on the mouth of the Pearl river in Zhongshan county, in Guangdong province, very close to Macao and facing Hong Kong. Zhuhai is somewhat behind Shenzhen in its development, but work is proceeding apace on industrial units, office blocks and hotels.

Arriving

There are no rail or air connections to Zhuhai: most people travel here from Hong Kong by hydrofoil, or there is a bus from Guangzhou. Hong Kong–China Hydrofoil operate three departures direct to Zhuhai daily at 7.45, 11, and 2.30, returning at 9.30, 1 and 4.45. The tickets can be obtained at Ticketmate outlets in most MTR (Mass Transit Railway) stations in Hong Kong for HK$70 one way. Alternatively, you can take the hydrofoil or jetfoil service which leave every 15min from Hong Kong to the Macao ferry pier and then take a taxi to the Zhuhai border gate 10min away. Visas valid for three days and for the Special Economic Zone only are issued on arrival.
Getting around Taxis are numerous, but charges are all too often arbitrary. You are recommended to make a reservation in advance for a limousine from the better hotels. Prepayment may be required.

Hotels

There are many hotels recently opened or still under construction. Those hotels recommended here are not quite up to international standard. You may wish to consider staying at the *Oriental* (¥¥¥¥¥) Ave da Amizade, Macau ☎ 567888 (AE DC MC V), from which it is easy to commute to Zhuhai.
Gongbei Palace (¥¥¥) Gongbei, Zhuhai ☎ 886822/886823 ⊠ 45638 • AE DC MC V. This is a short walk from the border gate and includes some attractive villas overlooking the sea. Facilities include swimming pool, tennis court, sauna, disco, snooker; also photocopying.

Zhuhai (¥¥¥) Zhuhai Shi ☎ 333718 ⊠ 45618, fax 332339 • AE DC MC V. This hotel managed by CITS has similar facilities to the Gongbei Palace.

Restaurants

For entertaining, the *Jade City Restaurant* (¥) in the Zhuhai Resort Hotel and the *South China Restaurant* (¥) in the Gongbei Palace, which serve Cantonese cuisine, are recommended. For informal dining, there is the Western-style *Lido* in the Gongbei Palace.

Relaxation

Zhuhai offers little of interest to the visitor, although the surrounding countryside of the Pearl river delta undoubtedly fulfils many visitors' image of China. Within China, in a day you can visit Guangzhou, Foshan with its potteries, and Zhaoqing where the scenery is comparable to Guilin. Macau is definitely worth a day or a weekend visit.

Local resources

Fortunately, Macau and Hong Kong are near enough to return to regularly; local facilites are limited. Interpreters may be obtained through the CITS office at the Zhuhai Resort Hotel ☎ 333718 ⊠ 45618, fax 332339 or the Special Economic Zone office at Xin Guang Li ☎ 22146, but you might be better advised to bring an interpreter from Hong Kong, fluent in both Mandarin and Cantonese.

HONG KONG

When Hong Kong reverts to China in 1997, its future will be inextricably tied up with the People's Republic. But, from the moment China made the first moves to open its doors to trade and investment from the outside world, Hong Kong has been used as a base by many firms wanting to do business in the world's biggest market.

Hong Kong may feel larger than it is, yet despite the spectacular contrasts which help create this illusion – soaring skyscrapers, overcrowded shantytowns, vestiges of British colonialism, smart department stores and chaotic street markets – the city's geography is quite easy to grasp. The main built-up area on *Hong Kong Island* is on the north side, tightly squeezed between the harbour and green hills which rise abruptly. The three areas most likely to be visited by business travellers are *Central*, the prime business area, *Wanchai*, where many small firms are located, and *Causeway Bay*, where the World Trade Centre and principal department stores are sited. A 10min ferry trip connects the Island with *Kowloon*, the densely developed peninsula on the mainland, containing shopping and entertainment districts, housing and factories; at its southern tip is *Tsim Sha Tsui*, the site of most of the tourist hotels. The remaining area of Hong Kong is known collectively as the *New Territories*, and includes the rural mainland north of Kowloon up to the Chinese border as well as outlying islands.

A much more detailed guide to Hong Kong is given in *The Economist Guide to South-East Asia.*

Hotels

Many business travellers prefer hotel locations on Hong Kong Island, in particular favouring the Mandarin, one of the world's top hotels. However, several of the best hotels are in Kowloon, within 20min of Central by the Star Ferry or the MTR(subway) system; the Regent is the pick of them. All hotels listed have business centres, except the Peninsula; 10% service and 5% tax are additional to quoted rates. All major credit cards are accepted.
Excelsior, 281 Gloucester Rd, Causeway Bay ☎ 5-767365 ☎ 74550
Furama Inter-Continental, 1 Connaught Rd, Central ☎ 5-255111 ☎ 73081
Hilton, 2 Queen's Rd, Central ☎ 5-233111 ☎ 73355
Hyatt Regency, 67 Nathan Rd, Kowloon ☎ 3-662321 ☎ 43127
Mandarin, 5 Connaught Rd, Central ☎ 5-220111 ☎ 73653

Park Lane, 310 Gloucester Rd, Causeway Bay ☎ 5-8903355 ☎ 75343
Peninsula, Salisbury Rd, Kowloon ☎ 3-666251 ☎ 43821
Regent, 18–24 Salisbury Rd, Kowloon ☎ 3-7211211 ☎ 37134
Royal Garden, Mody Rd, Kowloon ☎ 3-7215215 ☎ 39539
Shangri-La, 64 Mody Rd, Kowloon ☎ 3-7212111 ☎ 36718
Sheraton, 20 Nathan Rd, Kowloon ☎ 3-691111 ☎ 45813
Other hotels *Holiday Inn, Golden Mile*, 50 Nathan Road, Kowloon ☎ 3-693111 ☎ 56332
Holiday Inn, Harbour View, 70 Mody Rd, Kowloon ☎ 3-7215161 ☎ 38670
Hong Kong, 3 Canton Rd, Kowloon ☎ 3-676011 ☎ 43838
Lee Gardens, Hysan Ave, Causeway Bay, ☎ 5-8953311 ☎ 75601
Prince, Harbour City, Canton Rd, Kowloon ☎ 3-7237788 ☎ 50950

Restaurants

Ethnic restaurants are mostly too informal for business entertaining. Chinese executives will just as happily eat Western food, and the expatriate community prefers the more tranquil atmosphere of hotel dining rooms. Gaddi's, the Mandarin Grill and the Plume are considered the top three restaurants. Unless stated otherwise, Continental cuisine is offered. All restaurants listed accept major credit cards.

Eagle's Nest (Chinese), Hilton Hotel ☎ 5-233111
Gaddi's, Peninsula Hotel ☎ 3-666251
Hilton Grill, Hilton Hotel ☎ 5-233111 • closed Sun L
Landau's, 30 Harbour Rd, Wanchai ☎ 5-8912901
Mandarin Grill, Mandarin Hotel ☎ 5-220111
Man Wah (Chinese), Mandarin Hotel ☎ 5-220111
Margaux, Shangri-La Hotel ☎ 3-7212111
Pierrot, Mandarin Hotel ☎ 5-220111
Plume, Regent Hotel ☎ 3-7211211
Verandah Grill, Peninsula Hotel ☎ 3-666251

Good but casual (Chinese)
Cleveland, 6 Cleveland St, Causeway Bay ☎ 5-763876.
Fook Lam Moon, 35 Johnston Rd, Wanchai ☎ 5-8660663.
Luk Yu Tea House, 26 Stanley St, Central ☎ 5-235464.
Spring Moon, Peninsula Hotel ☎ 3-666251.
Sze Chuen Lau, 466 Lockhart Rd, Causeway Bay ☎ 5-8919027.

Useful addresses

American Chamber of Commerce, 10th Fl, Swire House, Central ☎ 5-260165.
Customs and Excise Department, 8th Fl, Harbour Bldg, 38 Pier Rd, Central ☎ 5-8523324.
Exports Credit Insurance Corporation, South Seas Centre Tower 1, 2nd Fl, 75 Mody Rd, Kowloon ☎ 3-7233883.
Federation of Hong Kong Industries, Room 407, Hankow Centre, 5-15 Hankow Rd, Kowloon ☎ 3-7230818.

Hong Kong Exhibition Centre, China Resources Bldg, Gloucester Rd, Wanchai ☎ 5-8318831.
Hong Kong General Chamber of Commerce, 22nd Fl, United Centre, 95 Queensway, Central ☎ 5-299229.
Hong Kong Trade Development Council, 31st Fl, Great Eagle Centre, 23 Harbour Rd, Wanchai ☎ 5-8334333.
Information Services Department, Beaconsfield House, Queen's Rd, Central ☎ 5-8428777.
Productivity Council and Centre, 12th Fl, World Commerce Bldg, Harbour Centre, 11 Canton Rd, Kowloon tel 3-7235656.
Trade and Industry Departments, 14th Fl, Ocean Centre, Kowloon ☎ 3-7222333.

Local resources
Business services

Hotels in Hong Kong are the best in Asia for business support and visitors will rarely need to seek outside help. The *American Chamber of Commerce* (see above) has office space for short-term rental and its business services include a reference library.

Photocopying and printing
Copykat, Printing Centre ☎ 5-226191
Secretarial *Margaret Sullivan Secretarial Services* ☎ 5-265946; *Lindy Williams Typing and WP Services* ☎ 5-8456777.
Translation and interpretation
Interlingua ☎ 5-430188; *Polyglot Translations* ☎ 5-215689; *Translanguage Center* ☎ 5-732728.

Communications

Local delivery *Document Express* ☎ 5-782341; *Evergreen* ☎ 3-903307.
Long-distance delivery DHL 24hr hotline ☎ 3-7644888.
Post offices Main offices: Connaught Pl, Central (by Star Ferry) ☎ 5-231071; 405 Nathan Rd, Kowloon ☎ 3-7808598; Beaconsfield House, Queens Rd, Central ☎ 5-230226.
Telex and fax *Cable and Wireless* 102A, Tower 1, Exchange Sq, Central (open 24hr) ☎ 5-8439439.

Planning and Reference

Entry details

China welcomes visitors and has considerably relaxed the rules that, only a decade ago, inhibited independent travel. Nevertheless, certain requirements must be observed, including that of obtaining an official sponsor for any business travel in the country. This also makes good business sense, since it is difficult to meet effective trade contacts without a sponsor to make the introductions.

Documentation

Visas All visitors to China must have a visa, but getting one is not usually difficult. Applications should be made to an embassy or consulate of the People's Republic of China, preferably in your own country (see *Embassies*). Forms and further information can also be obtained from specialist travel agents, who may be able to process applications for tourist visas, but not usually visas for business travel.

Visa application forms are now much simplified. Ordinary travellers need to provide details of the purpose of the visit, tickets, intended duration and itinerary. Those seeking a business visa must attach to the application form the original of a letter or telex of invitation from the host organization. Processing the applications takes from one to three weeks; some embassies give a swifter service to personal callers.

Hong Kong is the easiest place in the world in which to get a visa for China. Visitors of any nationality can call at the offices of the China International Travel Service (CITS) with their passport and obtain a visa the same day, provided they apply before noon. Business visas are readily granted. To obtain one, simply present a letter from your own company, or from your company's agent in Hong Kong,

stating that you wish to travel to China on business. CITS's head office in Hong Kong is 6th Fl, Tower II, South Seas Centre, 75 Mody Rd, Kowloon ☎ 3-7215317 ⓉⓍ 38449 fax 3-7217154. China Travel Service, which used to process arrangements for all visitors to China, now deals mainly with overseas Chinese.

If you are travelling directly to China from anywhere other than Hong Kong it is also possible to obtain a visa on arrival at Beijing airport (provided you have a letter or telex of invitation). The service is used by regular travellers whose records are already on file. In theory, even first-time visitors can use it, but there is always a risk that entry will be refused.

Visas are valid for a single journey and expire three months from your intended date of entry. Extensions can be obtained in China from local offices of the Public Security Bureau (Foreign Affairs Section). Officially, visas can be extended only twice and for a maximum of four weeks. In practice, you should not have difficulty in obtaining further extensions, particularly if the application is backed by your Chinese sponsor or host.

The authorities permit considerable freedom of movement within China. More than 430 cities and regions are completely open to foreigners, and those cities not yet declared "open" can be visited simply by applying for an alien's travel permit at the Public Service Bureau (Foreign Affairs Section) in any major city.

Driving licence Non-residents are not allowed to drive in China.

Health regulations

On arrival at their port of entry, visitors to China fill out a simple health declaration form stating where they have been in the previous two weeks. Anyone who has been in South America or Africa during this period must have a current yellow fever inoculation certificate. Visitors must also have a cholera certificate if they have stayed in an infected area during the two-week period. To be certain of what they need, and for advice about their own best interests, visitors should check with a vaccination centre at least two weeks before entry. You may wish to protect yourself against typhoid, malaria and hepatitis, as well as tetanus and polio, although you are not required to do so by law (see *Health care*).

Customs regulations
Visitors must complete a baggage declaration form on entry and declare watches, cameras and lenses, calculators, tape recorders and business equipment, gold and silver, jewellery and antiques, foreign currency and traveller's cheques. All of these and other goods may be imported duty free, provided that they are for personal use, in addition to two 75cl (26 fl oz) bottles of spirits or wine, 200 cigarettes or 50 cigars or 225 grammes (8oz) of tobacco.

When your baggage has been inspected you will be given a duplicate copy of your baggage declaration form, which must be stamped by the customs official. This is an important document which must be produced at the customs check at the point of departure. The purpose is to ensure that you have not sold possessions or made "unauthorized" gifts. At the point of exit, if you cannot produce the form or the items listed on it, you will be subjected to a lengthy cross-examination which may result in your being charged punitive duty – or, at the least, missing your flight. (For what to do if you lose the form, see *Lost possessions*.)

Prohibited items include weapons of all kinds, narcotics, radio transmitters/receivers, and a catch-all

category of "articles detrimental to Chinese political, economic, cultural and ethical values." There is no official list of what might cause offence, but in the past visitors have not been allowed to import Taiwanese publications, or anything that could be interpreted as pornographic. In particular, videotapes are treated with suspicion and must be declared. If you intend to carry promotional videos into China it is advisable to ask your host in advance for a covering letter describing their contents and purpose.

The rules concerning the importation of gifts and samples that you intend to leave behind in China are another grey area. Low-value items such as product literature, calendars, pictures and books are not likely to be a problem. However, calculators, watches, cigarette lighters and other goods of this kind must be declared as gifts and either you or the recipient may be charged duty. Also, the recipient will have to provide you with a letter of receipt. Experienced China traders recommend that you do not import new-looking devices or machines but rather items such as ties or fountain pens. Alternatively, buy your gifts in China, or express your thanks by hosting a banquet.

Chinese customs officials will scrutinize any item in your baggage the like of which they have not seen before. Questions such as "What is this?" and "How does it work?" do not necessarily mean that you are under suspicion of smuggling, merely that the official is curious. The best response is a simple, friendly explanation.

Climate
China's huge size and varied topography mean that climatic conditions may differ markedly from region to region.
Beijing and northern China
There are four distinct seasons. From December to February temperatures

rarely rise above freezing, with biting winds and occasional snow flurries. In the far north it is colder still, and for longer. Static electricity shocks can be an uncomfortable by-product of the very low humidity. Spring is mild but may be accompanied by dust-laden winds from central Asia. The temperature and humidity begin to climb from early June, to a possible high of 40°C/100°F during July and August. At this time, Beijing experiences three- or four-day cycles of rising heat, followed by a heavy thunderstorm which clears the air briefly until the next cycle begins. Autumn is dry, clear and sunny, and the best time to visit.

Central China The Chang Jiang (Yangzi) river delta region, centred on Shanghai, has a mild winter with average temperatures of 4°C/40°F, but temperatures occasionally fall well below freezing point. Even on warmer days, the city is overcast and damp. Spring is marked by rapid warming of the air, followed by rain in May and June. Shanghai summers are notoriously sultry, with high temperatures and humid weather interspersed with prolonged rain. Autumn is the pleasantest season, because then there are bearable temperatures and less rainfall.

Southern China South China, including the province of Guangdong with its capital at Guangzhou (Canton), has a subtropical climate. The temperature falls to around 10°C/50°F only during the first six weeks of the year, and rises rapidly thereafter to a very humid 30°C/86°F for most of the summer. Rainfall is very high during the spring and summer, but falls in heavy, sporadic downpours, rather than continuously. From April to August, typhoons are common in the coastal regions. September to early December are the most attractive months, when the humidity falls but the temperature remains in the upper 20s°C/70s°F.

Dressing for comfort Lightweight clothing is essential for the hottest regions of China, for air conditioning is rare outside the major hotels. In winter, northern China demands several layers of warm, padded clothing, lined footwear, gloves and headwear. Although hotels are comfortably warm, offices and factories are often so cold that visitors and host alike keep their outdoor clothing on.

Holidays

Apart from New Year's Day, Western holidays such as Christmas are not observed in China. The main

Average temperatures and rainfall

	Beijing			Shanghai			Guangzhou		
	°C	°F	mm	°C	°F	mm	°C	°F	mm
January	−4	24	3	3	38	44	14	57	39
February	−2	28	8	4	40	63	15	58	63
March	4	40	9	8	47	80	18	64	92
April	13	56	22	14	57	111	22	71	159
May	20	68	36	19	66	129	26	78	267
June	25	76	70	24	74	157	27	81	299
July	26	79	197	28	82	142	29	83	220
August	25	76	244	28	82	116	29	83	225
September	20	67	64	24	75	146	27	81	204
October	13	55	21	18	64	47	24	75	52
November	4	39	8	13	55	54	20	67	42
December	−3	27	2	6	43	40	15	59	20

Chinese holiday is the three-day Spring Festival (known as Chinese New Year in the West), a time of family reunions and gift-giving. The timing is variable, according to the lunar calendar, and the Festival usually comes in late January or early February. People in China take their individual holidays by arrangement with their employer; there is no period when businesses close altogether, other than the following public holidays:

Jan 1 New Year's Day
Late Jan/Feb Three-day Spring Festival
May 1 International Labour Day
Oct 1/2 National Day

Mar 8 (International Working Women's Day), May 4 (Youth Day), Jun 1 (Children's Day), Jul 1 (Anniversary of the Founding of the Communist Party of China) and Aug 1 (Anniversary of the Founding of the People's Liberation Army) are also marked or celebrated, but do not cause all business to stop.

Money

Local currency China issues special currency for visitors. Like the local currency, it is denominated in yuan but on the reverse is printed "foreign exchange certificate," to distinguish it from *renminbi*, "the people's money" used by Chinese nationals. The two forms of currency are usually referred to by the initials FEC and RMB. In 1986, the government announced that it was phasing out FEC, since so much was in circulation among Chinese that it seemed pointless to maintain the two currencies; however, no dates have yet been set for the change.

FEC and RMB are supposed to be identical in value, but FEC is in demand on the black market because it can be used to buy Western imports. Neither currency can be purchased outside China, except in the form of traveller's cheques issued by the Bank of China, and it is illegal to import Chinese currency.

Banknotes of both currencies are issued in denominations of 100, 50, 10, 5, 1, and 0.05 and 0.10 yuan. Yuan are known colloquially as *kuai*, tenths of the yuan as *mao*, and hundredths as *fen*. The 100 and 50 yuan notes are best avoided since taxi drivers, shops, restaurants and bars frequently have no change. You can ask for RMB when changing money, as well as FEC, and it is useful to have a small amount for use in street markets or restaurants where FEC may not be accepted.

Currency regulations When you arrive in China you must complete a form declaring how much foreign currency you are bringing into the country. You should produce this form whenever changing money, and when leaving the country you must produce it, together with all receipts of any exchange transactions, in order to prove that you have not changed any money on the black market. Any surplus FEC, if properly documented, can be exchanged at the currency checkout on departure (or, much less conveniently, at the Bank of China abroad).

Foreign currency The foreign currencies that are most widely accepted for exchange within China are those of Australia, Austria, Belgium, Canada, Denmark, France, West Germany, Hong Kong, Italy, Japan, Malaysia, the Netherlands, Norway, Singapore, Sweden, Switzerland, the UK and the USA.

Note that, in return for payment in a convertible currency, companies that have an agent in China are often glad to pay visitors' major bills out of RMB profits that they are unable to export.

Traveller's cheques issued by the major banks in any of the above currencies can be exchanged without difficulty. In addition, the Bank of China's branches overseas and in Hong Kong, Macao and China, sell traveller's cheques denominated in yuan, although there is no particular advantage in such cheques. Cheques issued by American Express have the advantage that their office in Beijing will quickly replace any that are lost or stolen, if you contact Shop D, Lobby, Jinglun Hotel, Jianguomenwai Dajie, Beijing ☎ 5002266 ext. 2244 (office hours Mon–Fri, 9–12, 1.30–5; Sat, 9–12).

Credit and charge cards It is unwise to rely upon credit or charge cards as a sole or even primary means of payment in China, though they can be used. A surcharge of 2% is nearly always added for card transactions. American Express has an arrangement with Bank of China branches in Beijing, Tianjin, Hangzhou, Guangzhou and Shanghai allowing cardholders to cash personal cheques up to US$1,500 or £600 a day, but this is not always easy to implement. Other cards accepted are Diners Club, MasterCard and Visa. Hotels may suspend acceptance of a particular card at short notice.

Changing money
Avoid unofficial transactions, no matter how favourable the rate of exchange, because you may have to account for all your currency dealings at customs on departure (see above). Instead, exchange foreign currency and traveller's cheques at your hotel or at branches of the Bank of China, record the transaction on your currency declaration form, and retain the receipt.

All hotels have a foreign exchange desk, usually run by the Bank of China. Rates are fixed daily by the Bank of China and do not vary throughout the country.

Tipping
Hotels and restaurants levy a 10% service charge. Elsewhere, it is not necessary to tip; the authorities disapprove of the practice.

Getting there
More than 20 international airlines offer a regular service to China (principally Beijing), although few

fly non-stop. Flights from Europe are via the Middle East, Pakistan or India and Hong Kong. From North America, flights over the Pacific stop over at Tokyo (or Manila or Bangkok), while Atlantic flights go via Europe and stop over more than once. Flights from Australia and New Zealand stop over at Hong Kong. In all cases the flight is long and tiring. Consequently, few travellers make the trip in one leg, preferring to transit a day or so to adjust to the time zones and climate. There are no flights to China from Taiwan or South Korea.

Across the Pacific Travellers to China across the Pacific from North America usually go via Tokyo. From here, the time to Beijing is around 4hr. There are several flights a week, operated by JAL, CPAir, Northwest Orient, PanAm and CAAC. JAL also offers a non-stop flight to Shanghai. However, some trans-Pacific travellers fly to China via Bangkok, or via Hawaii and Manila, where luxury hotel accommodation is significantly less expensive than in Tokyo or Hong Kong. Total flight time from Manila to Beijing, including a stopover in Guangzhou, is six hours.

Via Hong Kong The most popular transit point, Hong Kong has been dubbed the "gateway to China." Here, before entering China, you can catch up on the latest trade intelligence and talk to agents, banks and embassy commercial staff. Hong Kong also offers the greatest choice of destinations in China and the most frequent flights, operated largely by the Chinese national carrier, CAAC, with more limited services from Cathay Pacific and Dragon Air. There are direct CAAC flights from Hong Kong to Beijing, Guangzhou and Shanghai, and also to Chengdu, Fuzhou, Guilin, Hangzhou, Kunming, Nanjing and Tianjin. Typical flight times are 25min to Guangzhou, 1hr 50min to Shanghai, and 2hr 40min to Beijing. Travellers from Hong Kong to Guangzhou have the option of travel by rail or hovercraft, in addition to the three flights a day operated by CAAC (see *Guangzhou: Arriving*). Trains run the short distance from Hong Kong to Shenzhen very frequently.

Special itineraries The business traveller who needs an individually tailored itinerary should contact a travel company that specializes in China, such as China Travel Service or Voyages Jules Verne of London. Chinese National Tourist Offices will refer you to the commercial agencies.

Chinese National Tourist Offices
Frankfurt, Eschenheimer Anlage 28, D-6000 Frankfurt am Main-1 ☎ (069) 555292 ㏇ 4170360.
Hong Kong (CITS), Unit 601, 6th Fl, Tower II, South Seas Centre, 75 Mody Road, Tsim Sha Tsui East, Kowloon, Hong Kong ☎ 3-7215317 ㏇ 38449.
London, 4 Glentworth St, London NW1 ☎ (01) 935 9427 ㏇ 291221.
New York, Lincoln Bldg 60 E 42nd Street, Suite 465, New York, NY 10165 ☎ (212) 8670271 ㏇ 662142.
Paris, 51 rue Ste-Anne, 75002 Paris ☎ 42969548 ㏇ 612866.
Sydney, 33/336 Sussex St, Sydney, New South Wales, 2000 Australia ☎ (02) 2679674 ㏇ 73301
Tokyo, 6F Hanchidai Hamamatsu-cho, Minato-ku, Tokyo, Japan ☎ (03) 433 1461, office; (03) 452 6266, evening.

Getting around

All long-distance travel arrangements within China should be made well in advance of your visit with the assistance of your host in China or your agent. This will ensure that your time there is not monopolized by the lengthy process of booking, confirming and paying for tickets.

Within China, travel arrangements should be made through hotel travel desks or the China International Travel Service (CITS), which has branch offices in all major cities.

Air
The most practical means of travel between cities in this vast country is by air, using CAAC's extensive domestic network, which covers 166 routes connecting more than 80 cities. Many of its aircraft are old, and in-flight services are far from luxurious, but the fleet is being modernized as China becomes more tourist-oriented.

Reservations can be made and tickets purchased through hotel travel desks, the CITS, or at CAAC booking offices. When collecting tickets, you will need to show all your travel documents. Tickets are fixed or open: fixed ones are valid only for the date and flight on the ticket; open tickets are valid for 90 days. Typical fares are Beijing–Shanghai US$55 (2hr); Beijing–Guangzhou US$90 (4hr); Beijing–Hong Kong US$130 (4hr). First-class seats (see below) are available on these routes, but on most domestic routes there is only one class.

Reservations must *always* be made well in advance and reconfirmed 72hr before departure, or the reservation will automatically be cancelled. There are penalties for cancelling a reservation, although if notice is given up to 2hrs before the flight, the charge is negligible; after that it is 20% of the fare. Failure to arrive in time for a domestic flight results in cancellation of the ticket with no refund.

Advance booking of onward flights within China is highly unreliable, because domestic flight reservations are not yet computerized. Always reserve or confirm an onward flight as soon as you reach the city from which you intend to fly.

Standards Chinese airports are very basic. Refreshment areas serve beer, soft drinks and little else. Shops, where they exist, sell tourist knick-knacks. Flights are frequently delayed due to engineering faults or bad weather, so take a good book. On the plus side, airports are generally well signposted in English as well as Chinese and Japanese. Announcements are made both in Chinese and in English.

The arrangements for departures from Chinese airports also leave much to be desired. There are invariably long lines at check-in desks and for customs and security. Customs checks precede check-in on flights out of China. It is advisable to allow not less than 90min for checking in and boarding.

First-class seats, costing about 30% more than the standard fare, are available only on long-distance routes. The premium buys a bigger seat, more legroom and use of the VIP lounge at the airport, where comfortable seating is available, but not much else. In-flight services are negligible: passengers get a cup of tea and a bag of boiled sweets, and a picnic lunch only on longer flights. Smoking is not permitted on internal flights.

Train

The rail network is comprehensive, but as a general rule, train travel is worthwhile only if you have plenty of time to spare and want to see something of the Chinese countryside. Although trains are punctual, they are slow: Beijing to Shanghai 22hr; Beijing to Guangzhou 34hr. Train fares are on average 25% lower than the equivalent flight.

Reservations If you have not arranged tickets before arriving in China, you should do so at least five days in advance, because long-distance services are frequently full. The easiest way to buy tickets is through the hotel travel desk or the CITS, both of which will charge a small fee. Some stations, for example Beijing, have a separate ticket office for foreigners, but generally it is not

worthwhile going to the station yourself to wait in the inevitable long line before trying to explain your needs to a clerk whose English will almost certainly be very limited.

Standards Foreigners travel in deluxe or "soft" class (as opposed to "hard" or wooden seat class), in reserved seats or berths. Sleepers are clean, dividing into four-person compartments with tiered bunks. Cabin attendants will provide hot water and tea, beer and soft drinks (often not chilled), and will supply menus, take your meal order and escort you to the dining car when the meal is ready.

Station waiting rooms are generally crowded and station restaurants none too clean.

Car and taxi

Foreigners are not allowed to drive in China. Short, local journeys within China will usually be organized by your official host, who will provide a car and driver. If, however, you have free time simply to explore a city or the local countryside, you will find that taxis are readily available for short journeys or even day trips. It is simplest to order a taxi through your hotel, but often you can also contact local taxi companies directly (names and telephone numbers are given in the City by City section). Fares are calculated according to the cab model (newer vehicles with heating and airconditioning charge slightly more) as well as distance and waiting time, and you will be expected to pay for the driver's lunch if you are out for the day. In many cities it is advisable to fix the price in advance. The cost is seldom excessive: ¥6 is the typical fare for a short trip within Beijing; less in other cities; and around ¥300 for the 160km/100-mile round trip from Beijing to the Great Wall and Ming Tombs.

It is always sensible (vital in the less visited cities or if you are travelling to places other than tourist sights and hotels) to provide destinations written in Chinese characters and to make advance arrangements for the taxi to wait, no matter how long, unless you can be sure that a Chinese speaker will be able to summon you a taxi by phone.

There are no self-drive car rental facilities in China, but all the superior hotels can arrange chauffered limousines. Prices start at ¥80 per day plus mileage.

Bus

Travelling by bus is not recommended unless you can speak Chinese and are adventurous. Though cheap, local transport is often crowded, hot and slow.

Street names and addresses

Usually in this guide the Chinese (pinyin) name of a hotel, restaurant, site or road is given before any translation, eg Wansui (Coal) Hill, Heping (Peace) Hotel. However, only the translated name may be given if that is more commonly used among English speakers (eg the Garden Hotel, Friendship Store). For clarity, the nature of the place is given in English, eg Renmin (People's) Park, Wansui (Coal) Hill – except in the case of roads, streets and avenues, for here it is generally more useful to have the Chinese common noun as well.

Chinese addresses and street names may well be a source of confusion to a visitor, even though all streets also have signposts in pinyin. It is useful to know that *jie* is translated as "street," *dajie* as "avenue," *lu* as "road" and *hutong* as "lane." Many Chinese thoroughfares are designated "east," "west," "north," "south" and "central," for which the pinyin is *dong, xi, bei, nan,* and *zhong.* Thus Dongchang'an Dajie in Beijing may appear elsewhere as Chang'an Avenue East; Yan'an East Road in Shanghai is given as Yan'an Donglu.

Hotels

Things have changed radically in China since the 1970s, when the quality of its hotels was extremely poor. Travellers had to put up with half-finished buildings, rooms without furniture, plumbing that did not work and unmotivated staff. Improvements began when the Chinese invited international hotel chains to bid for contracts to run luxury-class hotels. Today, joint-venture hotels in the major cities and tourist regions can be as good as their counterparts anywhere in the world.

Reservations All the hotels listed in this guide accept reservations from outside China, directly, or through the central reservation system of the group that manages the hotel, or through travel agents. There is rarely a shortage of rooms but, to be sure of securing your first preference, it is advisable to make reservations a month in advance.

Styles and standards Traditional Chinese hotels are low-rise, often built around courtyards containing gardens and ponds. Many modern hotels are still built in this style, but, where land is at a premium, are likely to be high-rise buildings of more than 20 floors. Hotels in areas off the tourist track tend to be dreary blocks put up by the Russians during the 1950s.

Rooms in all the major hotels listed in the guide are equipped with a private bathroom and air conditioning, and have a desk, colour TV, radio and telephone. Increasingly, hotels have closed-circuit TV showing English-language films, and hotel radios in Beijing are tuned to the local English-language service.

The rooms in most of the hotels listed have minibars, but some of these are stocked only with beer and soft drinks. Everywhere you will be provided with a carafe of pre-boiled drinking water, and a thermos flask of hot water for making tea. Hotels in Guangzhou usually provide 24hr room service, but few do so elsewhere. Service during the day is provided by floor attendants, who usually keep stocks of tea, beer and soft drinks for purchase by guests, and handle laundry. Only the top, joint-venture hotels provide snacks or meals on room service. Most hotels have a choice of coffee lounges or snack bars, one of which will be open until midnight. Some also have hairdressing salons and the service almost always includes a head massage.

Standard to the major hotels are a post office, currency exchange desk, taxi procurement, and shops selling imported foreign wines, spirits, cigarettes, toiletries, camera film, newspapers and books.

Business facilities Hotels are the focus for East-West business in China. Of the 2,000 or so foreign firms with a permanent presence in the country, the majority have their offices in hotel rooms, sometimes leasing a suite or a whole floor. Resident companies will have all their own business resources on hand, and hotels otherwise generally make only basic provision for business visitors: a telex, fax and postal service and, more rarely, typing. The Garden and the China in Guangzhou, the Hua Ting Sheraton in Shanghai, the Hyatt in Tianjin, the Jinling in Nanjing and the Great Wall Sheraton in Beijing are exceptions, with business centres equipped and staffed for word processing, translation, photocopying and binding, plus telex, fax and meeting rooms. All of these services can be used by nonresidents.

Interpreters are always provided by the Chinese host. Secretarial assistance is more problematical. For this reason, draft contracts, letters of agreement, memoranda and so on should be prepared in advance of the visit.

Sports facilities Not many hotels yet have swimming pools, sports facilities or health centres.

Electric current in China is 220 volts, and visitors from countries with different systems should carry a transformer or variable voltage equipment. Plug types vary from region to region, but adaptor plugs

can usually be borrowed from floor attendants or the concierge, or purchased from hotel shops.

Hotel groups
There are no China-wide hotel groups as yet, though Holiday Inn has committed itself to opening 20 hotels by 1990. Most of these, however, will be tourist oriented. China's best hotels are usually managed under fixed term contract by Japanese, American and Hong Kong groups. The Sheraton group has led the way in setting standards. The Hua Ting Sheraton in Shanghai and the Great Wall Sheraton in Beijing are always full. The Hong Kong-based Peninsula Group, which runs the Garden in Guangzhou and the Jianguo in Beijing, runs a close second, providing comprehensive and reliable facilities without ostentation. Hilton International is opening in Shanghai and Beijing, and the Japanese Nikko chain, which runs the Jinglun in Beijing, plans further development.

Our recommended hotels
Hotels given full entries in the guide have generally been selected on the basis of being the most comfortable and stylish and the best-equipped for business travellers. Only hotels within reasonable distance of the business districts have been included.

Listed under "Other hotels" are establishments that do not achieve the standards of their competitors but which offer adequate accommodation, usually at a lower price than the hotels given full entries, and also hotels that were not yet open at the time of the guide's compilation.

The price symbols have the meanings given on the following page. These prices are those of the published tariffs of the hotels, but at periods of slack trade you may be able to obtain a discount, provided that you deal with the hotel direct (not through CITS, a travel agent or the hotel group reservation system).

¥	up to ¥200
¥¥	¥200–250
¥¥¥	¥250–300
¥¥¥¥	¥300–350
¥¥¥¥¥	over ¥350

These reflect the cost at the time of going to press for one person occupying a standard room.

Restaurants

Business entertaining in China usually consists of formal banquets. The Chinese sponsoring organization will generally host a welcoming banquet, and foreign guests reciprocate towards the end of their visit. All of the hotels listed in this guide reserve their grandest dining rooms for these banquets and have a range of special menus of up to 15 courses; but certain local restaurants are also very suitable.

The Chinese generally eat earlier than Westerners do. The lunch hour begins not at 1, but at noon; dinner is served from as early as 5.30, and orders are often not taken after 2 or after 8 or even 7.30.

Hotel restaurants

Foreigners generally eat in hotels, since most other restaurants are basic, noisy and crowded, and the menus are invariably written only in Chinese. The larger hotels have several dining rooms, each specializing in a different cuisine: expect to find at least one Beijing-style and one Cantonese restaurant. An increasing number of hotels offer European and Japanese menus, a buffet and a fast food restaurant serving pizzas, pasta and beefburgers.

Hotel restaurants are always busy: they have a captive market in the many staff who work for foreign companies based in the hotel, as well as those visiting from other hotels for a change of scene. The hectic periods are around 8am, 12–2pm and 7–9pm. If you do not reserve a table by telephone earlier in the day you should expect to have to wait. Your table may be given to someone else if

you arrive late. Many restaurants will not admit guests after 2pm or 9pm.

Each group of tables is attended by a team of waiters, each with a specific role: the captain takes orders and supervises the others, who will be variously responsible for serving drinks and delivering or clearing dishes. Learn to recognize their faces and roles; if you ask the wrong waiter, your order could be forgotten or ignored. Generally, though, waiters are friendly and attentive.

Local restaurants

Outside the hotels, excellent food can be sampled very cheaply, but frequently in simple or even scruffy surroundings. Here again, it is essential to make reservations early in the day, and often advance notice is needed for special dishes. Usually this can be done at the hotel's travel desk, and there will be a small charge for the service. If one of your party speaks Chinese, he or she can order the menu for you in advance, or write down the list of dishes you would like to try; or establish a price range with the restaurant management and let them devise the menu. Alternatively, you can simply point to dishes you like the look of on other people's tables.

Independent restaurants tend to close still earlier than those in hotels, though it varies to some degree from city to city. In Beijing, for instance, non-hotel restaurants often close at 7.30. Elsewhere it may be somewhat later, but still early by Western standards.

Our recommended restaurants

The restaurants given entries in this guide have been selected both for formal business entertaining and for more casual occasions. It will be clear from the description whether or not the quality of service, ambience, decor, reputation and, last but not least, the quality of food render the restaurant suitable for entertaining.

The price symbols used in the

guide have the following meanings:

¥	up to ¥50
¥¥	¥50–100
¥¥¥	¥100–150
¥¥¥¥	¥150–200
¥¥¥¥¥	over ¥200

These reflect the cost at the time of going to press of a typical meal, including half a bottle of house wine and coffee or tea.

Local cuisine

Chinese cuisine is not a single kind of cooking: in fact, the cooking of Mongolia differs as much from the cooking of Sichuan or Canton as that of Norway from the food of Greece or Turkey. The differences are based on climate, which affects the produce available and the type of agriculture; on social and religious factors, which may inhibit the eating of certain foods, and on the economic structure of the region, which may have permitted a "noble" cuisine to develop side by side with the normal peasant diet.

Visitors used to Chinese restaurants of the West, with several dishes of meat, fish and vegetables shared between the guests, should realize that what they are accustomed to eating would be a banquet for the ordinary Chinese. An agricultural or blue-collar worker's meal will consist of *fan* (boiled rice or other cereal) and a small quantity of *cai* to help the cereal down – this might be a small amount of fish or pickled vegetable, perhaps a small portion of chicken or other meat. These meals are packed in lunch boxes strapped to the back of bicycles, carried in students' satchels, or can be seen being eagerly demolished by hungry workers. Even the more elaborate family meals are often very simple – rice, a fish, a vegetable and soup. However, sophisticated and extravagant cooking does exist, and some of the restaurants recommended here will provide a gastronomic experience equal to anything available in Europe or America. But the coming of tourism has only slowly created a

new generation of talented cooks to replace those trained before the Revolution, and it is idle to expect anything more than good ingredients, cooked carefully enough, even in a first-class hotel.

Two points will immediately strike the first-time traveller. First, that except in the far northwest milk products are almost completely absent, perhaps because people of Chinese race develop lactose intolerance after weaning. The versatile soybean replaces dairy products – soy oil for flavouring, soy milk to drink and to make an excellent yoghurt (which is a sovereign preventative against gut infections), and even fermented soybean curd, which smells and tastes like a very high Roquefort. Second, if you visit any kitchen, you will not fail to notice the large jars of monosodium glutamate (MSG) and the abandon with which it is used.

The greatest regional differences are those between the colder, northern wheat areas and the subtropical, southern rice regions, and between the coastal provinces with their abundant seafood and the inland areas where fish must either be freshwater or preserved by drying or pickling. In many places preserving and pickling become very important, and this is reflected in the local markets and menus. Equally striking is the way in which every scrap of edible material is used; a duck banquet will include every imaginable and several unimaginable parts of the duck to produce course after delicious course. But travellers' tales of eating monkeys' brains, dogs and other exotic fare need not concern you. Most travellers will encounter nothing more exotic than sea-slugs (tastier than they sound), though it is easy to eat snake in Guangzhou. Shark's fin and bird's nest, both preserved products, appear rarely, because they are exceedingly expensive.

Southern (or Cantonese) cooking

Until recently, this cuisine was the

one most familiar to Westerners. The principal methods are stir-frying – cooking in a little oil in a wok over a fierce heat – and steaming, often in bamboo steaming baskets piled over a wok of boiling water. Both conserve fuel and retain freshness and nutritive content. All along the southern coasts of China, fish and shellfish are the dominant protein food, but pork, beef and duck are also found, often stir-fried with green vegetables, or with mushrooms. In Guangxi province, the hotter spicing of Hunan begins to show itself and Vietnamese influences can also be detected. Rice is the staple cereal. Oyster sauce and a sweet-sour bean sauce are often used with stir-fry dishes.

Eastern China and the Yangzi
The humid river plains of the east abound in freshwater fish and subtropical fruit and vegetables. The rich cities of the past, such as Nanjing and Suzhou, were centres of "court cooking" and still have excellent restaurants specializing in sophisticated dishes and elaborate presentations. Shaoxing wine – like a rather pungent sherry – is made here and appears in the so-called "drunken" dishes of meats marinaded in wine and spices and served cold. Wheat is grown in the north of the region and narrow noodles appear in soup. Savoury dishes will often seem sweet to the visitor as sugar mixed with soy sauce is a frequent ingredient. Frying of fish is common, and the famous, slow-cooked "lion's head" or minced meats should not be missed.

Northern China This is not rice country: the staples are wheat and maize baked into various kinds of bread, pasta and cakes. Vegetables are in short supply in winter and meat is a luxury for the common people. Beijing has a tradition of court cooking, based on elements from many regional cuisines. One dish not to be missed is oil-poached fish: fillets of flat-fish are gently cooked in hot but not boiling oil and served in a

wine sauce. Another that no visitor can escape is Beijing duck (see above, or *Beijing: Local restaurants*).

Western China This area, which includes the provinces of Sichuan, Yunnan and Hunan, has a style of cooking which has become familiar to the Westerner in recent years. Spiciness is the most striking feature – chili, garlic and Sichuan pepper are freely used. Rice and wheat are both grown and the forested hills abound in edible fungi and bamboo shoots. Yunnan is famous for its hams. Towards the west, where the economy is based more on nomadic herding, milk products can be found. Steaming is an important method of cooking and particular emphasis is laid on texture. Dishes are not copiously sauced, as they are in eastern China, but are carefully composed of elements chosen to impart "crispiness" or "chewiness."

Bars

There are no bars outside hotels, although in Beijing some of the embassies have them for staff and guests. The best hotel bars serve a comprehensive range of imported beers, wines, cocktails and spirits. Others are more basic and may serve only local beer, mineral water and soft drinks.

In the plushest hotel lounges, with waiter service, prices are uniformly high, even for local beers, but they stay open until midnight or later. In the less pretentious bars customers pay for drinks over the counter and can expect the bars to close by 11pm at the latest.

Drinking, and even mild inebriation, is not frowned upon in China, but any kind of loud behaviour and particularly flirtatiousness, no matter how mild, is strictly taboo.

Local drinks

Chinese beer is generally excellent: Qingdao (Tsing Tao) is a light, flowery lager brewed mainly for export but usually available in hotels.

Otherwise try Beijing Beer or Wu Xing (Five Star). Lao Shan mineral water (either still or sparkling) is also good, but the local carbonated orange juices, lemonade and cola drinks are not to everyone's taste.

Chinese wines, both red and white, are sweet and syrupy, although both the Great Wall and the Dynasty brands are light, medium-dry whites, the product of recent joint ventures between Chinese and foreign viticulturists. Most Chinese spirits, with the possible exception of brandy and vodka, are rough, raw and fiery.

Shopping

A decade ago, foreigners could shop only in Friendship Stores, using foreign exchange certificates (FEC); the idea was to force foreigners to pay high prices and to prevent local Chinese from acquiring a liking for the trappings of Western materialism. Today, foreigners can shop anywhere they like using FEC or RMB (see *Money*), and department stores are well stocked with locally manufactured products.

Friendship Stores and hotel shops Although Friendship Stores are still a useful source of Western cigarettes or spirits, hotel shops now stock a wide selection of imported goods, and also products which previously were rarely available outside Friendship Stores, such as the more expensive silks and jewellery. Prices in general are high; expect to pay at least double what you would at home.

Local shops General department stores are interesting if only as an education in the range of goods available to the average Chinese family. Much of what they sell is heavily ornate or old-fashioned in design, but there are some excellent bargains to be had, including silk scarves and ties, linen tablewear and inexpensive souvenirs such as army caps and T-shirts.

Specialist shops Many stores specialize in native arts and crafts. Here you can buy jewellery, silk,

embroidery, furs, rugs, ceramics, furniture, cloisonné, scroll paintings and woodblock prints. Prices are not necessarily lower than Hong Kong, or indeed back home.

Antiques Collectors of antiques will find a wide selection of small objects on sale in hotel lobbies and licensed antique stores. They will rarely be more than 100 years old (Qing dynasty), and visitors should not expect to find any bargains. However, some beautiful objects can occasionally be found; for example, hair ornaments made of exquisite blue kingfisher feathers, jade jewellery, ceramics, embroidery, and stone, wood and bamboo carvings. Ivory carvings are also sold. When you buy antiques check that they carry a red seal, indicating that they have been approved for export, and ask for the special customs declaration form that you will need to submit on leaving the country.

Items difficult to obtain Most of the comforts, medicines and hygienic aids to which Westerners are accustomed are now available in China, at least in the major cities. Tampons can be obtained in some hotel shopping arcades but not generally. There is no guarantee that you will be able to buy your favourite brand of toothpaste or soap. Bring your own if you are choosy. Stationery items such as Tippex or Sellotape are also often difficult to obtain; and, perhaps not surprisingly, Indian tea.

Opening hours Shops are open seven days a week, usually from 9 to 9 or later.

Prices are fixed and shopkeepers will not bargain with foreigners. Large stores have multilingual staff, but elsewhere much can be achieved through gestures, and shopkeepers will usually write out the price on a piece of paper.

Shipping Friendship Stores, hotel shops and large department stores can usually cope with a request to ship home large items. Otherwise, you can arrange this through one of the international airlines operating in

China, or by asking your hotel to put you in touch with a shipping agent. Small items can be mailed at the hotel, or at the main international post office (see **City by City**: *Local resources*).

Information sources
Business information

China is a notoriously difficult country in which to obtain information and published sources may use generalizations to cover up the lack of solid facts. The most informed people in China are undoubtedly Embassy Commercial Section staff, banks and specialist China trading companies.

Several Chinese foreign trade organizations are listed under the *Local resources* section for each city in this guide, and they will act as consultants and matchmakers between potential foreign and Chinese trading partners. They are useful as a source of information on whom to talk to in which company but rarely provide the detailed information that would enable anyone to draw up a business proposal. Information about the sort of trade agreements being struck – a good guide to Chinese spending priorities – can be gleaned from the *China Daily* and from Hong Kong-based publications such as the *South China Morning Post*, the *Asian Wall Street Journal* and the weeklies, *Far Eastern Economic Review* and *Asiaweek*, all of which can be obtained in hotel bookshops. See details of further relevant publications in the section *Business publications*.

Tourist information

Hotel travel desks, usually run by CITS, or CITS branch offices (see **City by City**: *Local resources*), will answer questions about transport and costs, attractions and events, but since their chief purpose is to sign visitors up for one of their guided tours they are not always helpful to those who want to make their own

arrangements. The best rule in China is to ask foreign residents for advice and guidance.

Crime

You are very unlikely to be the victim of crime during a visit to China. The Chinese are scrupulously honest, and overcharging is rare, let alone mugging or theft. A possible exception is Guangzhou where, under the influence of nearby Hong Kong, sharp trading practices and petty theft are beginning to spoil the previously trouble-free atmosphere. Sensible precautions should be taken to protect cash and valuables, which can be entrusted to a hotel safe.

Lost possessions

If you lose possessions, traveller's cheques or money, passports or airline tickets, inform the hotel at once. There is every chance that the finder will have handed it over to the concierge or floor attendant. If not, you should immediately seek the advice of your host or agent. Also, without delay, inform the issuing bank of lost credit cards and cheques. The loss of large amounts of money or items declared on your baggage declaration form will cause difficulties at customs, so you should report the problem to the Public Security Bureau (Foreign Affairs section) at the earliest opportunity and obtain a letter of explanation. Lost airline tickets may be replaced by the carrier, but not those issued for CAAC internal flights, or train tickets. Embassies will deal with lost passports and, in the last resort, are a source of assistance for problems you are unable to resolve yourself.

Embassies
In Beijing

Australia, 15 Dongzhimenwai Dajie ☎ 522331
Austria, 5 Xiushui Nanjie ☎ 522061
Belgium, 6 Sanlitun Lu ☎ 521736
Canada, 10 Sanlitun Lu ☎ 521475
Denmark, 1 Sanlitun Dongwujie ☎ 522431

Finland, Tayuan Diplomatic Office Bldg 1–10, 14 Liangmahe Nanlu ☎ 521817

France, 3 Sanlitun Dongsan ☎ 521331

Greece, 19 Guanghua Lu ☎ 521277

Ireland, 3 Ritan Donglu ☎ 522506

Italy, 2 Sanlitun Dongerjie ☎ 522131

Japan, 7 Ritan Lu ☎ 522361

Luxembourg, 21 Neiwubu Jie ☎ 556175

Malaysia, 13 Dongzhimenwai Dajie ☎ 522531

Netherlands, Tayuan Diplomatic Office Bldg 1–15, 14 Liangmahe Nanlu ☎ 521131

New Zealand, 1 Ritan Dongerjie ☎ 522731

Norway, 1 Sanlitun Dongyijie ☎ 522261

Philippines, 23 Xiushui Beijie ☎ 522794

Portugal, Tayuan Diplomatic Office Bldg 2–72, 14 Liangmahe Nanlu ☎ 523220

Singapore, 4 Liangmahe Nanlu ☎ 523926

Spain, 9 Sanlitun Lu ☎ 523520

Sweden, 3 Dongzhimenwai Dajie ☎ 523331

Switzerland, 3 Sanlitun Dongwujie ☎ 522736

Thailand, 40 Guanghua Lu ☎ 521903

UK, 11 Guanghua Lu ☎ 521937

USA, 3 Xiushui Beijie ☎ 523831

West Germany, 5 Dongzhimenwai Dajie ☎ 522161

In Guangzhou

USA, Dong Fang Hotel, Liuhua Lu ☎ 669900

In Shanghai

Australia, 17 Fuxing Lu ☎ 374580

Belgium, Room 314 Jingan Guesthouse, 370 Huashan Lu ☎ 538882

France, 1431 Huaihai Zhonglu ☎ 377414

UK, 244 Yongfu Lu ☎ 374569

USA, 1469 Huaihai Zhonglu ☎ 379880

West Germany, 181 Yongfu Lu ☎ 379951

Health care

Bring with you ample supplies of any medicine you take regularly, since it is unlikely that they will be available locally. Fresh fruit is often not obtainable and some travellers like to take vitamin tablets with them. You should only drink water that has been boiled, or mineral water.

Potential problems The two commonest complaints suffered by visitors are colds and upper respiratory infections, and minor stomach upsets. Mosquitoes are a nuisance in warm weather, and dry skin, cracked lips and chapped hands commonly occur in the cold, dry northern winter.

Pharmacies Hotel shops stock basic non-prescription drugs such as painkillers and cold remedies. Chinese pharmacies stock only herbal remedies. Prescription drugs are dispensed only by hospitals and are sold to foreigners at cost (cash only).

Doctors If you need medical attention, first ask at the hotel; all the top hotels have nurses on the staff or doctors on call who will visit your room if necessary. In any case you should arrange through the hotel to be referred to a hospital. Medical services are available in all major cities and Chinese doctors are also trained in Western medical practice, although you will need the assistance of an interpreter.

Dentists Dentistry in China is very backward, and most visitors prefer to live with their toothache until they return to Hong Kong or home. Embassies do have dentists for their own staff, and although they are not happy to be thought of as anything other than a last resort, they will help with real emergencies.

Emergency treatment In the case of serious illness your embassy should immediately be informed, and they will make appropriate arrangements. In any event, it is wise to take out medical insurance of the type that will repatriate you in a crisis, or fly you to Hong Kong where medical standards are high.

Communications

One of the main difficulties of doing business in China is the rudimentary communications network. Things are improving, but it will be years before the communications systems operate as efficiently as in most Western countries.

Telephones

Local telephone calls are usually free in China. Hotels have plenty of telephones in their lobbies as well as in rooms. Some hotels in the major cities now have IDD and their number will certainly increase, but IDD is still very rare. Hotels built within the last two years generally have IDD, but sometimes only to Japan and Hong Kong. In the absence of IDD, international and long-distance calls have to be arranged in advance through the hotel's English-speaking, long-distance operator. Sometimes you are required to complete a form, obtainable in the hotel lobby or from the floor service desk. Then you have to wait for the operator to call back to say your call has been connected. This may take an hour or more, although some hotels offer an urgent call service which takes priority over regular calls.

Long-distance or international calls are expensive, and the quality of lines can sometimes be very bad. When you put the phone down the operator will call back to check that you have finished and tell you the duration of the call. Soon after this (usually) the floor attendant will bring you the bill and ask you to settle up. You can, however, make reverse charge/collect calls or (provided you have informed the operator in advance) charge the cost to an ITU credit card.

Make sure that anyone calling you from overseas knows your room number and asks for that, rather than giving your name. This is important because even English-speaking telephone operators may have difficulty in understanding the pronunciation of a Western name.

Telegrams, telex and fax

The telegraph offices of major hotels offer various services, including domestic and international telegrams, international telex and, less frequently, fax. The offices supply self-explanatory forms and charge telegrams by the word, fax and telex by the minute. The rates are doubled for express services and even the regular service is expensive.

Incoming cables and telexes are not always delivered promptly to your room; if you are expecting a cable which does not arrive, try going to the hotel's telex room and asking for it in person.

Mail

All forms of mail can be dealt with at the postal desk in major hotels, including airmail, air parcel post and registered mail. Airmail to Europe or the USA from Beijing takes up to ten days, and from Guangzhou six days. Parcels should not be wrapped until they have been inspected by postal staff.

Incoming mail to China takes at least two, and sometimes as much as three weeks.

Couriers

Beijing is amply provided with courier services out of China, but Shanghai, Guangzhou and other cities are not. Perhaps this is because visitors rarely need to send items out with any urgency. Getting items in is another matter: spare parts, samples and documentation can all be sent into China by air freight but the experience of an agent or representative is required in handling the documentation and customs procedures on collection. Within China, local courier services are non-existent, and businesses established there employ their own full-time messengers.

International dialling codes

Before dialling the country's code, dial 00. International direct dialling (IDD) is rare and it may be some years before all the codes are available. Omit the initial 0 from the city code. The figures in brackets indicate how many hours the country is ahead or behind China. In Apr–Sep, clocks are put forward one hour.

Australia	61	(0–+2hr)
Austria	43	(-7hr)
Belgium	32	(-7hr)
Canada	1	(-11hr 30min–16hr)
Denmark	45	(-7hr)
France	33	(-7hr)
Germany (E.)	37	(-7hr)
Germany (W.)	49	(-7hr)
Greece	30	(-6hr)
Hong Kong	852	
India	91	(-2hr 30min)
Indonesia	62	(-1hr–+1hr)

Israel	972	(-6hr)
Italy	39	(-7hr)
Japan	81	(+1hr)
Malaysia	60	
Netherlands	31	(-7hr)
New Zealand	64	(+4hr)
Norway	47	(-7hr)
Pakistan	92	(-3hr)
Philippines	63	
Portugal	351	(-8hr)
Singapore	65	
South Korea	82	(+1hr)
Spain	34	(-7hr)
Sweden	46	(-7hr)
Switzerland	41	(-7hr)
Taiwan	886	
Thailand	66	(-1hr)
UK	44	(-8hr)
USA	1	(-13hr–18hr)

Conversion charts

China is moving towards the metric system but imperial measurements are still used by some. Travellers might also encounter traditional Chinese measurements.

Length

centimetres (cm)	cm or in	inches (in)
2.54	= in 1 cm =	0.394
5.08	2	0.787
7.62	3	1.181
10.16	4	1.575
12.70	5	1.969
15.24	6	2.362
17.70	7	2.756
20.32	8	3.150
22.86	9	3.543
25.40	10	3.937
50.80	20	7.874
76.20	30	11.811
101.60	40	15.748
127.00	50	19.685

Mass (weight)

kilograms (kg)	kg or lb	pounds (lb)
0.454	= lb 1 kg =	2.205
0.907	2	4.409
1.361	3	6.614
1.814	4	8.819
2.268	5	11.023
2.722	6	13.228
3.175	7	15.432
3.629	8	17.637
4.082	9	19.842
4.536	10	22.046
9.072	20	44.092
13.608	30	66.139
18.144	40	88.185
22.680	50	110.231

Distance

kilometres (km)	km or miles	miles (mi)
1.609	= mi 1 km =	0.621
3.219	2	1.243
4.828	3	1.864
6.437	4	2.485
8.047	5	3.107
9.656	6	3.728
11.265	7	4.350
12.875	8	4.971
14.484	9	5.592
16.093	10	6.214
32.187	20	12.427
48.280	30	18.641
64.374	40	24.855
80.467	50	31.069

Volume

litres (l)	litres or UK galls	UK galls
4.546	= l 1 gall =	0.220
9.092	2	0.440
13.638	3	0.660
18.184	4	0.880
22.730	5	1.100
27.276	6	1.320
31.822	7	1.540
36.368	8	1.760
40.914	9	1.980
45.460	10	2.200
90.919	20	4.399
136.379	30	6.599
181.839	40	8.799
227.298	50	10.998

Temperature

°F	32	40	50	60	70	75	85	95	105	140	175	212
°C	0	5	10	15	20	25	30	35	40	60	80	100

Index

INDEX

information: business 184;
tourist 184
infrastructure 8, 30–1, 32
Instrimpex (China National
Instruments Import/Export
Corporation) 49
insurance 45: for imports and
exports 63
international alignments 17
international dialling codes 187
International Finance
Corporation 29
International Monetary Fund
(IMF) 17
International Trust and
Investment Corporations
(ITICs) 70
introductions 80
investment certificates 53
iron ore 43
Islam 90
Italy 24, 25

Japan 8, 17, 24, 25, 86
Japan's Overseas Economic
Cooperation Fund (OECF) 28
Jiang Qing 78
Jiang Zemin 14, 15
Jiangsu 28
jobs for life 50
Joint Venture Law 52
joint ventures 51, 53–5:
taxation of 55–6

Ka Wah Bank 70
Kuomintang (Nationalist
Party) 13, 17, 85

labour, cost of 51
labour law 54
land ownership 53, 86
language 82, 93: spoken 93;
written 93
law, Chinese 12, 54
law, foreign business 52
law firms: Chinese 73;
Western 73
lawyers 73
Leading Groups 12, 34
leasing 60–1: companies 71
left wing 15
leisure 91
Li Peng 14–15
Li Ruihan 15
Li Xiannian 15
Liaoning 28
licensing contracts 61
lifestyles 89–91
literacy 20
livestock 19
London 29
Long March 9, 86, 88

Macao, return of 17
Machimpex (China National
Machinery Import/Export
Corporation) 49

machinery imports 36–7
magazines, business 75
mail 186
management 35, 46, 51
Manchu dynasty 8, 84–5, 88
manners 79, 83
manufacturing 36–9
Mao Zedong 8, 10, 13, 17, 26,
32, 86, 87
Mao suit (zhongshan) 37
market entry 58–64
market research 67: problems
67
markets, financial 72
marriage 90, 91
Marxism 10, 89, 90
medical treatment, emergency
185
meetings, business 80–3
metals 18, 43
"Middle Kingdom" 9
military 16, 38, 49
minerals 18–19, 43
ministries 11–12, 34, 48
Ministry of Aviation and
Space 38
Ministry of Defence 12
Ministry of Energy 41
Ministry of Finance 12
Ministry of Foreign Affairs 12
Ministry of Foreign Economic
Relations and Trade (MOFERT)
12, 23, 34, 37, 47, 48, 49, 53,
54, 55, 59, 60, 65
Ministry of Machinery and
Electronics 38
Minmetals (China National
Metals and Minerals
Import/Export Corporation)
43, 49
MOFERT, Foreign Investment
Commission 49
MOFERT, subsidiary
corporations 49, 59
MOFERT, Technology Import-
Export Bureau 61
money 174–5: changing 175
mothers, working 78
municipalities 12–13, 95

names: personal 80; of streets
178
Nanjing 140–1
National Defence Commission
for Science, Technology and
Industry 16
National Party Congress 10:
13th Congress 8, 9, 13, 14
National People's Congress
11
Nationalist Party, see
Kuomintang
nationalization 86
natural resources, see
resources, natural
negotiating 77, 80
Nei Menggu 13

neighbourhood committees
89
New China (Xinhua) News
Agency 75
New York 29
Ningxia Hui 13
Nixon, Richard 87
nuclear defence 16, 17
nuclear power 42
numbers 93

October 1986 incentives 56
OECD (Organisation for
Economic Cooperation and
Development) 63
oil 18, 40–2: corporations 41
OPEC (Organization of the
Petroleum Exporting
Countries) 23, 25
"open door" policy 8, 9, 12, 17,
26, 47, 58, 87
Opium War 8, 85
Overseas Chinese Affairs
Office 12
overseas funding 28–9

packaging 33
Patriotic Christian
Association 90
payment methods 59–60
People's Bank of China (PBOC)
22, 68
People's Communes 26, 28
People's Courts 12
People's Insurance Company
of China (PICC) 45, 70–1
People's Liberation Army (PLA)
11, 16
People's Republic 86–7
personal income tax 21
petrochemicals 44
pets 91
pharmaceuticals 44
pharmacies 185
phrases, key 94
Pinyin system of
transliteration 93
Plan, First Five-Year (1952–
57) 26
Plan, Seventh (1986–90) 27
planning 26–7
Politburo 10, 15, 77
politics 10–17: and society 89
population 9, 20, 50
ports 30
postal services 186
power, business 48–9
power, reins of 13–15
premier 11
president 11
price control 27, 46
private sector 27
processing 36–9
productivity 50
products: finished 37; foreign
36; light industrial output 39;
updating 35